In the Shadow of the Giants

In the Shadow of the Giants

Mountain Ascents, Past and Present

Tom King

San Diego • New York
A. S. Barnes & Company, Inc.
In London:
The Tantivy Press

© 1981 by A. S. Barnes and Co. Inc.

All rights reserved under International and Pan American Copyright Conventions. No part of this book may be reproduced in any manner whatsoever without written permission from the publisher, except in the case of brief quotations embodied in reviews and articles.

First Edition
Manufactured in the United States of America

For information write to:
A. S. Barnes & Company, Inc.
P. O. Box 3051
La Jolla, California 92038

The Tantivy Press
Magdalen House
136-148 Tooley Street
London, SE1 2TT, England

Library of Congress Cataloging in Publication Data

King, Tom, 1929-
   In the Shadow of the Giants: Mountain Ascents Past and Present

  Bibliography: p. 269
  Includes index.
  1. Mountaineering. I. Title.
GV200.K56   796.5'22   77-84572
ISBN 0-498-02186-6

1 2 3 4 5 6 7 8 9 84 83 82 81

Except where otherwise indicated, all photographs were taken by the author or member of his party, and sketches were prepared by him from previously published photographs and maps.

To
Tara, Mother, Bea & Mike

Contents

PREFACE	9
ACKNOWLEDGMENTS	11
1 Genesis: To the Top of Mont Blanc	13
2 The Matterhorn Revisited: In the Tracks of Whymper	48
3 The Bernese Trinity	84
4 On the Edge of Everest	115
5 A Pilgrimage on Fujisan	173
6 Excursions in the High Sierra	197
7 *La Haute Route:* Crossing the Western Alps on Skis	219
GLOSSARY	263
NOTES	265
SELECTED BIBLIOGRAPHY	269
INDEX	281

Preface

The epics of mountaineering—and of the pioneer climbers who made first ascents of the great peaks—represent a small but stirring chapter in man's ever-unfolding history. These past triumphs and tragedies formed an inspiring symbol of courage and will, of the quest to know, of an acceptance of nature's and our own self-imposed challenges, under the most trying conditions.

To tread in the footpaths of such trailblazers is to enjoy and experience, in some slight way, the rich and illustrious legacy created by them.

Here I have endeavored to undertake—and invite the reader to join—a smattering of present-day scrambles in the wake of the early explorations. Typically, the normal or easiest route is used, often with a guide, via a line that is nontechnical and may even largely be a hike or trek. Certainly the outings would present no problem or difficulty whatsoever for the serious mountaineer.

With proper motivation and training, virtually anyone who savors the exciting world of pinnacles and snow can readily make the same series of ascents.

T.K.

Acknowledgments

I wish to thank the following publishers for having given me permission to quote from published works:

George Allen & Unwin Ltd, for permission to quote from Claire Eliane Engel, ed., *Mont Blanc—An Anthology*, 1965.

Edward Arnold & Co., for permission to quote from Col. C. K. Howard-Bury, *Mount Everest—The Reconnaissance 1921*, 1922; and from Lt. Col. E. F. Norton, *The Fight for Everest: 1924*, 1924.

Basil Blackwell Publisher Limited, for permission to quote from A. W. Moore, *The Alps in 1864*, 1939.

E. P. Dutton & Co., Inc., for permission to quote from *The Conquest of Everest* by Sir John Hunt. Copyright, 1953, by Sir John Hunt.

Rupert Hart-Davis Ltd., for permission to quote from Heinrich Harrer, *The White Spider*, 1968.

Hodder & Stoughton Limited, for permission to quote from Sir John Hunt, *The Conquest of Everest* (published by Hodder & Stoughton under the title *The Ascent of Everest*), 1953.

Oxford University Press, for permission to quote from T. Graham Brown and Gavin de Beer, *The First Ascent of Mont Blanc*, 1957.

Special thanks are owing to friends Dale Vrabec, Dede Hilton, Henry Hilton, and Sylvia Vrabec for the valuable comments and suggestions made by them while reviewing the manuscript and proofs, and also to Erika Oller, whose exceptional talents produced the map of *La Haute Route* that appears in Chapter 7.

Adaptations of portions of this book appeared in *Summit* and *Carte Blanche* magazines.

1
Genesis: To the Top of Mont Blanc

> *Far, far above, piercing the infinite sky,*
> *Mont Blanc appears—still, snowy and serene*
> *Its subject mountains their unearthly forms*
> *Pile around it, ice and rock; broad vales between*
> *of frozen floods, unfathomable deeps,*
> *Blue as the overhanging heaven, that spread*
> *And wind among the accumulated steeps.*
>
> —Percy Bysshe Shelley, *Mont Blanc*

> *My most lively and pleasant sensation was to feel myself at the end of my uncertainty; for the length of the struggle, the recollection and the still vivid impression of the exertion it had cost me, caused me a kind of irritation... Still the grand spectacle I had under my eyes gave me great pleasure... that which I came to see, and now recognized with the greatest clarity, was the order of the great ranges of which I had so long desired to ascertain the grouping.*
>
> —Horace Bénédict de Saussure, *Voyages dans les Alpes*

A young medical doctor and a thickset peasant who hunts chamois and crystals for a living stumble onto the virgin summit of an all-too-immense snow dome. A menacing swirl of séracs and glaciers, of cataracts and fluted ridges, trails off toward the green valley below. It is 6:23 P.M.—the crowning moment of a bold exploit inspired by an aristocratic Genevan scholar-naturalist who has become entranced by the magnetic allure of the resplendent white peak.

Far below a crowd watches through telescopes. One of the onlookers, a German topographer, meticulously plots the climbers' progress from early in the afternoon and follows them, making notes, as they reach the apex of the ascent. On the crest it is bitterly cold. The doctor ties a red handkerchief to a staff as a marker and takes measurements with a barometer.

They have been climbing fourteen straight hours. After about thirty-five minutes they start the descent. Within days the comradeship and shared adventure of the heights dissolve. There are venomous recriminations and accusations. A fistfight ensues. The dispute grows. The peasant claims to have reached the top first and alone. The doctor, it is said, had to be aided like a child and was virtually pulled to the summit by his rugged companion well after the latter had completed the epochal initial ascent.

The legend dies hard. About fifty years later it is given wider credence by one of the eminent novelists of the era. More than a century passes. The diary of the topographer-visitor is found. An affidavit signed shortly after the climb is reexamined. Other vital details are uncovered. The full tale emerges, and the doctor, who lies half-forgotten in an unmarked grave, is vindicated.

Thus was unraveled the intriguing but true story of the winning of the highest mountain in Western Europe. The date was August 8, 1786—ten years after the American Revolution. The event sired a revolution of its own.

MONT BLANC, 15,771 feet. Not only the loftiest pinnacle in the Alps, but one of the most beautiful. A transcendent, ivory-sheathed mass that overtops the aiguilles, or needles, of Chamonix, France, in vast, inexorable furrows of bulging cornices and cyclopean glaciers. A world of ice and snow unto itself. The first great Alpine peak to be climbed.

Modern mountaineering—whether it represents a way of life, a personal evocation, a sport, an exploration, a quest for knowledge, a spiritual affirmation, a challenge, an adventure, or an escape—had its true genesis in the quiet, hidden vale of Chamonix at the foot of the Mont Blanc range, fifty-six miles southeast of Geneva. As surely as the Norsemen crossed to Greenland and the Wright Brothers took flight, the ascent of Mont Blanc in 1786, and the enthralling successes that followed, fired the imagination of Europe and opened up the pristine lure of the Alps to one and all.

Before then, most persons who rambled among the hills were chamois hunters, crystal searchers, and naturalists. A mountaineer, as

Mont Blanc (15,771 ft.) from the east

such, was unknown. Early travel publication warned of dragons and serpents that surely inhabited the fearsome peaks, cataloging and classifying the demons by canton and area. One creature, reported in the early 1700s, possessed "the body of a snake, the wings of a bat, and emitted sparks as it flew by"; another had a "red hairy cat's head, sparkling eyes, scaly legs, a tongue like a snake's, and a long hairy bifid tail." A residue of these superstitions lingered in the minds of the hill peasants more than a century later. Seventy years after the initial ascent, an English writer stoutly proclaimed that most of those who climbed Mont Blanc possessed a "diseased mind." Also, of course, the sophisticated climbing equipment so commonplace today was nonexistent.

The complete story of the conquest of Mont Blanc, and its ugly, embittered aftermath, reads like a Gothic yarn, with multiple subplots. Stripped to its essentials, it involved a handful of men who, in varying degrees, possessed an astounding degree of vision, diligence, curiosity, and courage—plus, in too many instances, a salty and unfortunate admixture of spite and envy. There were four protagonists:

Horace Bénédict de Saussure, a remarkably gifted youth who, at twenty-two, was elected professor of philosophy and natural science at the Geneva Academy. Through marriage into the Boissier banking family, he became one of the wealthiest men in the area. Of high standing, both socially and as a scientist, he cut a prominent figure throughout the continent.

Marc-Théodore Bourrit, an artist, writer, and precentor, also from Geneva, a talented but pathetic individual who, like de Saussure, devoted the whole of his being to the climbing of Mont Blanc and became its unofficial historian. His almost maniacal jealousies and deceits blinded posterity to the true happenings on the mountain for more than a century.

Michel-Gabriel Paccard, age twenty-nine, a diligent but modest, independent-minded Chamonix physician, whose meticulous studies and observations of Mont Blanc over several years finally yielded their reward.

Jacques Balmat, a powerful, five-foot-three-inch, twenty-four-year-old peasant and crystal hunter from the nearby village of Les Pélerins. Cocky, bold, and not well liked, he was the porter on the final assault.

Without doubt, the ascent of Mont Blanc was directly traceable to the enterprising gifts and inspirational genius of that latter day Renaissance man, de Saussure. His was the dominant influence in the relentless pursuit of what was then believed to be beyond the reach of human aspiration.

De Saussure was blessed with extraordinary talents. He properly may be regarded as both the father of Alpinism and a founder of modern geology. A ranking member of the patrician class, he lived in an era when the city-state of Geneva often stood alone in a vortex of fluctuating political currents that continually scorched the continent. A strict Calvinist oligarchy, Geneva then had a population of only about 25,000. Yet, as the home of Voltaire and Rousseau, and as a cultural and social capital, its influence was widely felt. A sensitive and devoted family man, de Saussure occupied the finest and most luxurious estate in the city. But his eyes and soul were forever fixed on the Alps—a love affair that spanned some thirty-six years.

Chamonix already was a tourist center when de Saussure first visited it in 1760 at the age of twenty. Two Englishmen, William Windham and Dr. Richard Pococke, had come to Chamonix in 1741, and it was Windham's letters, together with those of Pierre Martel, that first made the Mer de Glace and the other glacial wonders of the region well known. Martel probably is responsible for having named Mont Blanc, which at one time had been known locally as Mont Maudit, or the Accursed Mountain.

DeSaussure came to Chamonix in search of plants. In those days the trip from Geneva to the Savoy, then under the rule of Sardinia, was an achievement in itself since the road to Sallanches, and the mule path to Chamonix, were not entirely free of brigands and smugglers. DeSaussure walked most of the way. In all likelihood he was the first outsider to reach the top of Le Brévent, the granite buttress that rises opposite the sprawling Mont Blanc massif.

Mer de Glace—with Grandes Jorasses in the rear

Mont Blanc was the consuming passion of de Saussure's life. "It became for me a kind of illness," he stated. "I could not even look upon the mountain, which is visible from so many points around, without being seized with an aching of desire." He posted notices in three local parishes offering an attractive reward (equal to about two pounds sterling, later increased) to whoever found a way to the summit. It was his fondest dream that once the trail was blazed, he could conduct extensive experiments from this, the crowning Alpine peak, thereby enhancing his standing as a scientist and naturalist. De Saussure traveled widely, recording his many climbs and explorations in his monumental four-volume work, *Voyages dan les Alpes*. His investigations were manifold: he sought explanations for the movements of glaciers, the formation of medial moraines, and of so-called red snow, which is created by one-celled red organisms. He constantly checked the depth and temperature of lakes. He climbed Mount Etna, as had the Roman Emperor Hadrian, and in later years was so fascinated by the Matterhorn that he made a special trip to the Théodule Pass to fix its height by use of a chain and sextant. Probably his finest achievement was spending eighteen straight days making observations on the origins of rain and electrical, meteorological, and related atmospheric conditions, at the 11,000-foot level, on the Col du Géant, which he christened. During another season he spent five weeks touring the Monte Rosa region and, at fifty-two, climbed the 12,750-foot Kleine Matterhorn.

Bossons Glacier spilling toward the heart of Chamonix

De Saussure's well-to-do wife was not entirely enamored of his ceaseless wanderings, and he once wrote her: "You would like better—God pardon me—to see me as fat as a canon, asleep all day in the chimney corner after a good dinner, than to see me gain immortal fame by the most sublime discoveries at the cost of a few ounces of weight and several weeks of absence."[1]

As a result of de Saussure's instigations, numerous attempts on Mont Blanc were made, none reaching higher than the Dôme du Goûter at 14,800 feet. De Saussure even wondered aloud whether it would be possible to use "air carriages" to reach such inaccessible peaks.

Basically, two approach routes were pioneered. The first and most popular was from the northwest side, which spills out over Chamonix in massive, streaming pylons of snow and ice forming the Bossons and Taconna glaciers; these drop about 10,000 feet over a five-mile path, straight into the heart of the valley. Townspeople habitually watched parties as they struggled up a long, prominent rock buttress, the Montagne de la Côte, which sprouts in the vale and rises in steep steps, like an intruder, to the lower snowfield or Jonction. For another 1,500 feet icy berms and séracs intercede to the base of a narrow crest of rocks that, like the sharp, curved back of a marlin, sits squarely in the midst of the heaping snow expanse, neatly dividing the Bossons glacier on its left (or east) from the Taconna on its right. This granite protrusion, known as the Grands Mulets, extends above 10,000 feet.

From here the difficulties grow more severe. Gaping crevasses and twisting icefalls, dangerous and ever-shifting, lead to and beyond the twin terraces of the Petit and Grand plateaus, at about 13,000 feet. At this point the snowfields angle up sharply, forming a natural playground for avalanches and slides, and reach two parallel lines of rock, readily discernible from Chamonix, called the Rochers Rouges. A maze of snow walls and ice steps, this forms one of the stiff last barriers to the top.

The early climbers, once attaining the Grands Mulets, tended to veer to the right (or west), avoiding the perils of the Grand Plateau and Rochers Rouges, and traversing the ridge to the Dôme du Goûter, which itself squats immediately to the west of the crown summit. Here they invariably were stymied—by weather, avalanches, fatigue, altitude sickness, fear, and a last, seemingly infinite procession of sheer snow cornices.

The first serious effort on this northwest flank, facing Chamonix, was undertaken in 1775 by four peasant guides who ascended much of the way up the Grands Mulets. This gave impetus to further reconnoitering. Paccard and Bourrit once tried the route together, but the timid Bourrit, whose aspirations invariably outstripped his abilities, never budged beyond the safe rocks of the Grands Mulets, while Paccard and the others proceeded to explore the Jonction.

In June of 1786 Balmat, a rugged but vain man, tailed along with a party of local guides in an effort that reached the Dôme du Goûter. When separated from the rest of the group, he bravely slept alone on the mountain, probably well above the Grands Mulets, thereby showing that, in the face of foul weather and at high altitude, a well-conditioned person could survive a night on the mountain. He also claimed to have discovered a new route through the Rochers Rouges. This episode later was to provide a point of friction in determining who first discovered the ultimate path of ascent.

The second main approach to Mont Blanc emanated from Saint Gervais, farther to the west. It involved ascending the gentle hills to the Tête Rousse, crossing the snout of the Bionnassay Glacier, and then tackling the long, precipitous rock pitches of the Aiguille du Goûter,

Westerly flank of Mont Blanc, displaying the Dôme du Goûter (center) and Aiguille du Goûter (right)

also culminating at the Dôme du Goûter.

The energetic Paccard himself pioneered the initial attempt from the Saint Gervais side. When Bourrit learned of it, he anxiously rushed out to try the same approach himself but attained only the Tête Rousse, while two guides, Jean-Marie Couttet and Francois Cuidet, reached the Dôme du Goûter. Later, de Saussure, with Bourrit, the latter's son Isaac, and a group of guides, again made this attempt, but de Saussure and the Bourrits could manage only part of the way up the Aiguille du Goûter.

Deliberately ignoring Paccard's feat, Bourrit used his position as a journalist to broadcast the claim that he personally had found the Saint Gervais route. A mediocre climber who to his dying day was never able to scale Mont Blanc, Bourrit later argued that his discovery triggered renewed efforts to find a way that would be closer to, and immediately benefit, Chamonix, and thereby was partly responsible for the final victory. In fact, the churlish Bourrit became intensely envious of Paccard and launched what in due time became extremely poisonous attacks upon the doctor. The underlying reason for this is unclear. It may have originated when Paccard witnessed Bourrit's tremulous refusal to venture onto the Jonction in their prior joint attempt from the northwest, or when Paccard found the opening from Saint Gervais, which threatened to rob Bourrit of the only glory left to him. Perhaps it was simple jealousy: that an unknown small-town doctor could steal such a valued prize was more than Bourrit could bear.

In any event, Bourrit, while enjoying bursts of flowery eloquence when extolling Mont Blanc, spent years propagating malicious half-truths and distortions about the mountain's history, with Paccard the prime victim of his sharp verbal stiletto. Tall and dark complexioned, possessing strong likes and a sentimentally poetic style, Bourrit was often in financial trouble and, as one acquaintance noted, talked incessantly—mostly about himself. James D. Forbes said that he conveyed the "simplest facts through a medium of unmixed bombast." Toward the latter part of his life Bourrit acquired the habit of sleeping under a walnut tree in his garden. His genuine adoration of the Alps was marred by his own petty conceits and small-minded vindictiveness. Douglas W. Freshfield summed him up in this manner: "If he loved the Alps well, he loved Bourrit still more. If Mont Blanc was his idol, he looked on himself as its high priest, and was jealous of any intrusion on the shrine."[2]

Despite breaking the new ground from Saint Gervais and also having tried a futile approach from Montenvers on the east, the indefatigable Paccard was not satisfied. From the Brévent, directly across Chamonix from Mont Blanc, this son of a local notary, a recipient of a medical degree from the University of Turin, had for several years been studying the ice and snow patterns near the crest, and concluded that still another route, also from the northwest, was feasible. Almost every knowledgeable observer in the area was shackled to the idea that the path to the top lay via the Dôme du Goûter. It was the prevailing gospel to all—except Paccard and perhaps Balmat.

The doctor had learned of Balmat's solitary bivouac on the mountain and was impressed by it. Accordingly, the educated Paccard induced the peasant Balmat to make still another attempt. Their motives differed: Paccard longed to climb the mountain but also was absorbed in scientific observations; for Balmat the monetary reward offered by de Saussure, and a grand chance at fame, were uppermost. Their provisions and equipment were incredibly rudimentary, typical of the era: nine-foot shafts or alpenstocks, a blanket, bread, cold meat, and a few instruments such as a barometer (for determining altitude), thermometer, and compass.

The pair set out late on August 7, 1786, following the usual way up the northwesterly flank and proceeding along the girth of the Montagne de la Côte, where they bivouacked overnight at about 7,640 feet. At 4:00 A.M. the next morning they resumed, moving through the white wastes of the Jonction and onto the long, crusty spine of the Grands Mulets. Up to this juncture they were following well-traveled ground.

Here, instead of tending to the west, toward the Dôme du Goûter, Paccard persuaded Balmat to attack the snow slopes of the Petit Plateau

The Mont Blanc massif (the author's climbing route followed the skyline from right to left)

and then the steep, forbidding Grand Plateau. As far as is known, never before had this region been penetrated. It was now about 3:00 P.M. Paccard was determined to forge a new route between the rock outcroppings of the Rochers Rouges, which was to become known as the lower Ancien Passage. Because of the multiple perils of slides and crevasses, this section previously was thought to be impassable. The slope is long, and though it actually sits at only about a thirty-two-degree slant, it is barricaded by a succession of ice pillars. Four times they broke through hidden abysses. Yet, in about an hour and a half they had forced the Rochers Rouges and now were plodding doggedly past the Petits Mulets up the flank of the snow crown. Once they had to flop on their bellies to avoid being swept over by the piercing winds.

At 6:23 P.M., on August 8, 1786, exhausted, eyes swollen, Paccard and Balmat lurched onto the summit of Mont Blanc. They had climbed over 8,000 feet in about fourteen hours—itself a formidable accomplishment.

Mont Blanc—summit of the Alps. The original Paccard-Balmat route in 1786 followed the Montagne de la Côte, the prominent ridge in the lower right; the Grands Mulets, the slanting, almost vertical line of snow-covered rocks in the upper middle; and the Rochers Rouges, the two parallel lines of rock outcroppings below the top. The arrow points to the railway tunnel through the mountain. *Courtesy French Government Tourist Office.*

The two men remained on the top for little more than a half-hour. Paccard took notes and made measurements, and each proceeded partway to the Mont Blanc de Courmayeur, the lower of the mountain's twin peaks. On the lengthy descent both suffered frostbite, and Paccard, partially snowblinded, had to be assisted by Balmat. Again they passed the night on the Montagne de la Côte and the next morning returned in triumph to Chamonix.

The flawless melding of inspired trust and teamwork that, remarkably, had enabled two daring but vastly different individuals to venture into the unknown, and survive, deteriorated almost as soon as their footsteps resounded in the valley. If mankind's spirit was ennobled and uplifted by the conquest, it shortly was to crumble against the baser human reefs of greed, distrust and acrimony. The resultant controversy lasted for generations.

Frustrated, almost enraged by Paccard's masterstroke, Marc-Théodore Bourrit, the self-proclaimed official chronicler, produced a pamphlet entitled "Letters on the First Journey to the Summit of Mont Blanc," which decried Paccard's role in the climb. Balmat was a simple man, and the feat clearly turned his head; he provided the grist for Bourrit's fabric of falsehoods.

In brief, Bourrit and, necessarily, Balmat claimed that the Ancien Passage actually had been discovered by Balmat, not Paccard, during the former's lonely overnight vigil earlier in the year; that Paccard had not paid Balmat for his labors much less his leadership on so ambitious an enterprise; and, most notably, that Paccard had collapsed before reaching the summit, Balmat had pushed on alone to the top, then had to return and, rousing Paccard, was compelled to drag the inept doctor the last few hundred feet up. The point was that Paccard was said to be a parasite and an ingrate whose role, in all significant phases of the ascent, was secondary, while Balmat had been alone and the first on the summit. Bourrit once even indicated that Paccard never attained the top at all, but finally retreated from such an extreme accusation.

When the doctor announced that he would author a book, Bourrit promptly countered:

"I learn now that Dr. Paccard hopes to reap the fruits of his expedition; that he has announced himself at Lausanne, and that he has made himself to appear to be the conqueror of Mont Blanc . . . while the poor Balmat, to whom he owes this discovery, remains unknown, and does not know there are Journalists, and Journals, and that it is possible by means of these literary trumpets, to obtain from the public a kind of admiration."[3]

For lack of subscriptions, the doctor's book on this, one of the most epic of all mountaineering achievements, was never published, and the manuscript for it was never found.

Mont Blanc's twisting glaciers

Stirred by the ascent, the ardent de Saussure set about making plans. On August 1, 1787, he assembled a company of seventeen guides, Balmat, a personal servant who never had set foot on a slope before, and a pack mule. Bourrit wanted to join the party, but de Saussure put him off. His baggage consisted of: green spectacles, a black veil, white clothes, waistcoats, blankets, a bearskin mattress, a small stove, copper dishes, tents, heavy shoes with iron screws to grip on ice, a seven-foot shaft with a metal tip, a geologist's hammer, a barometer, and other gauges. Following Paccard's suggestion, poles were placed across crevasses to help the professor, supported by his guides. It was, in a sense, mountaineering's first "expedition." De Saussure attained the summit on August 3, 1787, via the upper Ancien Passage, which lies immediately above the Rochers Rouges. As usual, he busied himself as soon as he arrived, testing magnetic variations, checking pulse rates, measuring the temperature of boiling water, and carefully reading his barometer, thermometer, hygrometer, and electrometer.

Although this constituted the third ascent of Mont Blanc (Balmat and two guides made the second via an eastern ridge), it proved to be a truly Olympian event. De Saussure's prestige and notoriety, coupled with the widespread publicity heralding the feat, actually enabled it to eclipse in importance the virginal Paccard-Balmat conquest. Western Europe was entranced by the respected scientist's ascent of its highest peak. Measured by its influence on the evolution of mountaineering, it undoubtedly is one of the most significant single climbs ever made.

Mont Blanc
(from northwest)

Solid line: original Paccard-Balmat route.
Dotted line (below summit): De Saussure's variant via upper Ancien Passage.

1 — Bossons glacier
2 — Montagne de la Côte
3 — Jonction
4 — **Grands Mulets**
5 — Grand Plateau
6 — Rochers Rouges
7 — Summit (15,771 feet)
8 — Mont Maudit
9 — Mont Blanc du Tacul
10 — Dôme du Goûter
11 — Chamonix

Horace B. de Saussure and party descending from the Col du Géant. *Courtesy, the British Museum.*

Meanwhile, the myth of Balmat's leading part in the first conquest was perpetuated by Bourrit's successive editions on the history of the mountain—and by de Saussure's inexplicable silence on a matter that only he, by virtue of his position, could have clarified.

The reserved Paccard took few steps to defend himself publicly. But he did obtain an affidavit, signed by Balmat and witnessed by two Chamoniards, which was to play a key role in his vindication. Balmat later claimed he was tricked into signing the document in blank. Indeed, in July of 1787, the doctor and the peasant—whose Herculean efforts had made them the "space men" of their age—engaged in a street fight over the affair. When Balmat implied forgery, Paccard promptly knocked him to the ground, thereby coming out much the better here than in his literary jousts with Bourrit. While the validity of the affidavit was never determined with certainty, it still constitutes a significant piece of evidence. It stated:

> When Dr. Paccard was planning yet another of his attempts on Mont Blanc, I learnt about this, and knowing that Dr. Paccard's guide was away, I volunteered to go with him.
> On learning that Dr. Paccard proposed to take a route by the Montagne de la Côte, I did not believe that he would succeed,

because we had considered this route to be impracticable at the attempt on June 8, 1786. Dr. Paccard, however, told me that he had examined these places with his telescope for three years.

I declare that we could not have reached the summit but for the steady way in which Dr. Paccard climbed; that he never ceased from encouraging me; that he shared my tasks from time to time by taking some of the load which he had given me to carry; that when I wanted to go back to my wife, as I had promised to help her, and also to my sick child (who in fact died on 8th August), M. Paccard said that these were just excuses.

He would not take the route which we had taken on the last attempt, but continued directly up to the middle of the plain which is above the Glacier des Bossons. He himself showed me the way up his new route by going first up a steep slope at the base of the Grand Mont-Blanc. Because he had always said that we should bivouac on this cone, he told me to look for a place when he had reached the top of this slope, whilst he himself went on up to examine some rocks; when no place for a bivouac was to be found, he resolved to go up to the summit that same evening; he called me, I followed. At that same moment I saw his hat blown away by the strong wind.

The doctor continued to climb nimbly; we reached a little rock behind which I sheltered from the wind, whilst M. Paccard examined it and loaded himself with some stones. We were near the summit; I went to the left to avoid a steep slope of snow, which the said M. Paccard tackled bravely to reach the summit directly. My detour delayed me, and I had to run in order to reach the summit nearly at the same time.

On the summit he made experiments and observations, which he wrote down; he set a mark on it, and we descended together in our tracks, taking turns to find them. When we reached the Montagne de la Côte, M. Paccard lay down on the side open to the glacier.

He fed me, he paid me, and he handed me the money which had been given to him for me.[4]

Almost fifty years later, in 1832, Alexandre Dumas came to the valley and interviewed Balmat, the latter's memory now fancifully embroidered by the lapse of time—as well as several bubbly bottles of wine. The upshot was that Dumas gave credence to Balmat's version in what was then considered to be an authoritative account included in his *Impressions de Voyage* (London: Peter Owen Ltd., 1958). Balmat, he proclaimed, was the Christopher Columbus of the Alps—and by this latest reckoning, Balmat spent not two but four nights in the snow. Conveniently, Paccard already had passed away by then.

A few snippets from this interview, which took place at the Hotel de

Rock spire seen from Aiguille du Midi

la Couronne on the corner of the Place de l'Englishe, will make the point.

"In those days I really was something worth looking at," Balmat is quoted as saying. "I had a famous calf and a stomach like cast-iron, and could walk three days consecutively without eating." Concerning his dreams of making the big climb: "I was like a lizard on a wall." On the first night on the Montagne de la Côte: "I carried a rug and used it to muffle up the doctor like a baby." Reaching the top: "I had come alone, with no help but my own will and my own strength. I was the monarch of Mont Blanc. My subjects below saw me, and were gazing up at their king." When being retrieved, the doctor supposedly said, "Where can I lie down and go to sleep?" Starting the descent: "Paccard was like a child, no energy or will." The second night: "I rolled my baby in his rug and put him to bed under a shelter of rock."

Freshfield, writing in the *Alpine Journal,* labeled the Dumas interview "a monstrous farrago of nonsense."[5] Said Charles Edward Mathews: "Even a benevolent critic, on carefully considering Balmat's story, must feel disposed to put the tongue of incredulity into the cheek of derision."[6] Other researchers, including H. F. Montagnier, Ernest H. Stevens, and, to a lesser extent, the ubiquitous Edward Whymper, raised doubts.

Still, it was not until the discovery and publication by Dr. Henrich Dübi in 1913—127 years after the original ascent—of a detailed diary kept by an eyewitness to the event that Paccard was elevated to his rightful niche and the matter laid to rest.

When Paccard and Balmat made their great climb, it so happened that they were watched graphically, almost step by step, through a powerful telescope by a German baron, Adolf Traugott von Gersdorf, of Görlitz. Von Gersdorf was a topographer and an incurable notetaker. In the company of a friend, he had visited Bourrit in Geneva a few days before the ascent and obtained directions to Chamonix. Carefully he eyed Paccard and Balmat as they proceeded up, changed to higher ground to get a better view, and followed them as they reached the Petits Rochers Rouges, about a half-hour's distance from the top. From there, wrote the baron, they moved upward, about 100 steps apart, both pausing often; then they proceeded from some small rocks, the Petits Mulets, to the summit itself. The baron also made detailed sketches of the ascent, accurately depicting the route pursued.

Glaciers and crevasses

The diary thus belied Balmat's claim, spurred by Bourrit, that Balmat had first achieved the top alone and then had to return to carry Paccard to the crest.

Today, it is generally acknowledged that Paccard discovered the novel route through the Rôchers Rouges and led the first successful assault supported by his porter, Balmat. In their exhaustive and absorbing work *The First Ascent of Mont Blanc,* T. Graham Brown and Gavin de Beer flatly state that Balmat's claims are false and conclude that, based on the evidence, his "whole later story of his heroic and solitary first ascent of the mountain is utterly destroyed." The only "clean incident" in the whole venture, they point out, was the climb itself. On the mountain, removed from the heady pressures of an imperfect world, Balmat "was only a strong young porter, half afraid and half eager, but willing to brave the unknown perils with Dr. Paccard alone."[7]

On reflection, it may be that subsequent researchers overtipped the scales. The hard fact is that Balmat played a vital and even indispensable role in the first great Alpine ascent, and much is to be said for the proposition that he actually discovered the original route. If Balmat was an unlettered liar and an egotist, he also was a relentless climber; he was a member of each of the first six parties to reach the summit. While modern accounts may be more accurate, it is possible that all questions have not yet been fully and fairly settled.

Such is the chronicle of one of mountaineering's most momentous deeds.

Perhaps poet William Blake had the conquest of Mont Blanc in mind when, in "Gnomic Verses," he wrote:

> Great things are done when men and mountains meet;
> This is not done by jostling in the street.

* * *

Now let the reader join in the wake of those intrepid pioneers by following a party in a contemporary ascent of Western Europe's highest peak by a popular route.

The sleepy village of Saint Gervais was writhing out of its snow-caked slumbers when our toylike cogwheel train began its run up Le Prarion, through the dry green pastures of the Col de Voza and Bellevue, and on to the trough of the tumbling Bionnassay glacier. Here Paccard, Bourrit, and de Saussure had made some of their important early explorations. It was late September and already the early snows blanketed the slopes. Norbert Bozon, my husky young guide, and I had spent the early hours foraging among the small shops of Chamonix, collecting enough foodstuff for the two-day trip. Now, from 7,000 feet, the climb abruptly began.

A broad gentle path, populated with early-morning walkers and sightseers, wound through a network of multicolored rocks and flowers. Our party of four quickly hit the snowline, and soon the path emptied, with only two or three hikers continuing to plod ahead. We proceeded to the left side of the glacier, staying above and away from it.

I had long been assured that the ascent of Mont Blanc was merely a long, interminable slog.

"It's not technically difficult," said Desmond, a Britisher now living in Uganda. "In fact, it's mostly a walkup. But it's bloody exhausting, and before you're there you'll think your lungs need an asbestos lining." Desmond, who had made the ascent once before, had been climbing since he was a tot and comes to the Alps each summer to link up with Henri, his guide of longstanding. A leg injury prevents him from skiing, but he is an able climber.

"Let's move," said Norbert, ever in a rush. Chamonix guides live—and die—by this credo. Like their counterparts throughout the Alps, they also seem to delight in killing off Yankee novitiates—and have been engaging in such pleasures ever since Drs. Jeremiah von Rensselaer and William Howard made the first American ascent in 1819.

Our objective was to climb the upper section of Mont Blanc, above the Refuge du Goûter, by moonlight. Actually there was no choice. Norbert and Henri simply ordered it. A guide does not ask his client's approval—he just moves out. Norbert in particular wanted to take advantage of the full moon that was going to blossom. As a precaution, he planned to use a miner's lamp—another standard bit of Alpinism.

Slowly we trudged up the thin twisting path, amid a foot or two of snow, feeling free and exuberant. The sun's golden streams refracted radiantly off the wide, creamy canvas. On our flanks boiling avalanches crushed wantonly down, depositing their fury on gray-green glacial carpets.

Two hours later, still strong, we paused at the Refuge de Tête Rousse, at 10,390 feet, for lunch. At this tiny hut, from which many famous ascents have been launched, we made a fire, warmed a bucket of snow into water, and consumed tea, consommé, salami, cheese, and bread. From here climbers can scale the treacherous north face of the Aiguille de Bionnassay or, like us, pursue the huge rock struts that guard the Dôme du Goûter and the higher reaches of Mont Blanc. I recalled that on his initial effort from Saint Gervais, Bourrit reached only the Tête Rousse.

The sweeping snowfields that initially fanned out above the Tête Rousse could form a prime setting for a ski area. We sank in deeply, but a broken trail helped. Shortly, we reached the toe of the Aiguille du

Goûter, whose alchemy gradually changed from slanting bluffs of snow to a soaring ridge of steeply banked boulders covered with thick pockets of ice and slush.

Monotonously the harsh clean whacks of the ice ax grated against the heavy crust, spewing chips of crystal over the glistening slopes.

"Too much ice," said Norbert. "We must crampon up from here."

Now we traversed an enormous couloir that formed a natural pipeline for falling stones and slides. An overhead wire, suspended about ten feet above the ground, spans the gully. Norbert roped us up, slinging one end over the wire, so that if the slope avalanched, the high-strung rope would provide a convenient lifeline. The ground was slippery and Norbert became slightly discombobulated when I stopped in the middle of the funnel to snap a picture. He had the quaint idea that an exposed snow corridor was not the most propitious place to perform experiments with a camera.

My eyes now were riveted on the stark granite buttress that

Beginning of the Mont Blanc climb—up Aiguille du Goûter

plummeted down to us, the Aiguille du Goûter, the hulking watchtower that guards the secluded upper ramparts of the massif.

"The best way to dispose of your enemies is to force them to climb Mont Blanc," someone announced flatly. Actually, I was greatly buoyed by the prospect of the ascent.

As we moved forward, I glanced down at the sprawling, glaciated valleys that encircle the Chamonix-Saint Gervais-le Fayet-Mègeve complex, and pondered that first ascent made by Paccard and Balmat almost two centuries ago. It transfixes the imagination. With no rope between them, no railway to drop them off conveniently at the foot of the glacier, no refuge to protect them in a storm or other crisis, no support parties or trained guides to assist, no safety lines, no organized rescue squad, no antibiotics or other modern implements of first aid, no oxygen to combat an attack of pulmonary edema; and with meager food, scanty clothing, and only rough homemade "crampons" to bite into the shifting qualities of snow and ice; with no precise bearings on the staggering range of snow and ice blocks that abound for miles around, nor even a definite fix on the myriad approaches that a single ridge can offer; with the most primitive of equipment—in short, with about as much relative background and technical know-how as Columbus possessed when he caught the westwinds to the Bahamas, these two men, mere microbes in the context of the vast crucible they explored, persevered and won.

If Bourrit made scant progress on his first try, and neither de Saussure nor Paccard ever went higher than the Aiguille du Goûter by this westerly route, they cannot be faulted. For Paccard even to have uncovered the approach was itself a considerable accomplishment.

From that vantage point one evening de Saussure wrote: "The restfulness and the utter silence reigning in the vast spaces spread out before my eyes, which imagination pictured vaster still, inspired in me a feeling akin to terror; I seemed to be the sole survivor of the universe, and that it was its corpse I saw stretched beneath my feet. Sad as such ideas may be, they possess an attraction which the mind resists with difficulty. My eyes kept turning to those dark solitudes more often than towards Mont Blanc, where snows gleaming with a sort of phosphorescent light suggested thought of movement and life."[8]

As we climbed the heavy rocks, I indeed found it difficult to fathom that the great Paccard-Balmat conquest truly came to fruition under such conditions, made all the more striking in light of the pedestrian, commonplace attitude that today is marked by the hundreds who stalk the massif to its very limit, often with little risk or worry. Often—but not invariably.

"Mont Blanc can be the most gentle—or most wicked—of mountains," Desmond pointed out.

On a balmy, clear day, it offers a gorgeous, breathtaking outing that lulls one into a deep sense of fulfillment and contentment, while still demanding the utmost in conditioning. Scores have made the top in a single day; indeed, Edward Whymper asserted that by 1910 some 2,510 recorded ascents had been completed. But if the weather breaks—as often it does—and storms or avalanches gyrate over those rolling slopes, then few mountains in the world are as dangerous as Mont Blanc. It can, in a twinkling, turn into an inferno, and the consequences are frequently disastrous. Many lives have been claimed by such an abrupt metamorphosis. Mont Blanc waits calmly and patiently, but, once disturbed, it strikes with the deadliness of a rattler. In angry moments, said Leslie Stephen, when it puts on its robe of clouds and mutters with its voice of thunder, no mountain is so terrible.

The fates are capricious; never should they be taken for granted. Fortunately, when we climbed they were in good humor, and we enjoyed two buoyant days of sunshine.

Approaching Aiguille du Goûter

Our party was now working its way up the Aiguille du Goûter. Halfway up I felt strong, but then the effects of the altitude hit, and the thighs began to burn, so that every step became an act of will. To Norbert, however, it was a breeze, and he could not comprehend why his companion did not simply float up those rock pitches as though filled with helium.

I was still laboring, tiring considerably, halting frequently, when at 5:00 P.M. we attained the Refuge du Goûter, at 12,674 feet. A Hilton penthouse could not have been more welcome. The view was sweeping—Geneva, the Arve Gap, and, most impressively, the north face of the Bionnassay. One had the feeling of being in the Arctic—not a remote corner of southeast France.

"We pass the evening here," said Norbert, "but will set out before dawn." I really do not think he wanted to stop at all.

"I'll just pass out—period," I rejoined. My legs wobbled with fatigue, and my head ached from lack of oxygen, so I flopped into the sack.

Norbert practically forced me to swallow some tea and cheese. One loses his appetite when tired, but fuel is vital and one has to eat. Desmond felt fairly sharp (how jealous I was!), but generously distributed high-altitude (dextrose) pills, which he warranted would help cure the growing nausea and dizziness. Back in the States, I assured him, medicine men gave out snake oil the same way.

"How will it be climbing here in the dark?" I asked.

"Invigorating. Refreshing. It's surprising what sheer snowbanks you can surmount then, which in daytime would psych out even an experienced climber."

But the major factor was safety. If we encountered foul weather, there would be more daylight to find shelter. Also, fewer avalanches occur at night and in the early dawn, before the hot sun begins to loosen the snowpack.

"Are the upper slopes very rugged?" I continued.

"Steep. Endless. But not really hard. Just keep pushing ahead like a damn burro!"

There was a subdued atmosphere in the hut that evening. A half-dozen parties quietly made preparations for the next morning's climb to the top, each checking gear, fixing a small hot supper, exchanging sugar or salt for tea, but otherwise largely keeping to themselves. A three-man Italian contingent was feeling quite optimistic.

"No problem," they said.

I was not so sure.

Several trim-looking Korean students lay prostrate in their bunks. They had started out at 6:00 A.M. that day and taken twelve long hours to make the trip up and back to the refuge—double the time normally required for that segment of the climb. Now they planned to recuperate by spending another night there.

"Altitude sickness," their young leader repeated in slow deep breaths. "Very long climb." He had tackled more than a hundred peaks, many of them more perilous, but none more exhausting.

The beds were comfortable and warm, but cramped, leading one to curl up tightly beneath the covers. The air was chilly except in the main room where everyone lounged and a crisp fire burned.

I crawled into a bunk, beneath a thick pile of woolen blankets, at about 7:30 P.M. Norbert wanted to get up at 1 A.M., but I prevailed on him to start an hour later. Going to sleep was a different matter. For a couple of hours I tossed about, thinking about tomorrow. Would I feel better? What would it be like scratching up those long ramparts in the middle of the night? How icy would it be? Would the weather stay clear, or would a storm descend upon us, wiping out our chances? And how would I do? Would I enthusiastically swing into the climb, or drag up slowly? Would the equipment be suitable? Would the aching muscles in my legs simply halt in protest? Worse, would I hold the others back, or would I even make it?

The robust guides preferred to move fast; Desmond was reliable and steady, as though climbing were part of a natural law. The jumble of questions kept rattling through my mind, magnified by all the doubts that one typically senses the night before the ascent of a major peak. Only now it seemed to be worse. Conscious that I was overwrought, I finally lay back, tried to relax, and told myself to cheer up, for the morrow just might bring one of those truly memorable experiences. And so I sank into a kind of light trance.

At 2:00 A.M. Norbert shook me out of bed. I felt as if I had gotten no rest at all. Hastily I buckled on my boots and pack, downed some jam and coffee, and before 3:00 A.M. we all lurched out into the frosty night. Sure enough, the moon was plastered in the sky like a high-voltage searchlight, and the broad, crystalline snowfields were clearly visible, rippling with a dark, eerie grandeur. The shadowy outline of soaring Alpine summits and ridges was faintly discernible behind us. Ahead, ghost white, welling up in wide precipitous bluffs, perched the highmost tiers of Mont Blanc. Alone on the slope, we slogged up, cresting one cataract after another, suffused by the early-morning chill.

No wonder poets and artists have found an almost rhapsodic inspiration in Mont Blanc and the Alps. Seen as sunrise follows moonlight, their awesome, slumbering majesty can scarcely be matched. As our axes bit sharply into the rigid ice sheets, one by one, like countless amoebas quivering to life, the distant hamlets and vales began

Dawn streaks the upper tiers of Mont Blanc

to stir and glow. The shimmering darkness gradually surrendered to pale streaks of citron yellow, turquoise, and dark almond that friskily etched themselves against the dawn, offset against fragmented palisades and low-hanging cumulus. To our left, ominous and solitary, loomed gigantic blue ice blocks and séracs.

Except for the steady crunch of our boots and axes, we seemed to be in an icy vacuum. A few dim lights filtered up in the haunting silence.

"Chamonix," Norbert said, nodding toward the valley.

One of the oldest and most princely of Alpine settlements, it is also the most storied. The list of literary and even political lions who extolled its virtues is truly exceptional: Goethe, Percy and Mary Shelley, Victor Hugo, Charles Dickens, Jean-Jacques Rousseau, Alexandre Dumas, John Ruskin, Mark Twain, Samuel Taylor Coleridge, William Wordsworth, George Sand, François Chateaubriand, Théophile Gautier, William Windham, and, when he was not annexing Transvaal and the Fijis, Benjamin Disraeli. (Many of their essays and odes have been conveniently collected by Alpine writer Claire Eliane Engel.)

Indeed, I recalled the familiar refrain from Lord Byron's *Manfred* (1.1) from my schooldays:

> Mont Blanc is the Monarch of Mountains
> They crowned him long ago
> On a throne of rocks, in a robe of clouds
> With a diadem of snow.

From a nearby moonlit col, de Saussure was inspired to write:

> The crests that towered above us, and the intervening snows, put on the loveliest shades of rose and carmine. Over Italy a broad bank of purple extended along the whole horizon, and above the band the full moon rose in queenly majesty, vermillion-tinted. The air around us was as pure and perfectly limpid as Homer imagines that of Olympus to have been, while the valleys, filled with the vapours that had formed there, looked like abodes of the deepest darkness.
> But how shall I find words to describe the night that followed on this lovely evening, when the twilight ended and the moon shone in solitary glory, pouring floods of silvery light upon the immense amphitheatre of snow and rock that encircle our humble shelter. These fields of snow and cliffs of ice, too dazzling to be looked at in the day, what a wondrous and enchanting spectacle they present under the soft beams of the torch of night![9]

Goethe was almost cosmic:

> It shone through the night like a glow-worm and we realized at last that it was none other than Mont Blanc. It had a strange, supreme beauty, it covered us with light and the stars were massing around it. It had not their twinkling glimmer, but it looked like a vast shining body, belonging to a higher sphere. It was difficult to believe that it had earthly roots.[10]

Ruskin wrote:

> I was never dazzled by moonlight until now; but as it rose from behind Mont Blanc du Tacul, the full moon almost blinded me; it burst forth into the sky like a vast star. For an hour before, the aiguilles had appeared as dark masses against a sky looking as transparent as clear sea, edged at their summits with fleeces of clouds breaking into glorious spray and form of white fire. A meteor fell over the Dome as the moon rose; now it is so intensely bright that I cannot see the Mont Blanc underneath; the form is lost in its light.[11]

The romantic Hugo regarded the mountain as a being incarnate:

> He [Mont Blanc] can unsheathe a blizzard like a sword, and lakes tremble under his mist. He dips the blazing saw of lightning into the massive darkness of night. Immensity stoops down to kiss his brow and takes him for her lover. He is crystal azure and diamond sea. His mane of icicles, worthy of the polar lion, spreads

out like a terrifying cloak over his fierce shoulder. His precipices are too deep for chamois; on his sublime side, the twelve months are strung one above the other. He is higher, purer, grander than all of us and, were we men, we would insult him![12]

In contrast to such vivid hyperbole, Professor John Tyndall, caught in a blizzard with Alfred Wills and Auguste Balmat on the peak, described a serious case of frostbite with all the realism of an organ transplant:

> The idea that I should be in some measure the cause of [Balmat] losing his hands was horrible to me.... At length returning sensation in one hand announced itself by excruciating pain. *"Je souffre!"* he explained at intervals—words which, from a man of his iron endurance, had a more than ordinary significance. But pain was better than death, and, under the circumstances, a sign of improvement. We resumed our descent, while he continued to rub his hands with snow and brandy, thrusting them at every few paces into the mass through which we marched. At Chamouni he had skillful medical advice, by adhering to which he escaped with the loss of six of his nails—his hands were saved.[13]

The historian Jules Michelet was notably grim:

> Passersby ... went up the Prarion and took a look at Mont Blanc. But what a terrible sight it was! One is very near it, within a stone's throw. It does not look—as it does from afar—like a huge corpse laid out with its head and its feet resting on other Alps. Seen from near and from below, it stands alone, like a huge white monk swathed in a cope and cowl, dead and yet standing. Others see in it a splinter or a piece of that dead star, the pale and terrible moon, a planet of death above our own planet.
> Its wide snow cap looks like a cemetery. The monuments are dark pyramids, contrasting with the snow. Those aged daughters of the fire object to the ice; according to them, this white pall is nothing in comparison with the dark fathomless world below it.[14]

In *A Tramp Abroad,* Mark Twain wrote of a caravan of eleven persons who perished above the Grands Mulets, stating:

> They had wandered around and around in that blinding snowstorm, hopelessly lost in a space of only a hundred yards square, and when cold and fatigue vanquished them at last they scooped up their caves and lay down there to die by inches, unaware that five steps more would have brought them into the

Mont Blanc as seen from Courmayeur side

Huge iceblocks en route up Mont Blanc (upper section)

right path. They were so near to life and safety as that and did not suspect it. The thought of this gives the sharpest pangs that this tragic story conveys.[15]

Thus, Mont Blanc inspires romanticism, awe, extravagance, beauty, terror, sensitivity, mystery, excitement—almost every edge and aspect of human experience.

Chamonix itself, now seen from the upper slopes, sat in a small pocket among the giants. It was almost strange—like a tiny bassinet cast adrift among the swells that envelop it. Founded in 1091, originally called Le Prieuré, the town was once a scene of slavery and thought to be inhabited by heretics, sorcerers, and children eaters, some of whom were put to death for the suspicions they aroused. Large, confiscatory-type levies were extracted by the priory before the local populace, after buying its independence, detached itself from the Kingdom of Sardinia and, by an overwhelming vote, became a part of France on March 24, 1860.

Chamonix once could be called a quaint village. Today it is neither quaint nor a village. It is, instead, a busy, elbow-bruising city, a forest of shops, tourists, and screeching autos. It has as much charm as an avalanche. Still, it is the birthplace of mountaineering. My later visit to the little cemetery, not far from the Mer de Glace station, confirmed it. There lie Louis Lachenal, conqueror of 26,504-foot Annapurna, who perished in 1956 when he plunged into a crevasse while skiing the Vallée Blanche; Lionel Terray, killed in 1965 in a climbing accident at the Vercors, whose firsts included Makalu and Jannu in the Himalayas and who, with Lachenal, achieved the second ascent of the north face of the Eiger; Charles Bozon (Norbert's cousin), a world champion skier who died in 1964 when an ice slope avalanched while he was leading a party of student guides on the Aiguille Verte; Edward Whymper, the indomitable victor in the race to reach the summit of the Matterhorn in 1865; and many others.

We continued to move up in the dead of the night. Gaining height rapidly, smartly stepping up the long, angled snowfields, I felt much fresher, my doubts having faded into the cold night air. Henri and Desmond took the lead, keeping a steady pace. At first we walked slowly, just trying to loosen the muscles, the breathing coming heavily, then the pace quickened. Occasionally we paused to study the distant silhouetted crests, offset by that monstrous moon, asked how everyone was doing, and then plunged on. The talk was sparse, and not merely because of the slight language barrier. Each of us concentrated single-mindedly on the task at hand—actually a long stroll by many Alpine standards, and certainly a routine outing for the guides—but the intensity was now heightened, at least in my impressionable mind, by the stiff wind and chilly night air.

The lambent dawn crept upon us almost unnoticed. A thin patch of light eerily poked through the horizon, a splendid precursor that flecked and streaked playfully over the dark clouds that were arrayed in the distance. I could not see too many peaks distinctly, so I returned to the plodding and scrambling. I wondered where were all the enormous ice blocks about which I had heard. We had merely bypassed them in the darkness. I saw them—as big as houses, overpowering in their glazed, iridescent presence—on the way down.

We now reached the airy, tapered slopes of the Dôme du Goûter, which for so long was the frustrating high point for the Chamoniards. Briskly we dropped to the Col du Dôme and then ascended a steep snow cliff to the Vallot, which, at 14,312 feet, forms the last main shelf before the long, zigzag pull to the crown; it also is the crossroads for the route that comes up from the Grands Mulets.

It was 6:00 A.M. A grinding fatigue possessed me, and I promptly disgorged most of my breakfast, causing Norbert to remark that I was blotching up the landscape and damaging the ecology. This prompted me to deliver up the balance of the previous day's cuisine. Earlier in the summer I had spent two days hiking up to the 14,494-foot crest of Mount Whitney in the High Sierra, via the mountaineer's route adjoining the east face. This experience spawned the naive notion that I was amply prepared for this business on Mont Blanc. How mistaken I was! A snow-and-ice climb of 14,410-foot Mount Rainier, near Seattle, Washington, which I did later via the Emmons Glacier, would have been a more suitable preparation.

A climber, I informed Desmond, is simply a stubborn animal who can tolerate everlasting frustration. None of these hallowed "because it is there" preachments here.

We now attacked the Bosses ridge, a swirling succession of crescent-shaped embankments, festooned with bulbous cornices stacked like chalky turrets beneath the fortress summit. The Rev. Charles Hudson, who died on the Matterhorn, pioneered the Saint Gervais route with E. S. Kennedy, making the initial ascent of this soaring ridge in 1855. Twenty years later it was climbed in mid-winter. The heady prospect of reaching the top kept me ploughing on. The ice axes clinked hard into the snow and we clambered up steadily, the minutes dragging.

Once my crampons struck a piece of flat rock, and in a flash I went reeling on my back, skidding and tumbling, frantically trying to flip on my stomach and brake the fall by digging my ax into the metalliclike ice. This action whirled me around, and I was still sliding when the rope jerked taut. Norbert had struck a quick belay around both himself and his ax.

"We must go," he said flatly as, somewhat giddy, I shook off the slush. Without another word, we did.

We cut a jagged line up the arête, passing the shattered wing of an Air India plane that had crashed on Mont Blanc years before. The Bosses is very exposed, but it forms a more direct and quicker access to the summit than the Corridor or the Ancien Passage on the northwest side.

Like layers of a flocky blanket the snowfields unfurled, undulating brightly in the morning's rays. On several occasions, much to Norbert's consternation, I came to a dead halt, nearly suffocating (or so I thought) in the rarefied atmosphere.

Protruding cornice-tongues now presented themselves in a startling series of false summits, so that as I surmounted one, thinking I was *there,* the way was opened to another cavalcade of still higher slopes and bulges. I began to call these "falsies," and I heartily urge aspirants not to be misled by them. At last—it seemed like we had been climbing forever—a long arc of snow fluted out before us, gradually leveling into a broad, tablelike expanse.

Tired and happy, we jauntily planted ourselves on the summit of the Alps. It was like standing on a balcony overlooking all the roofs of Western Europe. For once I stared down, not up. It was 7:30 A.M.

Before us, an enormous black shield, austere and forbidding, was the dizzying north face of the Grandes Jorasses, whose Walker Spur presents the most classical climb in the Alps. A vast mosaic of minarets,

On the summit of Mont Blanc (Author, right, with Norbert Bozon)

ridges, and glaciers burgeoned up—the Grépon, the stylish Dru, the Dent du Géant, the Aiguille Verte, the Grand Charmoz. The rugged Frêney and Brouillard pillars, two of the most difficult of some twenty approaches up Mont Blanc, lay below. The northeast skyline was fractured by the sturdy bulk of the Grand Combin, and behind it, forty miles away, shooting up in sharp, steepled purity, reposed the Matterhorn.

One could now begin to grasp the enormity of the Mont Blanc massif. About three miles high and ten miles wide, it stands astride three borders, looping from Martigny in Switzerland to Saint Gervais—a distance of some thirty miles. From afar it looks akin to a massive camel stretched at length; atop it, one is entranced by the limitless voids and thin, craggy needles that abound, and the prodigious scale of its inimitable bulk.

An observatory was once erected on the summit spine; lacking a rock foundation, it fitfully broke up and sank into the ice.

Nonsensically I prowled around looking for Paccard's and Balmat's footsteps, or the sitzmark that de Saussure happily must have created when he finally puffed his way up here. After other such irreverent antics, we started down. I led, followed by Norbert. It was a long trek, the snow having deteriorated into soft, wet slush. The Grands Mulets provides the fastest avenue of descent, so naturally we backtracked all the way to Saint Gervais.

Grandes Jorasses north wall

45

The spectacular range of Mont Blanc. *Courtesy Office Du Tourisme, Chamonix-Mont-Blanc.*

"Like swimming in slop," I said, sinking in to the kneecaps. At other times I almost sprinted down.

We met the Italians as we reached the Vallot. One of them had turned back because of the effects of altitude; the other two had not yet ceased putting one foot doggedly in front of the other, and they eventually reached the top.

Lower down we altered course and traipsed onto the Bionnassay glacier, carefully steering around fearsomely deep chasms and crevasses, and ducking beneath a torrent of wind-chiseled séracs. The cool air was a delightful spur, and, after hours trailed by, we came onto easy red-rock crags that signaled we were near the station.

At 2:30 P.M., after almost twelve straight hours on the snow and ice, we shook hands and passed around a winebag.

Thoughts of that first ascent in 1786 still lingered. Back in Chamonix, I noted that the handsome commemorative statue in the center of town depicts de Saussure and Balmat. One looks at length for a monument to the neglected Paccard, which is found embodied only in an obscure plaque hung in the entrance of the old Hotel de Ville. A street also has been named after him.

Balmat, of course, enjoyed much acclaim during his lifetime. The king of Sardinia permitted him to use the title "Balmat dit Mont Blanc," and Napoleon Bonaparte promoted him to the post of tax collector. He came to a mysterious end in 1834. Ever active, he disappeared while searching for gold ore near the Glacier des Fonds. His body was never found and foul play was suspected. Paccard died peacefully in his hometown in 1827, at the age of seventy.

As for the illustrious de Saussure, although he was a moderate, the boiling aftermath of the French Revolution swept away most of his personal fortune and helped wreck his health. For a brief period he served as president of the Constituent Assembly. Riots and insurrections were common. A threatening mob once held him and his family at bay in his home for a week. Disabled by several strokes, no longer able to wander among his cherished mountains, and ensnared by political events, he spent his last years completing his classic, *Voyages dans les Alpes.* On January 22, 1799, shortly after his beloved Geneva forfeited its independence and was annexed by France, he passed away.

Ironically, the following year his widow and son personally entertained Napoleon at their lodge in Geneva when the future emperor was en route to the Great Saint Bernard Pass, through which he led 30,000 troops to the victorious battle of Marengo—a decisive event that helped shape the course of history and propel him to the leadership of the French empire.

2

The Matterhorn Revisited: In the Tracks of Whymper

> *When the enigma is solved the sphinx dies. Let a man but know that one of his fellows has succeeded in performing any action, and that action appears less difficult. The real merit is his who first does the deed.... He had thought himself the Matterhorn's master; thenceforth the Matterhorn was master of him.*
>
> —Guido Rey, *The Matterhorn*
>
> *A momentary negligence may destroy the happiness of a lifetime.*
> —Edward Whymper, *Scrambles Amongst the Alps*

Zermatt nestles like a piece of Meissen china in the lap of the Pennine Alps. It is unique, timeless. Yet the face of the tiny hamlet has experienced many changes in its 700-year history.

Only a little more than a century ago its hardy dwellers salvaged a meager living out of hunting chamois, separating curd from whey to make cheese, herding goats and cows over the vast bare hillsides, and serving as porters for tourists who trekked high over the Théodule Col to Italy. As for the astounding rings of peaks that hovered over them, these were warily treated as the abodes of demons, monsters, and dragons. Tumbling avalanches that spewed their fury over glaciers and snowfields were regarded as the devil's own handiwork. Mountains were to be feared, not climbed.

Today, a sparkling, vibrant town has emerged in the Valais, one its forebears would scarcely recognize. Neon signs flicker along the main street, itself often so clogged as to be virtually impassable. Bars and discotheques abound. There are more tourists than permanent residents. Skiing, not climbing, dominates, bringing with it the exuberant clatter of the latest in fiberglass skis and highback boots, in summer as well as winter. No longer do visitors and townsfolk gather in the church square to follow climbing parties through a powerful telescope. Indeed, a clear view of the famous, arching ridge that looms directly above the valley is partially obscured by the bespangled facades of new buildings. Automobiles are still prohibited, although they may be parked below. In the spring, fields of orange and blue tents sprout nearby, where hundreds of backpackers and wayfarers congregate. The once-invincible peaks are strung over with more than two dozen trams and lifts, boasting capacities of 18,000 persons per hour, serving 42

Winter cloaks the magnificent east and north faces of the Matterhorn (14,689 ft.); Hörnli ridge is in the center

pistes covering 60 miles in three distinct areas. The cumulative vertical drop for the skier is more than 13 miles. Another 200 miles of hiking trails lace the landscape.

The statistics—like the Alps—overwhelm.

There is one constant, unchanging, ageless aspect of Zermatt: the Matterhorn.

Twenty years before I had visited the area and, one bright crisp dawn, climbed to the summit of that staggering, flamboyant 14,689-foot cathedral of ice and snow.

Inevitably, I returned to Switzerland's Valais.

The green-dirty switchback trail swung high, leaving Schwarzsee and the furious rumblings of the Mattervisp gorge whispering behind. It all looked vaguely familiar. Charlie Brown, my companion who I had just joined on the Winkelmatten tram, adjusted his rucksack and emptied a wine flask. We both settled into the leisurely gait that in two hours would take us to the Hörnlihütte at the base.

A veteran mountaineer, Charlie, from Denver, had scaled more than a dozen 14,000-footers in the States. This, his first trip to Europe, had been frustrating. A storm thwarted his plans to attack the flank of the Eiger, and a try for the Jungfrau misfired when his guide was called away on an emergency search for two climbers. So he left the Bernese Oberland and migrated to inimitable Zermatt.

The notorious challenge of the Matterhorn, and the rich, intriguing tapestry of its Alpine history, still make it one of the most tantalizing lures in Europe. It remains, at once, one of the grandest and most awesome of sights—a rock fang slashing into the sky like an imperious giant, nature's masterful testimonial to itself. Even though hundreds parade up and down it every season, it still looks savage, untouchable, unspoiled. People, it has been said, attempt it mainly because it *is* the Matterhorn.

Naturally, Charlie wanted to know why I was interested in making the try again. Why indeed? For several years I had not scaled anything higher than a barstool. Although I had skied considerably, I certainly was in no shape to climb—a wholly different physical endeavor. Arriving in August to enjoy easy glacier schussing on the Plateau Rosa, I had no thought of traversing any further than a T-bar would pull me. But the Matterhorn, looming there day after day in solitary, pyramidal grace, silently drew me in. Soon I was inexplicably standing in the bergfuhrers' office, had rented a pair of vibrams and crampons, slipped into khakis, and headed up. It was like hypnosis. I mean, could I reject the idea without a try? I well remembered the lung-searing thrill of that first climb, and here I was—again.

Charlie moved evenly, without effort, as I cheerfully related that '51 experience. I had gone with two University of Oregon classmates, Herb Nill and Bill Byrd, the latter then a guide in the Grand Teton National Park. We planned to rope on with Johnny Churchill, a wiry, glue-fingered daredevil who flashed up sheer walls with lynxlike suppleness. Once Johnny had ventured part of the way up the Matterhorn by moonlight. This feat scarcely endeared him to the local pros who felt they had enough potential problems handling rescues by day much less by searchlight. At first Johnny was to lead us but, having previously made the ascent and incurred the wrath of the guides because of his unorthodox antics, he changed his mind. When Bill suffered a sprained ankle, I enlisted a guide, Franz Perren, who escorted me up in a vigorous nine-hour workout. Later Bill also made it. The next season Johnny, who invariably pushed himself to the outer limit, fell and was killed in the Alps.

The day we had arrived in Zermatt those many years ago, with Bill

High on the ridge of the Matterhorn

assuring us that many neophytes had attained the summit and not to worry, Otto Furrer, one of the most renowned of all Swiss mountaineers and a world-champion skier, perished on the mountain. A rope broke while he was taking an American girl up the Italian side—an ugly reminder that the Matterhorn can be vengeful. Somberly we watched the long procession that bore his remains across the gorge to a final resting place.

As we wended past the edelweiss line and purple gentian, Charlie and I inevitably reflected that the originator of the whole Matterhorn obsession—the intrepid Englishman Edward Whymper, then only twenty-five years old—had trod this same route when spearheading the initial conquest on July 14, 1865. The ill-fated party had experienced the most exhilarating of successes, narrowly beating an Italian rival, Jean-Antoine Carrel, who was waging a simultaneous assault from the opposite side. It was one of the last great Alpine peaks to fall, Mont Blanc already having been conquered seventy-nine years before. Tragedy struck when four members of the Whymper party fell 4,000 feet to their deaths during the descent—an accident wrapped in mystery to this day.

"Some say it is the corniest mountain in the world," I remarked to Charlie. "But it's a heck of a climb. Anyhow, just think of all those who *haven't* scaled it."

"Like who?"

"Marco Polo, for one. Now we know *he* never traveled this way."

"True. Nor Caesar nor even Hannibal and his elephants."

"And how about Gandhi, Lady Godiva, and Toulouse-Lautrec. Failures all. Just think: Alexander conquered the world but never the Matterhorn—even though it was right here the whole time."

By the time we blasphemously eliminated everybody right down through Tiny Tim, Steve McQueen, and Spiro Agnew, we were at the Hörnlihütte, nestled on a 10,758-foot ledge at the base of the mammoth obelisk. It was 5:30 P.M., and the Alpine sunset was a sweeping polychrome of cerulean blue, magenta, and pale gold. Zermatt, tucked in the vale like a string of silver pearls, lay a mile away as the stone drops. The Hörnli ridge, and the great north and east faces, rose 4,000 feet straightaway, now ghost-lost in the late-afternoon mist. Noble as it appears from a distance, at firsthand the igneous crystalline spire is an ugly clump—"a heap of rubble glued together with ice," as someone described it.

There was little activity at the hut. Most of those who had climbed that chilly day already had departed. Striding directly toward me was my guide, Richard Lehner, about six feet two inches, a young, hard, no-nonsense sort who quickly inspected his latest recruit. Since I had

The Matterhorn by twilight

made the assault before, the head of the bergfuhrers mischievously assigned me one of their strongest guides.

"Many go to 12,000 feet without difficulty, then the thin air is felt," Richard said in unadorned English, laying out all the problems in advance. "It was not good today—icy. We use crampons from above the Solvay." The inference was that I would be fortunate not to wilt after a couple of hours.

"You rent the boots," he noted. "The soles are light—you will tire. Do you climb recently? To climb well one must climb much."

"Made it before," I said. Richard stared at me incredulously and disappeared into the kitchen. I did not see him again until morning.

"That," I nodded to Charlie, "is one tough hombre. The Vince Lombardi of the Alps."

Charlie's guide, Georges, was a sackful of laughs by comparison. He held a similar five-minute drill and pronounced Charlie and his equipment fit. Then he too evaporated into the kitchen.

Supper that night would not have exactly shamed Maxim's—two bowls of pea soup, a rib steak that resisted to its death the prospect of being sliced up, a handful of hard bread, and warm tea. Most of the talk centered on the day's efforts. It had been unusually arduous. No one had started before 6:00 A.M. because of the thick fog and ice, and several did not return for eleven or twelve hours—a long time to be

53

Hörnli ridge—as viewed from the hut near the base

scrambling around on that big peak. Dark clouds often converge in the afternoon, after the morning's rays, which focus directly on the ridge, burn off the ice, and turn snow to slush. The object is to reach the crest and come down fast and early.

Jim, a young schoolteacher from Seattle who had been climbing for several years, returned triumphant but near collapse after a painful eleven-hour pull—the realization, he said, of his life's ambition. He looked as though he had come off a torture rack and scarcely could prop himself up to eat. Rather than take the two-hour traipse back to Schwarzsee, he chose to rest another night at the hut. Chatting with him, I knew a similar encounter awaited, but for some unfathomable reason I was eager to get at it.

One of the guides spoke of an English girl who had lost her life in a 2,000-foot fall to the Matterhorngletscher two weeks before. A good climber, she had come to the hut alone, met an American, and they decided to share the same rope. When they reached the Solvay refuge, about halfway up, the American was tired and did not proceed. A tricky couloir billows up from that point—not terribly difficult but a pitch that demands caution and where the exposure is considerable. Still feeling strong, the girl elected to go on. A moment after she and her companion split up, she slipped and plummeted all the way to the glacier.

At 9:00 P.M. the lights went out in the dorm. Charlie was calm, organized, confident—and hopeful that the fickle weather would hold.

"There is no predicting it," I said. "Twenty years ago we had to make three trips up to this hut—a four-to-five-hour hike in those days since there was no tram to Schwarzsee. The weather was clear at 3:00 A.M. on two of those occasions—and then, within minutes, a heavy storm broke in unseen from the south. No one could climb. We got so discouraged that we left for a couple of weeks, bummed around, and came back before finally making it on the third attempt. It's all luck."

Charlie sorted out his pack, laying in an ice ax, nylon rope, crampons, gloves, sweater, raisins, and cheese. We knew it was important that the ice melt off the lower sections.

"Whatever the conditions," he observed, "one has to respect the mountain."

Kids and elderly ladies have scaled the Matterhorn. The first woman to accomplish it was Lucy Walker, at age forty-five, in 1871. A television program was even held on its summit to mark the hundredth anniversary of the Whymper ascent. Yet the cemetery is lined with headstones of guides and climbers, each ominously designating the date and circumstance of a fatal slip. The Matterhorn is a chiseled staircase, but one mistake can be serious. More persons—an estimated 150—probably have been killed on its escarpments than on any other mountain in the Alps, with the possible exception of Mont Blanc. It is not untypical for the toll to reach a half-dozen per year, particularly since many aspirants are not well prepared.

The massive bulk of Monte Rosa (seen from the Matterhorn)

The usual wakeup is at 3:00 to 3:30 A.M. Unable to sleep, I heard sporadic stirrings and boots being laced. Finally I dozed off. Three Japanese students had in fact gotten up at 2:00 A.M., readied all their gear, and waited uncomplainingly for two hours for their guides to arise.

"It's 4:20," I heard Charlie say. I dashed into the room where the guides were skein coiling some rope. Richard was fuming. "The wakeup overslept," someone muttered. Later I found that a couple of the guides were tired from the previous day's long effort and wanted the extra sleep.

After surviving a visit to a men's room that undoubtedly had not been fumigated since World War II, I swallowed a roll and tea downstairs. Several parties already had left, although the Japanese kids were still sitting patiently. Charlie was all set.

"Twenty years ago I didn't need these," I told him, pointing to the crampons.

"I've heard all about 1951," he replied. "But this isn't *that* year."

The arête was barely perceptible in the early dawn—like a flickering candle that could not quite light up. A piercing wind whipped at us. But the sky was flawless—no clouds, no storms, just a luminous canvas of stars and a fading half-moon.

Richard linked me up with a bowline, and at 5:00 A.M. we started out—up the path behind the hut and onto a low scree terrace that leads to the sword-shaped ridge. We edged around a few initial rock ribs, easy corners that still had to be handled delicately since the mountain was dew-wet and I was not confident of my boots.

"You have not climbed in long time. I can tell—here where it is simple," he said, no doubt cursing whatever fate had ordained that my life be placed in his keeping for the day—especially since I was insistent that we go all the way.

The slope now spun out broadly, glittering, crag faced, a streaky mixture of intricately sculptured spikes and creases. Each move presented a minute confrontation, a fixed challenge to be met and solved, followed by another, featuring its own unique twists and variables, demanding utmost concentration.

"We start late," Richard said. "We must go fast, not stop. Sitting and resting do no good. We find they do not make you less tired." This curious theory is, in fact, largely true.

Richard was a veritable bull, thick muscled yet nimble. He was not drawing a deep breath. The mountains obviously were his element, and he loved the beauty of the climb. He also was relentless.

"Go up—not to side," he exclaimed, buffeting me with advice. "We never reach summit if you move sideways all day!" Another pitch. I shinnied up on belly and knees.

"You climb this way?" he observed in puzzlement. "You sure it was the Matterhorn." It was not a question; it was a proclamation.

"Short steps," he ordered. "Long steps make you tire. Always three points of contact." I only grimaced.

We passed a party that had commenced much earlier—a phenomenon that was to repeat itself throughout the climb. I was glued to Richard's butt.

About 200 feet above us I spotted Charlie crawling up a jagged flange, with Georges belaying ahead of him. They were moving at a rapid clip. Of course, so was I, since I had to be within a rope's length of Richard.

Looking directly down the spine of the Hôrnli arête

Slowly and inexorably the dank, glossy morn crept upon us, like a fine rosé filling an empty glass, drop by lazy drop, until the warmth and fragrance were spread throughout the undulating hills and meadows. Hazily etched peaks now sprang into bright, radiant relief. The ridge itself pulsed with the scratchy sound of boots and ice axes, and firm but intermittent voices. The Matterhorn was, it seemed, now fully awake.

Shifting onto the vast east face, we fell into a consistent pace, working one problem at a time, around protrusions, up gullies, veering back and forth as my guide sought solid footings and holds, and invariably found them. Even as the route steepened, and Richard let out some cord, there was ample room for maneuver. The early sun caressed my back. I was actually overdressed.

Ranged above us were many of the fifteen or so parties that were tackling the mountain. The Matterhorn flamed up in infinite ceramics of tawny, ruffled outcroppings and precipitous bluffs. The Monte Rosa's ermine saucer and the green bowels of the Valais were light years away. Trying to ignore the chronic fatigue was itself a chief problem. Only the brief pauses when Richard surged ahead fifteen to thirty feet gave partial relief. Yet we continued to pass many climbers, and I could only conclude that my guide was aiming for the track record—or to punish me for some imagined evil I had perpetrated by merely presenting myself in the first place. Stamina and persistence—not technical expertise—are the keys to the ascent.

An hour passed, and a piece of the second. The ridge and face were a complex of jutting edges that in turn swirled into a catena of uplifted cones. We surmounted a long rock strut called the Eseltritte and then a turret leading to the throat of a narrow combe that spewed forth a pesky series of stonefalls. I recalled that, in addition to the overhang below the top, there were two thorny couloirs—one just before and the other above the Solvay. I recognized the channel as we nudged up it, gingerly planting my vibrams on tiny nodules, scratching my shins and face, clinging to whatever fixture the mountain could spare. We achieved the Solvay shelf and I promptly sprawled out, hoping that fate might somehow liberate me from the duty of ever having to stir again.

"We take two minutes," called Richard, generously passing out time as though it were one of his personal belongings. He also offered some cold Chablis—a small sign that he now considered me worthy to be hitched to the same rope.

There was a brief respite at the Moseley slab while a couple of parties worked it. The pitch is named after an American doctor who, climbing unroped, fell from the spot in 1879. Thinking of the English girl, I studied the glacier and pondered the slight difference—an inch or

On Matterhorn's long upper snowfields

less—that had so abruptly snuffed out her young life. As Whymper wrote, "A momentary negligence may destroy the happiness of a lifetime." Richard yanked me back to the matter at hand.

Verglas appeared now, and a heavy snowpack loomed ahead. Even in mid-summer the upper tiers of the mountain lie shrouded in snow. The thin glass-ice was treacherous now, and when I slipped a few times—perilously enough to startle—Richard snapped the lifeline taut, remindful of a sleek barracuda striking at bait. Fitfully, the real danger came from falling stones and snow loosened by the sun or cast down by climbers above—plus any individual's own single instant of carelessness.

Far to our right a party was attempting the north face, making solid progress. Together with the Grandes Jorasses, Eiger, Cima Grande, and Piz Badile, this forms one of the elite north faces in the Alps, first ascended by two German brothers, Toni and Franz Schmid, in 1931, and not climbed in winter until 1962, then by the Swiss, Hilti von Allmen and Paul Etter, with a pair of Austrian and German teams right behind them. In February 1965, during the one hundredth anniversary year of the first ascent, Walter Bonatti, from Turin, made Alpine history by conquering the face solo, in winter.

As we passed an enormous red abutment—the Roter Turm—and embarked on a large snow expanse, we sat down (glorious rest!) to attach our crampons—a siesta that was virtually more than my leader could bear. I fumbled with my straps, adjusted and reset them, switched them from one boot to the other, dawdled, and otherwise nursed every precious second out of that luxurious pitstop. Still my legs felt like petrified logs. I also lost a glove, which trickled down the slope and doubtlessly spent a quiet winter resting in the séracs below. I did not need it.

"We climb or we sit," mused Richard. We lurched again.

The crampons were of incalculable help, whether on snow, verglas, or even rock.

The panoply of cracks and wedges crunched underfoot as we clambered toward the vertex of the ridge. The ice and snow also grew firmer.

At last we attained the shoulder that flares out dramatically about 700 feet below the top, and crossed over to the north side, to the fearsome, invincible-looking Tête du Cervin and a series of fixed ropes. When Whymper climbed, this convex overhang posed by far the most sinister challenge, forcing lengthy traverses; this may still be done but consumes considerable time, hence the ropes. A truly busy situation was now presented, for claiming a rope was akin to waiting for an escalator on ladies' night at Dodger Stadium. You needed reservations. But nothing deterred Richard. We crisply swept by climbers who had started an hour earlier, some because they were three or four in a party, but primarily because my bergfuhrer conceived himself to be the Mario Andretti of the Hörnli freeway. We cut lines, and if they were occupied crawled parallel with them.

Again I slithered, now throwing Richard off-balance. A spontaneous static belay around a pointed bollard slammed me stiff and I finally grabbed an ice step. This adroit maneuver by Richard averted a ticklish problem, not to mention the personal embarrassment of our becoming candidates for permanent residency in the little cemetery near the church.

The Rochers Rouges featured about half a dozen ropes altogether, and I vividly recalled that hoisting one's weight up them at that altitude (14,000 feet plus) was the most grueling part of the whole affair. Nor was my memory faulty. We tugged and scrambled, loosely flapping around above a grim mile-high void, feathered by a light breeze, finally reaching a small saddle. Pausing, I gazed across at the white-flecked massifs that rimmed the valley, and at the Plateau Rosa where an anthill of skiers was beginning to form. The rest, I knew, was a clear strike up the Unter Dach to the top. We plunged up a wide reach of snowfields. There was a crackling sense of anticipation. Charlie was sitting over to

The author atop the Matterhorn (second ascent)

the side with Georges, both having just preceded us to the crest.

"Fifty steps," they called. It was hard to figure. The cornice seemed to spiral austerely upward without end. But in moments the entire horizon whirled and we came onto a thin, gnarled spur that buckled up sharply, curved, and then suddenly flattened—the Matterhorn summit. There was, in short, nowhere else to go. Only 350 feet long, the top is blade-thin, ragged, and magnificent. It also looked unchanged from a vividly remembered moment twenty years ago.

Directly athwart us was the cross that marks the slightly lower Italian crown, a flag whipping smartly in the breeze. It was 8:40 A.M. Wave after wave of bright, alabaster peaks—the Mishabels, Lyskamm, the Dent Blanche—bobbed up stunningly in all directions. We could almost reach out and touch the whalelike hump of Mont Blanc and the tentacles of the Weisshorn; to the north the Eiger stood clear. It was a richly sculptured masterwork.

Fellow climbers rest and enjoy the view from just below the summit. From left, Richard Lehrer, Charlie Brown, and Georges.

Classic view of Matterhorn's east face, Hörnli ridge, and north face (left to right).

Shortly, we joined Charlie and Georges just below the pinnacle.

"So," Richard said finally, "Why do you climb here again?"

Silence. Charlie nibbled at a chicken leg. "Just trying to retrieve his misspent youth."

Richard shook his head, no doubt figuring some willow-headed Yank was off on a tangent again. "You won't find it here," he announced. "Try a discotheque."

"My eternal thanks for telling me now," I retorted. We all leaned back to savor the dazzling scenes that stretched out interminably from our perch.

"The Whymper party slipped over there," stressed Richard as we made the descent of the Tête du Cervin.

We glissaded the snowfields, backed down the ropes, cautiously worked through a long series of shafts and gullies, retracing nearly each step taken the way up.

"This is different than the Grand Teton," observed Charlie. "There you rappel part of the way down."

The Japanese were just reaching the ropes when we passed them. In view of the late hour and the fact that weather was forming, we did not think they would make it but later learned they did.

Charlie and I alternately led the way, off the snow cornice, onto ice, then late-morning slush and bare quartz and shale, all fanning out in a fabric of tortuously plunging strands. After almost three hours the Hörnli hut could be discerned, seemingly minutes away. Virtually another hour passed, each turn revealing another string of crags and buttresses, those we had surmounted on the ascent posing different problems on the way down. The hut appeared to be as far away as ever.

For many, a descent is the most troublesome, since one faces outward, toward a far valley, and vertigo often sets in. Viewed from Zermatt, the Hörnli ridge looks almost vertical, yet in profile it really slopes at about forty-five to sixty degrees. But such knowledge, while shakily staring out at endless vistas, can prove quite useless, especially to the inexperienced. My own reaction was the opposite; coming down those long ramparts was far less physically demanding. Concentration was, as ever, the major concern. After more than seven hours, staying alert and insuring the precise placement of each hold, no matter how obvious, was not automatic. My feet often insisted on fastening onto spots different from where ordered. Richard was at times almost apoplectic.

At last we slid down a bluff and onto a slight knoll where kids were playing tag and others were lounging in chairs, their binoculars trained on that huge classic arête. Across the way, the Théodule Pass was lined with hikers coming up from both Zermatt and Cervinia. We walked into the hut at 12:15 P.M.

The lower section of Hörnli ridge

Clouds now clustered around the mountain, sealing off the upper sections. It was hard to accept: the Matterhorn climb was over.

In fact, neither Charlie's intestinal system nor mine had quite accepted it yet. Thoroughly dehydrated, we disposed of boundless quantities of beer and juice—which, as Charlie said, was "like trying to fill a washbasin with an eyedropper." No drink was safe from our reach.

As for Richard, he was now semicontent with the effort. A slight smile—his first of the day—crossed his face as we shook hands and parted.

Like hundreds of others, we had climbed. And I, alas, had done it (or to be more precise, outlasted it) twice. But despite the comings and goings of the multitudes, the Matterhorn will forever be Edward Whymper's mountain. Never before has one man's fate been so indissolubly linked with one mountain.

* * *

Edward Whymper was an intense, wiry individual, square-jawed and broad shouldered, who graduated from a career as an artist and illustrator to become the most noted climber of his age. Born in London on April 27, 1840, the second of Josiah Whymper's eleven children, of Dutch extraction, he left school fourteen years later to become an apprentice to his father, a tradesman specializing in art and wood engraving. Whymper was essentially a loner. But his proficiency in drawing attracted the attention of a publisher, William Longman, who commissioned him to visit the continent to make illustrations for a book being prepared on the Alps. The assignment changed Whymper's life, and the course of mountaineering history.

When he first glimpsed the Matterhorn in 1860, he described it casually in his diary: "... it may be compared to a sugar loaf set on a table; the sugar loaf should have its head knocked on one side. Grand it is, but beautiful I think it is not."[1]

Came the summer of 1861 and Whymper was back in the Alps with another commission. Originally his publisher had wanted him to make some renderings of 12,973-foot Mont Pelvoux in the Central Dauphine Alps, to record a climb by another Englishman. When that attempt failed, Whymper made the ascent himself with a party of five, thereby embarking on a new career.

Mountaineering's Golden Age traditionally is said to have been launched in 1854, with the conquest of the Wetterhorn by a party led by a young English lawyer, Alfred Wills. In rapid succession, the Mönch, Dom, Grand Combin, Dent Blanche, Lyskamm, Grandes Jorasses, Taschhorn, Monte Rosa, plus scores of others, were climbed. Of the remainder, the Weisshorn and Matterhorn were acknowledged to be the biggest prizes. When Professor John Tyndall topped the Weisshorn, Whymper fastened his attention on the giant obelisk of Zermatt. It was widely thought to be completely inaccessible. To Whymper its conquest became an abiding, irresistible challenge. It was an era of "firsts" in mountaineering—and he must be the first to claim the Matterhorn.

In his celebrated account, *Scrambles Amongst the Alps,* Whymper was later to write lyrically:

> There seemed to be a *cordon* drawn around it, up to which one might go, but no farther. Within that invisible line djinns and effreets were supposed to exist—the Wandering Jew and the spirits of the damned. The superstitious natives in the surrounding valleys (many of whom firmly believed it to be not only the highest

Edward Whymper—conqueror of the Matterhorn.
Courtesy Swiss National Tourist Office

mountain in the Alps, but in the world) spoke of a ruined city on its summit wherein the spirits dwelt; and if you laughed, they gravely shook their heads; told you to look yourself to see the castles and walls, and warned one against a rash approach, lest the infuriate demons from their impregnable heights hurl down vengeance for one's derision. Such were the traditions of the natives.[2]

As for the Matterhorn, it "looks equally imposing from whatever side it is seen. It never seems commonplace; and in this respect, and in regard to the impression it makes upon spectators, it stands almost alone amongst mountains. It has no rivals in the Alps, and but few in the world."[3]

Often Whymper was sardonic or whimsical. Of one guide he said: "The man smiled when called a liar, shrugged his shoulders when referred to as a thief, but drew his knife when spoken of as a pig." On

Italian inns: "It is commonly said amongst Alpine tourists that goat-flesh represents mutton, and mule does service for beef and chamois. I reserve my opinion upon this point until it has been shown what becomes of all dead mules. But I may say, I hope, without wounding the susceptibilities of my acquaintances among the Italian inn keepers, that it would tend to smoothen their intercourse with their guests if requests for solid food were less frequently regarded as criminal."[4]

On the same visit Whymper encountered for the first time Jean-Antoine Carrel, then thirty-two, a brawny stonemason from the Italian village of Valtournanche, whose driving ambition to conquer the Matterhorn (or Mont Cervin, as it is also called) equalled his own. The destinies of these two men, who became both friends and rivals, were to be forever interlocked. A first-rate rock climber, Carrel was absolutely fearless. Though not a professional guide, he had been attempting the Matterhorn since 1857, during the first of which exploits he unceremoniously wound up stumbling into a crevasse. Whymper's initial impression was vivid. Carrel was the "cock of his valley," a well-made, resolute-looking fellow, with a certain defiant air that was rather taking.

Whymper sought to retain him as a guide, but when Carrel insisted on a comrade of his joining the party, Whymper demurred. Instead he set out with another party from Breuil on the south, ascended the Col du Lion, which leads to the Italian ridge, then a rock staircase up to a difficult chimney, at about 12,650 feet; it was swept with falling stones. By chance, Whymper met Carrel on the same climb, and the latter, with his uncle, Jean-Jacques, reached an altitude of 13,230 feet—the highest point yet attained.

Up to that time, there had been only a handful of attempts, almost all from the Breuil side. From there, the southwest (or Italian) arête rises in a succession of tiers that, in due course, became known as the staircase, the Tête du Lion, the Col du Lion, the Great Tower, the Crête du Coq, the Cravate, and Pic Tyndall, the last major shoulder below the summit.

The Matterhorn is like a four-pointed star, perched squarely on the Swiss-Italian frontier. To the north, toward Switzerland, the Hörnli ridge splits the north and east faces; the Zmutt ridge spins off in an elongated spine to the northwest, while the precipitous Furggen drops southeasterly to glacial ice fields. The fourth major ridge, the southwest, plunges directly into Italy. Excepting only the three Parker brothers, who in 1860 and 1861 made lone but rather remarkable efforts up the east face from Zermatt, no one had undertaken attempts from the Swiss side.

The reason was simple: the massive Hörnli arête and the adjoining east face, as viewed from Zermatt, look almost vertical. In contrast, the southwest ridge appears to slope at a much gentler angle. So virtually every assault had been made from the southern flank, and the denizens there became anxious that success be achieved from Italy, not Zermatt, in the expectation that Breuil would emerge as a favored tourist center in the Alps.

No one was more sensitive to this than Carrel. He had twice fought in the army for the glory of Italy, believed fervently in its efforts to wrest its independence from the Austro-Hungarian Empire, and was locally known as *Il Bergsagliere*, the mountain soldier. Making the first ascent was, for him, nothing less than a patriotic duty—provided it was from Breuil.

In 1862 Whymper returned once more to the scene. Within three weeks he mounted five attempts, two of them with Carrel, one alone.

On this solo effort, Whymper, carrying a crude grapnel claw and a wrought-iron ring as his equipment, reached 13,400 feet, above the Great Tower and Crête du Coq, on the southwest ridge. Going down,

Jean-Antoine Carrel—the stonemason from Valtournanche. *Courtesy Swiss National Tourist Office*

while rounding a corner, Whymper slipped and fell 200 feet in a tumble of seven or eight bounds, at one juncture spinning headlong 50 to 60 feet through the air, finally braking himself within a few paces of an 800-foot drop. He returned to the valley shaken and temporarily beaten—but still determined. He had in fact scrambled higher on the peak than any man before him.

Within a week he was off again with a hunchback guide, Luc Meynet, but after inching high on the Cravate he was thwarted by a series of smooth walls. Whymper felt that he should return to obtain ladders to surmount some of the steep parts—and link up again with Carrel.

Ironically, he now learned that Professor Tyndall, with J.J. Bennen acting as the guide and Carrel as a porter, had attained 13,970 feet, to the final shoulder, before being turned back by a deep cleft. Apparently Carrel was aware of a possible way around the problem. But when queried about it, Carrel, with characteristic independence, said, "We are porters, ask your guide." So, by a throw of luck, Tyndall and Carrel himself were probably deprived of the victory that later came to Whymper. It is clear that Carrel personally—and unswervingly—intended to lead the successful assault, and would settle for nothing less.

In 1863 Whymper made his seventh attempt, again with Carrel, but violent lightning and a snowstorm defeated them.

The ascent of the Matterhorn was no longer merely a deeply felt ambition. It became an unshakable obsession—for Whymper as well as for Carrel, though for different reasons. For Whymper, the mountain represented not a sporting challenge, but an arrogant enemy that must be defeated, by any route and any means. Carrel, on the other hand, regarded the Matterhorn as his personal preserve; he felt that the first ascent must be his simply because he and, even more, his native Valtournanche were entitled to it as a matter of right. Thus the lines were drawn.

The following two years Whymper made a spectacular series of climbs with Michel-Auguste Croz, a respected and highly accomplished Chamonix guide with whom Whymper formed a close and lasting attachment. Of all the guides with whom he ever traveled, stated Whymper, Croz was the one most after his own heart. With Croz, Whymper made numerous and impressive first ascents: Les Écrins, Aiguille d'Argentière, Aiguille de Trélatête, west summit of the Grandes Jorasses, Mont Dolent, Grand Cornier, and several original traverses of high cols. Together they scaled the Dent Blanche—his most difficult climb, Whymper was later to say.

In 1865 another attempt by Whymper on the Matterhorn, this time by a new route up a couloir to the south of the Furggen ridge, with Croz, Meynet, a prominent guide named Christian Almer, and Franz Biener,

**Matterhorn
(from southeast)**

1 — Col du Lion
2 — Great Tower
3 — Cravate
4 — Shoulder
5 — Tyndall's farthest
6 — Summit (14,689 feet)
7 — Furggen ridge
8 — Hörnli ridge
9 — East face

was stalemated. So Whymper trekked to Courmayeur, from where Croz had to depart due to a prior engagement. Whymper, with Almer, Biener, and a surveyor, Anthony Adams-Reilly, were able to achieve the virgin ascent of the vaunted Aiguille Verte—a feat that created much resentment among the Chamonix guides since none of them had partaken in the effort. In eighteen days Whymper had mounted an astounding campaign, scaling 100,000 vertical feet, much of it over new ground.

But not the Matterhorn.

By now Whymper's sharp artist's eye had caught the fact that, even in summer, the upper terraces of the Matterhorn's east face were encased in snow. He observed that, when viewed in profile, the east face tilted at only forty to forty-five degrees, a much shallower angle than the sheer verticality it appears to possess when seen head-on. Whymper also was aware the mountain was composed of layers of stratified beds, and noted the rock structures tilted downward, toward the climber, on the Italian ridge, making the route difficult, even though the angle of ascent did not look steep.

It was not until after my repulse in 1863, wrote Whymper, that I referred the particular difficulties of the southwest ridge to the dip of the strata; but when once persuaded that structure and not texture [of the rocks] was the real impediment, it was reasonable to infer that the opposite side, that is to say the eastern face, might be comparatively easy.... This trivial deduction was the key to the ascent of the Matterhorn. The point was, did the strata continue with a similar dip through the mountain? If they did, then this great eastern face, instead of being hopelessly impracticable, should be quite the reverse. In fact, it should be a great natural staircase, with steps inclining inwards; and, if it were

The granite obelisk of the Matterhorn as seen from Théodule Glacier on the southeast side

so, its smooth aspect might be of no account, for the smallest steps, inclined in this fashion, would afford good footing.[5]

Now Whymper went to Valtournanche and sought out Carrel, persuading him to join an attempt on the east face, failing which Whymper, as a concession, offered to return and make another try from Breuil. Carrel agreed, at which point Whymper discharged his other guides, Almer and Biener, neither of whom would have any further part of a mountain they judged impossible. "Anything but the Matterhorn, dear sir," said Almer.

By happenstance, while proceeding down to Valtournanche to visit an ill friend, Whymper ran into Carrel, who was leading a party up the path toward the mountain. In response to questions, Carrel gave evasive answers, explaining to Whymper that he was stuck with a prior engagement that now had to take precedence. Although he was not explicitly told so, Whymper thought Carrel was merely taking some harmless hikers for a stroll among the flora and fauna. In fact, Carrel was preparing to take a powerful, well-organized party up the southwest arête. When foul weather caused Carrel to turn back for the night, the men's paths again crossed. Whymper and Carrel, with the latter's brother, Caeser, sat up together until midnight imbibing wine and heartily recounting their former experiences. Carrel said nothing about his plans.

A couple of days later Favre, the owner of the inn in Breuil where Whymper was staying, admitted that Carrel had clandestinely set forth at the head of a formidable party to scale the peak. Whymper, feeling double-crossed in light of Carrel's previous promise, was stunned.

"Then I saw in a moment that I had been bamboozled and humbugged; and learned, bit by bit, that the affair had been arranged long beforehand,"[6] he related. This was not merely a hyperactive imagination at work.

Quintino Sella, the country's minister of finance, an engineer, geologist, and a mountain lover as well, had decided that the last great victory in the Alps must be Italy's. He organized a formal expedition to tackle the southwest ridge and placed a friend, Felice Giordano, in charge. Carrel, whose talents as a stonemason were thought to be indispensable to solving the final buttress above the shoulder, was enlisted to lead the assault. (Giordano even contemplated the use of explosives!) Carrel was forced to take an oath of secrecy—hence his evasiveness when encountering Whymper.

Letters from Giordano to Sella, found later, are revelatory of the unspoken struggle that was forming. On July 7, 1865, he wrote, in part, from Turin:

"Let us, then, set out to attack this Devil's mountain, and let us see that we succeed, if only Whymper has not been beforehand with us."[7]

On July 11, 1865, the day of Carrel's departure from Breuil, Giordano wrote from the Mont Cervin Hotel:

> I am head over ears in difficulty here, what with the weather, the expense, and Whymper.
>
> I have tried to keep everything secret, but that fellow, whose life seems to depend on the Matterhorn, is here, suspiciously prying into everything. I have taken all the competent men away from him, and yet he is so enamoured of this mountain that he may go up with others and make a scene. He is here, in this hotel, and I try to avoid speaking to him.[8]

Whymper was at the end of his tether. No other guide could be found, not even a porter to help him ferry his baggage over the Théodule Pass to Zermatt. At this point fate again interceded, adding another in the procession of twists and quirks that inexorably led to the ultimate tragedy.

Around midday, into Breuil walked Lord Francis Douglas, brother of the Marquis of Queensberry, who, although only eighteen, had just made an impressive ascent of the Gabelhorn. With him was Joseph Taugwalder, son of old Peter Taugwalder of Zermatt, who recently had been on the Hörnli arête and thought it was perhaps climbable after all. (Only forty-five, old Peter was so called to differentiate him from another son, young Peter.) When Whymper explained his quandary, both he and Douglas agreed to join forces, traverse the pass to the Valais, find old Peter Taugwalder, and formulate the attempt from there.

The confluence of coincidences did not abate. Arriving in Zermatt, Whymper was pleasantly surprised to find Croz on the village street. Croz's client in Chamonix had turned up ill, so he had been engaged by Rev. Charles Hudson. They had come to Zermatt to climb the Matterhorn—by the Hörnli route.

Hudson, thirty-six, was a strong and experienced climber, perhaps the most able amateur of his time. Tall, solid, now the vicar of Skillington, Lincolnshire, he had served as an army chaplain in the Crimea and once walked eighty-six miles in twenty-four hours. Hudson had made the first ascent of the Dufourspitze (highest summit on Monte Rosa) and the initial guideless climb of Mont Blanc; with Croz he also had just completed the second climb of the Aiguille Verte. With him was a young, sallow-cheeked lad of nineteen, Douglas Hadow.

By chance, Hudson entered the Monte Rosa Hotel where Whymper and Douglas were dining that evening. Two separate parties on such an untrod peak would not do. So the pact was sealed. They all would go as

Matterhorn seen from Cervinia, Italy

one. How about Hadow? He had very little climbing background, practically none on steep rock. A few polite inquiries—none too penetrating—were made, and Hadow was admitted to the party. It was all agreed upon rather quickly. Perhaps too quickly.

Pondering the fickle turn of events that brought the entire group together, Whymper noted that "if any one of the links of this fatal chain of circumstances had been omitted, what a different story I should have to tell!"[9]

On July 13, 1865—two days after Carrel left Breuil—Whymper and a party of seven left the valley and climbed fast, reaching the base of the Matterhorn in six hours, and eventually locating a suitable bivouac on the east face at 11,000 feet. They were transporting three ropes: 200 feet of strong Manila; 150 feet of a stouter and probably even stronger rope; and 200 feet of lighter and weaker hemp (actually sashline). As for the climbing, they had been astounded. They found no difficulties at all.

Members of Whymper's 1865 Matterhorn party. *Courtesy Swiss National Tourist Office.*

After fixing the bivouac, Croz and young Peter Taugwalder reconnoitered the face, returning after several hours in high spirits; no problems had been encountered, and they felt that they could have reached the top that very day. Enthusiasm was boundless. Commented Whymper: "Long after dusk the cliffs above echoed with our laughter and with the songs of the guides, for we were happy that night in camp, and feared no evil."[10]

The ascent resumed about 3:30 A.M. The party now consisted of

Whymper, Hudson, Douglas, Hadow, Croz, and old and young Peter Taugwalder. (Joseph Taugwalder, serving as a porter, returned to Zermatt). Within a few hours they had attained 14,000 feet, keeping mainly on the east face, off the ridge. (Whymper felt that snow gullies and faces invariably were to be preferred to ridges.) Subsequently they reached the perilous overhang that is seen so prominently from Zermatt, and crossed over to the north side. Croz was leading, followed by Whymper and Hudson. The Tête du Cervin was slick and tricky.

"Now for something altogether different," said Croz. Even so, the huge snowfield seemed to lay at an angle of no more than forty degrees. Yet the exposure was marked; to fall meant an unimpeded 4,000-foot drop. They crisscrossed this section, veering out horizontally for 400 feet, then back toward the ridge. Everyone climbed well—except Hadow. Repeatedly he required help. A 200-foot snowfield now opened up above them—the last pitch. Thoughts of Carrel and the Italians buzzed through their minds. Had they been beaten after all?

At 1:40 P.M. on July 14, 1865, Whymper and Croz raced in unison to the summit. "Hurrah!" wrote Whymper. "Not a footstep could be seen."

Flushed with victory, Whymper finally spotted Carrel near the Cravate, some 1,250 feet below. To attract his attention, Whymper and Croz yelled loudly and tossed down stones. Carrel, recognizing Whymper by the familiar white trousers he wore, turned and retreated. Yet Whymper experienced a tinge of regret:

> He [Carrel] was *the* man, of all those who attempted the ascent of the Matterhorn, who most deserved to be first upon its summit. He was the first to doubt its inaccessibility, and he was the only man who persisted in believing that its ascent would be accomplished. It was the aim of his life to make the ascent from the side of Italy, for the honour of his native valley. For a time he had the game in his hands; he played it as he thought best; but he made a false move, and he lost it.[11]

On July 15, 1865, the vexed Giordano wrote to Sella:

> Yesterday was a bad day, and Whymper, after all, gained the victory over the unfortunate Carrel. Whymper, as I told you, was desperate, and seeing Carrel climbing the mountain, tried his fortune on the Zermatt slope. Every one here, and Carrel above all, considered the ascent absolutely impossible on that side; so we were all easy in our minds. . . . However, yesterday, as I saw some men on the Matterhorn, and was assured by every one that they were our party, I sent off the telegram to you, bidding you to come up.

The first ascent of the Matterhorn, on July 14, 1865, as depicted by artist Gemälde von G. Dóre. *Courtesy Swiss National Tourist Office.*

And further:

> Yesterday the Val Tournanche was already *en fete* thinking that we were victorious; today we were disillusioned. Poor Carrel is to be pitied, the more so as part of the delay was due to his idea that Whymper would not be able to ascend from Zermatt. I am trying to act like Terentius Varro after the battle of Cannae.[1,2]

The moment of tragedy on the descent, when Croz, Hudson, Douglas, and Hadow perished. Also rendered by Dóre. *Courtesy Swiss National Tourist Office.*

Giordano was, at the time, unaware of the tragedy that already had unfolded on the north face.

The Whymper party remained about an hour on the summit. Croz tied a blue shirt to a flagpole, and it was seen in both Breuil and Zermatt; the natives of each thought their respective parties had been triumphant.

Now came the descent. It was agreed that Croz, the strongest climber, should proceed first, followed by Hadow, the reliable Hudson, Douglas, and then old Peter Taugwalder. Since no one had remembered to leave names in a bottle on top, as was the custom, Whymper, who had been making sketches, went back up to attend to the matter. The party already was slowly picking its way down the north face when he caught up with it. Whymper tied on behind old Peter Taugwalder, with young Peter last. Whymper claims he suggested the use of a fixed rope on the steep part, but in the joy and confusion such protection evidently was forgotten or thought unnecessary.

Around three o'clock that afternoon, fifteen-year-old Friedrich Taugwalder, old Peter's youngest son, dashed into the Monte Rosa Hotel in Zermatt and told owner Alexander Seiler that he had seen an avalanche fall from the top of the Matterhorn to the glacier below. It was thought to be an idle tale. It was not.

At just that moment Croz had set aside his ax and was grabbing the unsteady Hadow by the legs and placing them, one at a time, in position. As Croz turned to resume his own steps, Hadow, without warning, slipped and fell backward, striking Croz in the small of the back. Croz issued a startled cry and they both went sprawling, dragging Hudson and Douglas with them down the ledge, over crags, into nothingness. Old Peter and Whymper braced themselves, and the former even had a split instant in which to belay a slack portion of the rope around a projecting boulder. Wrote Whymper:

> Old Peter and I planted ourselves as firmly as the rocks would permit; the rope was taut between us, and the jerk came on us both as one man. We held; but the rope broke midway between Taugwalder and Lord Francis Douglas. For a few seconds we saw our unfortunate companions sliding downwards on their backs, and spreading out their hands, endeavoring to save themselves. They passed from our sight uninjured, disappeared one by one, and fell from precipice to precipice on the Matterhorn Glacier below, a distance of nearly 4,000 ft. in height. From the moment the rope broke it was impossible to help them. So perished our comrades![13]

Whymper and the two Taugwalders remained in a state of paralyzed disbelief. Finally Whymper asked to see the broken strand and was aghast to discover that it was the weakest of the ropes they were carrying; it was intended to be used only as a spare. The good Manila rope had been used to link up the first four climbers. Between Douglas, the fourth member, and old Peter, the fifth, the latter had used the weak hemp or sashline—about the thickness of one's little finger. Some

150 feet of strong rope was still available, but unused. Why? How did it happen? Had old Peter deliberately employed the hemp to save himself in just such an emergency? Would the stouter line have held?

These questions tortured Whymper as he and the Taugwalders made their slow, agonizing descent. The Taugwalders, Whymper indicated, were in a state of uncontrollable panic and, trembling, had to be led down almost like children. To Whymper's exasperation, they claimed to be concerned about the fact that they had not been paid; more specifically, he said, they asked him to make an entry to such effect, apparently to enhance their stature with tourists who might, in view of the inevitable publicity that would result, seek them out as guides in the future. The Taugwalders denied any such thoughts, but Whymper, infuriated beyond measure, virtually stopped speaking to them. The three of them bivouacked on a small bluff that evening, and the next dawn descended into Zermatt. Whymper strode directly to the hotel where he met Seiler.

"The Taugwalders and I have returned," he said.

The bodies of Croz, Hudson, and Hadow were found on the glacier, smashed apart, and each ultimately was removed for burial in the local cemetery. No trace was ever found of Douglas.

Immediately there was a strong outpouring of grief and criticism. The London *Times* raised doubts about mountain climbing as a sport, and Queen Victoria was called upon to ban it.

A dark cloud of suspicion hung over old Peter. Wild accusations were made that he had cut the rope at the instant of the fall. This, of course, was patently absurd; to have done so he would have had to possess the quickness and adroitness of a magician. Moreover, Whymper was braced right behind him, and undoubtedly would have observed such a heinous act.

Much more grave was the issue of how the lightest rope came to be used between Douglas and old Peter. In the furor that ensued, a board of inquiry was established and a series of questions addressed to both Whymper and old Peter on July 21 and 23, 1865. Certain of those posed to old Peter were framed by Whymper. While Whymper never learned of the answers, after his death the report was published in the *Alpine Journal*. It was not very helpful. Queried why the hemp cord was used between Douglas and himself, old Peter simply said that the first rope (Manila) was not long enough. Never was he directly asked why the stronger remaining line was *not* employed. And so the mystery remains, unresolved, to this day.

In the aftermath of the accident, other pointed questions were raised:

(a) Why was Hadow, an unknown quantity as a rock climber, taken along on such an admittedly adventurous and risky expedition?

(b) Was the placing of seven men on a single rope (or, to be more precise, on two linked ropes) far too many and unwieldy for safety, and was the order of descent correct?

(c) Was old Peter told about the purpose of the hemp sashline, and not to use it for tying up?

(d) Did a vacuum in clear-cut lines of command create a fatal flaw?

There were, after all, three possible leaders—Hudson, Whymper, and Douglas. It appears that no one took full charge. There also was the matter of a language barrier. Neither Croz nor old Peter, the two chief guides, spoke the other's tongue. When a life-or-death situation is measured in the thinnest fractions of inches and time, it is impossible to assess the exact ramifications of these factors.

A few hard facts emerge. A fatal slip occurred on dangerous ground by a member of the party (Hadow) known to be the least experienced; the rope snapped and possible saving precautions (different order of descent, fixed rope, use of stouter line, etc.) were not taken; and, according to old Peter, if the rope had held, the tragedy could have been averted.

The key point is, of course, why the weak hemp was employed when the heavier rope was still available. Taugwalder and Croz were paid professional guides, and normally the task of insuring that a party is properly roped falls to them. On the other hand, the lines of responsibility undoubtedly were blurred by reason of the presence of climbers of such stature as Hudson and Whymper. Hudson regarded himself as equal to a guide, a not immodest evaluation in view of his credentials. However, even if it is conceded that the guides must select and check the safety of the ropes, it is unclear whether they were informed of the precise purpose of carrying the hemp along—or who, for that matter, was transporting the heavier rope (although presumably the guides were). Still, all were acutely aware that they were descending the most perilous section of the mountain. On virtually every climb where death or injury occurs there are, with benefit of rear-view vision, steps that, if taken, might have prevented the mishap. Here, on balance, the harsh but inescapable verdict seems to be that, in the turmoil of victory, there probably was carelessness by the two head guides (at least by Taugwalder), and by the other lead climbers as well.

Still the critical question nags. Did old Peter, a man of first-rate ability and impeccable reputation, intentionally insert the weak link to protect himself in the event of a fall. There is no evidence to support such a proposition, and recent writings have tended to come forcefully to his defense. What is the truth then? After being compelled to leave Zermatt and having lived in the United States for several years, old Peter Taugwalder returned to the Valais and passed away at the Schwarzsee near the base of the Matterhorn, in 1888. The answer lies interred with him.

As for Carrel, with whom Whymper later climbed the 20,498-foot

Chimborazo in Equador, he expired from exhaustion, at the age of 62, while leading a party down his beloved Matterhorn in 1890. Whymper, the old lion of the Alps, died alone in a Chamonix hotel room in 1911. His body lies at the head of the center row of the cemetery there.

Thus was the denouement of mountaineering's greatest triumph and tragedy.

Other memorable ascents of the Matterhorn were achieved. In 1868 the irrepressible Tyndall made the first traverse from Breuil to Zermatt. A. F. Mummery, whose name resounds repeatedly in any accounting of Alpine annals, mastered the difficult Zmutt ridge in the company of three guides in 1879. But a thirty-foot overhang at the top of the Furggen arête proved to be the most vexing. So difficult was this treacherous stretch that, in 1890, the intrepid Guido Rey engaged in the somewhat dubious—if not ludicrous—spectacle of dropping a rope ladder over it, walking down it and then back up; he was, he said, the first "explorer." This quaint ritual left the projection's reputation fully intact, if not enhanced. Finally, in 1941, Louis Carrel, Giacoma Chiara, and Alfredo Perino made a direct ascent of the Furggen ridge, overhang and all.

Historic climbs of the Matterhorn, including the Hörnli ridge. *Courtesy Swiss National Tourist Office.*

There were other notable firsts on the Matterhorn, for such feats of originality were, and occasionally still are, the animating force behind many climbs. None, however, ever compared—in scope, daring, or impact—with the virgin conquest of the "impossible mountain" in 1865.

The next morning—my last in Zermatt—I saw an elderly man marking crevasses on the Plateau Rosa with flags and lines, and recognized him as my former guide, Franz Perren. The years had treated him kindly. He was heavier, but still hard and ruddy looking. After about thirty-five years as a burgfuhrer, he was now in charge of checking the safety of the glaciers near the ski areas. Franz truly devoted his life to the Matterhorn, having scaled it countless times.

"There used to be more than a hundred full-time guides," he said. "Today there are not so many. Now you go again? How long do you take?"

"Three hours and forty minutes to the top."

"Too fast," he said, shaking his head. "Before I think it was more for the fun—about five hours up and four down."

His face lit up as he looked at the mountain. "It is," he said, "a great climb still."

On the tram up from Furri that day I met a couple from Pittsburgh that was going to Schwarzsee to relax and enjoy the view.

"Do you think you'll be attempting the Matterhorn?" they asked, unaware of my previous day's effort.

I reflected a moment. "Yes—exactly twenty years from now."

Sure enough, after returning to the States, I received a long letter from Charlie with an expected postscript:

"See you at the Hörnlihütte, August 5, 1991—you'll only be in your early 60s!"

3
The Bernese Trinity

> *Eastmost, the Eiger with his rigid stare*
> *Furrows the sky. The Monk is next in place,*
> *Not all unfitly named. The cowl hangs down*
> *Over its ample brow. The folded snows*
> *Are sleeves and trailing garments. But the*
>   *Maid!*
> *O crown of beauty! If the Savoyard*
> *Is called the king of mountains, surely thee*
> *All hearts pay homage to, and hail as queen.*
>
> —Nathaniel L. Frothingham,
> *Eiger, Mönch, and Jungfrau*

However good he may be, and however favorable the conditions of his ascent, anyone who returns from the Eigerwand cannot but realize that he has done something more than a virtuoso climb: he has lived through a human experience to which he had committed not only all his skill, intelligence and strength, but his very existence.

—Lionel Terray, *The Borders of the Impossible*

Throughout this ascent, this snow and this storm, we had come to recognize from the bottom of our inmost hearts a great sense of fulfillment: of a life closely linked with the elements, a sense of comradeship, a taste for things which, when you have once tasted them, can never be replaced.

—Gaston Rébuffat, *Starlight and Storm*

The Mönch stands like an arbiter between two great contenders in the Bernese Oberland. To its east rises a gigantic, brooding tombstone, the Eiger. Opposite sits the enchanting Jungfrau in a morass of overhangs and projections, basking beneath a shawl of deep crystal that covers its head, shoulders, and arms, leaving only a hooded face exposed.

This marvelous trinity—the Virgin, Monk, and Ogre—dominates the sprawling gems of the Bernese Alps in Switzerland. There probably are few if any places in the world of mountains where such a striking juxtaposition occurs.

The Eiger is the lowest of the three, but by far the most notorious. It is a voracious killer. If the Matterhorn and Mont Blanc are the most notable peaks in the Alps, the Eiger surely is the most infamous.

This is because of the Wall.

Dark and ominous, the Wall sweeps up with chilling abruptness from the gentle fields that converge on Grindelwald, Wengen, and Lauterbrunnen. It is 6,000 feet of frazzled, crumbling limestone, loose crags, steeply slanting icefields, and above all an unholy patchquilt of chutes and gullies that, machine-gun style, regularly fire down volleys of rocks, boulders, ice, and snow on all who accept the challenge. Twice the height of Yosemite's El Capitan, the greatest single face in the Alps, it has been a bastion of terror for climbers over the years.

The Jungfrau casts a different sort of spell. It is winsomely handsome, as elegant as a queen.

Eiger, Mönch, and Jungfrau (*left to right*)

85

The Mönch squats monumentally between these, the Beauty and Beast of mountains.

I took the early train from Wengen to the Jungfraujoch. Alfred Fuchs, my guide, thoughtfully brought along the long gaiters and heavy gloves I would need. The railroad is a wonder in itself. The highest in Europe, it took 16 years of blasting and boring before it became functional in 1912. From Wengen to the Joch takes about one hour and forty-five minutes. At Kleine Scheidegg, where we changed lines, the Eigerwand looms up as if on a public stage, as indeed it is. Spectators, curiosity-seekers, journalists, hikers, guides, climbers, and simple hangers-on looking for a thrill are constantly stalking the huge blank face with their binoculars and telescopes, following the familiar line of attack, scanning it for parties that might be trying it again. If there is a climber in trouble, the faithful converge on the small hotel there like a convention, enjoying the comfortable sunshine, sipping wine, relaxing in folding chairs, watching intently—while on the face, seemingly a few steps away, a drama of life—or death—is acted out amid a turbulence of storms, avalanches, rockfalls, and snowslides.

The Wall is fearsome. But it is also history. One cannot gaze upon it without harking back to the hair-raising, almost crazed races by the first aspirants in the 1930s, supposedly in honor of the "Fatherland"; the tragedies and daring rescues; the memorable German-Austrian success in 1938; the well-formulated winter ascent in 1961; and finally, five years later, the solution of the "ultimate problem," the "direttissima," following the rigid John Harlin route from base to summit.

The train halted at the Eigergletscher station, at 7,612 feet, before plunging into the innards of the Wall. Far to the other side, toward Lauterbrunnen and Mürren, one sees the vertical cliffs gouged out by the glaciers of the Ice Age, eons ago, creating a deep chasm that forms the Lauterbrunnen valley. In a pastoral setting, not unremindful of Yosemite, one is scarcely aware of the surging crenelations of glaciers that thrive higher up.

Then the train entered a tunnel scoured out of the hard rock and pulled in to the Eigerwand station that, at 9,400 feet, sits like a flyspeck smack in the middle of the north face, and from which numerous escapes and rescues have been effectuated over the years. Looking out of its windows, one sees nothing but a relatively narrow frame of snow and rock, and the mind cannot grasp the true nature and immensity of the Wall. Further on came the Eismeer station, and then the train emerged at the Jungfraujoch, at 11,333 feet.

The Jungfrau received its name from the Augustinian monks and nuns of Interlaken. Clothed in white themselves, they were constantly attracted by the neatly carved snow mantle that jutted up to such

The enchanting Jungfrau; Mönch is on the left

dazzling heights in the distance, and christened it the Virgin. At 13,642 feet, it is not the loftiest of the Bernese. That mark belongs to the Finsteraarhorn, at 14,022 feet. But many regard the Jungfrau as the loveliest mountain in Switzerland.

The conventional route up the Jungfrau today is not challenging, and the peak itself is sufficiently isolated and eye-catching that it cannot escape one's notice. But in 1811 its first conquerors had difficulty in locating it, or knowing exactly where they were, or, for that matter, what they had climbed.

Johann Rudolf Meyer II, his younger brother, Hieronymous, and three servants set off from Aarau on July 29, 1811. Theirs was a singular family—proud, daring, gifted, athletic in the extreme. They disdained carrying scientific instruments, claiming it hindered "adventurous climbers." They reached the Grimsel Pass, crossed it, and made their way up to the Gletschetstafel via the Beich Pass. Here a couple of chamois hunters joined them.

After bivouacking on the Glosser Aletschfirn, they embarked on a reconnaissance and, it has been claimed, originally mistook the Gletscherhorn for the Jungfrau. In any event, they got to within 600 feet of some summit when heavy winds forced a retreat.

On August 3, 1811, they started out "as the first rays of the sun reddened the rocks of the Jungfrau close before us,"[1] and by 8:00 A.M. reached a saddle. The gulfs of glacial terrain that they never suspected existed—such as the Oberaar, the Finsteraar, and Lauteraar glaciers—were confusing, but the climb, except for some deep crevasses, had not been overly difficult. At least not for the Meyers. They used a rope but no ice axes or nailed boots. They were not even particularly tired when, at 2:00 P.M., they impaled a flag on the Jungfrau summit.

Matters changed on the descent. One of the party almost collapsed from exhaustion and, snowblinded, had to be led by a rope with his eyes covered. Two days later they recrossed the Grimsel and recorded their journey in the visitor's book at the Hospice.

Since no one had seen the flag, some questioned whether the Meyers actually had scaled the Jungfrau, although the 1811 climb is accepted today as an authentic first ascent. To eradicate any lingering doubts, another member of the restless clan, Gottlieb Meyer, son of Johann Rudolf II, scaled the Jungfrau on September 2, 1812, with two guides, Alois Völker and Joseph Bortes. Gottlieb rammed in a flag so securely and with such gusto that, according to one observer, it was still visible in 1842—thirty years later.

There now was no doubt that the Meyers—or one of them—had made the maiden ascent of the Jungfrau.

It was here in the Bernese Oberland that the so-called Golden Age of Mountaineering was born. Twenty-eight-year-old Alfred Wills, with four guides, scaled the Wetterhorn from Grindelwald on September 15, 1854, and touched off a furious spate of activity and first ascents— mostly by Englishmen—that was finally crowned by the Whymper conquest of the Matterhorn approximately a decade later.

Wills's climb of the Wetterhorn was not even a first. But the popularity of his *Wanderings Among the High Alps* (London: Richard Bentley, 1856), and the enthusiasm and lucidity with which he wrote, helped convert mountaineering from an unsystemized scramble into an organized and scientifically conducted venture that received broad acceptance.

Of his triumph, Wills wrote:

> Suddenly, a startling cry of surprise and triumph rang through the air. A great block of ice bounded down from the top of the parapet, and before it had well lighted on the glacier, [Ulrich] Lauener exclaimed, *"Ich schaue den blauen Himmel!"* ("I see blue sky!") A thrill of astonishment and delight ran through our frames. Our enterprise had succeeded! We were almost upon the actual summit. That wave above us, frozen, as it seemed, in the act of falling over, into a strange and motionless magnificence, was the very peak itself! Lauener's blows flew with redoubled energy. In a few minutes a practicable breach was made, through which he disappeared; and in a moment more, the sound of his axe was

heard behind the battlement under whose cover we stood. In his excitement, he had forgotten us, and very soon the whole mass would have come crashing down upon our heads. . . . As I took the last step, [Auguste] Balmat disappeared from my sight; my left shoulder grazed against the angle of the ice embrasure, while, on the right, the glacier fell abruptly away beneath me towards an unknown, an awful abyss; a hand from an invisible person grasped mine; I stepped across, and had passed the ridge of the Wetterhorn![2]

Wills later became a judge and presided over the trial that resulted in the conviction of Oscar Wilde.

The first ascent of the Mönch, in 1857, was a signal event. A Viennese doctor, Sigismund Porges, made the climb with three first-rate guides, Christian Almer and Ulrich and Christian Kaufmann. They were forced to bivouac twice, and Porges thought the steep sections were more forbidding than the Jungfrau or Monte Rosa.

The honor almost fell to a woman—a Rumanian countess, Hélène Kolzow-Massalsky, who used the pseudonym of Dora d'Istria—in 1855. Her concept of mountaineering was quaint. She had four guides cart her by chair to the edge of the Mönch, after which they tugged and pushed

The Bernese trinity: Eiger, Mönch, and Jungfrau *(left to right). Courtesy Swiss National Tourist Office.*

her, fore and aft, up the slopes. She reached the foot of the last ridge but there, in a state of complete collapse, had to abandon the attempt with victory in sight. Nevertheless, she wrote a book describing how she had arrived on top where she kissed the Rumanian flag and raised her heart to God. Unfortunately, her legs never reached as high as her hopes. Three of the guides gave her a testimonial confirming a first ascent. But the honest Almer knew that it was not authentic and refused to be a party to the ruse—even to please female royalty. The guides, certainly one of Almer's ability, no doubt could have made the climb on any sunny day, but never bothered. It is not unlikely that they were simply saving the market for foreigners who were willing to pay a neat price for the privilege of a "first."

Shortly thereafter, on August 11, 1858, Charles Barrington, a colorful Irishman who knew far more about horses and steeplechases than mountains, accomplished the initial ascent of the Eiger in the company of two local guides, the ubiquitous Christian Almer and Peter Bohren.

He gave a vivid account in a letter to his brother: "On Thursday, August 5, 1858, I left Grindelwald about 4 o'clock P.M. and walked up the glacier to a small hut, in which we spent the night. It was occupied by a goat-keeper. I was eaten up with fleas. Next morning I started with my two guides, Almer and Bohren, and a French gentleman, and crossed the Strahlegg to the Grimsel, where we arrived on Friday evening, the 6th."[3]

Here he relates that he scaled the Jungfrau. In Grindelwald, he met some climbers and stated that he did not "think much of the work I had done."

"Try the Eiger or the Matterhorn," they said.

"All right," replied Barrington, and went to sleep with "a beefsteak on my face."

He wrote:

> In the evening of the next day, the 10th, I made a bargain with the same guides for the Eiger, and walked up to the hotel on the Wengern Alp, stopping to play cards for an hour on the way, and found it quite full at 12 o'clock at night. Threw myself on a sofa, and started at 3:30 A.M. on Aug. 11 for the Eiger. We took a flag from the hotel. When we came to the point where one descends into a small hollow I looked well with my glass over the face of the Eiger next us, and made up my mind to try the rocks in front instead of going up the other side, which had been tried twice before unsuccessfully. Almer and Bohren said it was no use, and declined to come the way I wished. "All right," I said, "you may stay; I will try." So off I went for about 300 or 400 yards over

some smooth rocks to the part which was almost perpendicular. I then shouted and waved the flag for them to come on, and after five minutes they followed and came up to me. They said it was impossible; I said, "I will try." So, with the rope coiled over my shoulders, I scrambled up, sticking like a cat to the rocks, which cut my fingers, and at last got up say fifty to sixty feet. I then lowered the rope, and the guides followed with its assistance. We then had to mark our way with chalk and small bits of stone, fearing we might not be able to find it on our return. We went up very close to the edge, looking down on Grindelwald, sometimes throwing over large stones to hear them crash down beneath the clouds. We got to the top—the two guides kindly gave me the place of first man up—at 12 o'clock, stayed about ten minutes, fearing the weather, and came down in four hours, avoiding the very steep place, as, looking down from above, we found out a couloir, down which we came, and just saved ourselves by a few seconds from an avalanche.

I was met at the bottom by about thirty visitors, and we went up to the hotel. They doubted if we had been on the top until the telescope disclosed the flag there. The hotel proprietor had a large gun fired off, and I seemed for the evening to be a "lion."

Thus ended my first and only visit to Switzerland. Not having enough money with me to try the Matterhorn, I went home. Nothing could exceed the kindness of Almer and Bohren. I am sorry to hear the latter has passed away. Both were splendid mountaineers, and had I not been as fit as my old horse "Sir Robert Peel" when I won the "Irish Grand National" with him, I would not have seen half the course. I may add that when leaving Grindelwald for the Eiger I was surprised to see the families of the guides in a state of distraction at their departure for the ascent, and two elderly ladies came out and abused me for taking them to risk their lives.[4]

It remained for a tireless, plodding dentist from Zurich to achieve the most incredible record in the Bernese Oberland. Hans Lauper was a former Latin scholar who cherished the Alps so much that before becoming a dentist, he took a job as a mapmaker so that he could spend all his time among them. In a period of eighteen years he made a like number of major first ascents, an astounding feat. These included north faces of each of the Bernese trio, the Mönch, Jungfrau, and Eiger.

The north face of the Mönch is both impressive and difficult. In 1921 Lauper and Max Liniger struggled wearily with an infernal ice crack leading to a long ramp that slashes across the face. After a perilous fifteen-hour battle they gained the summit. In 1926, with

The Mönch north face

Pierre de Schumacher, he solved the puzzling grab-bag of gendarmes and subsidiary peaks that guard the tricky, though less fearsome, north face of the Jungfrau.

Finally there was the Eiger—by far the most arduous of the three. Its north side is divided into two sections, the northeast and northwest faces. It is the latter, the Eigerwand, that represents the most treacherous climb in the Alps. The northeast face was, however a formidable obstacle. The thoroughgoing Lauper studied it patiently for nine years before he undertook the attempt with a friend, Alfred Zurcher, and two Valais guides, Alexander Graven and Josef Knubel.

The key to the northeast face was an elongated rock spur that preceded a steep slope of ice and rock outcroppings sweeping down from the Mittellegi ridge; the latter was a tough nut itself that had been scaled in 1921 by Fritz Amatter, Samuel Braward, Fritz Steuri, Sr., and a Japanese tyro, Yuko Maki, who thirty-five years later led the successful attack on 26,760-foot Manaslu in the Himalayas.

Lauper and his party launched their assault before 2:00 A.M. on August 20, 1932, crossing from the Kleine Scheidegg railway to the base of the big tower. Traversing a dangerous couloir that was rattling with ice and stonefalls, they attained a long chimney and then went onto an extremely steep ice slope, one of the trickiest passages any of them had ever attempted. Each was acutely aware that one slip—by anybody—surely would be fatal.

Knubel was almost tiptoeing along this death trap. "We are all of us a bit crazy,"[5] he announced succinctly.

They reached a ledge where they took a forty-minute breather. Then they continued up another reef of rocks, and, after a fierce struggle, Graven was able to pull himself over a seemingly unbeatable overhang. Now only a gentle snow climb separated them from the top.

The northeast side—though not the dreaded Wall—had been mastered in one day. Lauper and his friends never tried the northwest face. That, they felt, was out of the question.

* * *

A long, narrow tunnel disgorged Alfred and me onto the snowfields on the north flank of the Jungfraujoch. By now, two Italian fellows, Roberto and Don, had joined us. Our luck held, and balmy temperatures prevailed. However, a heavy blizzard had hit the Alps earlier, and the terrain was frocked with a thick white coating. Alfred took the lead as we shuffled, heavy footed, through the drifts toward the easterly edge of the Mönch, following in the lee of its base. Two skiers had

Climbing the Mönch

tramped up a long snowfield and were preparing for a multimile cross-country descent.

Seen from below, the Mönch was almost nondescript, without character. Weighty brown and red layers of rock swung up in a befuddled, patternless line, most of them lathered with crusty swatches of snow, often tilting at a bewildering variety of angles, yet basically simple. The Mönch, from here, was an undistinguished hump.

Caught between the alluring, almost bewitching beauty of the Jungfrau, and the ferocity of the Eiger, the Mönch does indeed stand somewhat neglected, perhaps unappreciated. At 13,449 feet, it is less than 200 feet lower than the Jungfrau (13,642 ft.), and several heads taller than its other flamboyant neighbor, the 13,026-foot Eiger. Hence, the Mönch, though bulkier, is neither so high or attractive as the Jungfrau, nor so renowned as the Eiger.

We circled at length around the lower buttresses and, after a forty-five-minute romp, edged onto some scaly rock pitches.

We now roped up. The Mönch seems to tumble skyward in random layers of rock and snow. The arch of its arête presented a long string of scythelike shapes, each linked to the other, first baring a lengthy slice of rock, then dissolving into thick snow fields and cornices, now revealing another gently inclined row of boulders, and so on. Most of the bouldering and rock sections were not too hard, but higher up there were delicate points. On one granite ledge, the exposure was such that one seemingly could jump off and land in Adelboden. Here we carefully belayed each other, climbing what appeared to be a veritable ladder of loose rubble. There were many of these rock fences—but I noted that throughout the climb few couloirs and gullies were encountered, so that the objective risks were minimal. It is, for instance, unlike the Matterhorn, much less the Eiger, where one is subjected to a constant pounding of small missiles, as though the peak were alive and taking regularly scheduled target practice.

As the snow deepened, we affixed our crampons and became strung out on the slope. It was, however, mainly a ridge climb and, although we moved fast, the ridges never stopped coming.

Of the three amateurs, Don seemed to be the most at home on the rock. He was large-boned and muscular, particularly in comparison with the corpulent Roberto. He moved far more gracefully than any of us. Yet, after about two hours, the altitude got to Don and he stopped dead in his tracks, sat down, drank some water, and announced he would wait there while the rest of us completed the ascent. Once again, lack of adequate oxygen was the great leveler.

We now reached a procession of sharply angled cornices, sticking close to the edge of them, following Alfred step by step. When it steepened, he carefully hacked out toeholds and I fairly ran up to him, my crampons biting well, after which he would slowly pull ahead for another fifty feet, and once more I would bound up. Roberto followed steadily and moved well in the mirror-clear morning.

From the cornices the snowdrifts fell away at a keen slant, forming large pockets of glacial cavities, and we were careful not to stray too far from the upper lane; otherwise one could readily lurch, head over canister, into an involuntary somersault, and wind up atop, or beneath, deep mounds of névé that were splattered over the crosshatch of chasms.

As we continued up, the curtains of the Alps now parted, revealing a spectacular, all-encompassing perspective of peaks and valleys extending the entire breadth of Switzerland and into France. The Matterhorn and

En route up Mönch

Mont Blanc were as conspicuous as urban skyscrapers, and the other nearby uplifts—the Monte Rosa, the Piz Bernina near Saint Moritz, the Gran. Paradiso — were equally well defined. I had never seen anything so grand and comprehensive, unrivaled except perhaps by the sight from the Diablerets glacier above Gstaad.

The icefields now tilted at an acute sweep, and we more or less nitpicked up them, along thick lines of overhanging snow flutes, around cracks, moving smartly.

Three hours flew by and another snow ridge bulged up ahead. It was the last. Briskly we stepped onto the summit, a spacious, pentagonal flattop, but extremely cold and windy.

From the mountain's apex, the Eiger looked harmless enough. A soft, sheeny wrap of ermine lay draped over its backside, surging downward in gentle, wide folds. It appeared to be focusing its attention elsewhere, as indeed it was, for its face—*the* face—looked off to the north, away from us. As for the Jungfrau, from this vantage it looked somewhat disheveled and frumpy, rising in labyrinthine piles of ice and snow, not quite the striking enchantress that shows itself from afar.

Near at hand were the Wetterhorn, 12,142 feet, the Schreckhorn, 13,380 feet, the Finsteraarhorn, 14,022 feet, and the Breithorn, 12,409 feet.

From atop the Mönch we were conscious of staring at history. After Lauper's ascent of the northeast side in 1932, each flank of the Eiger had been scaled—except the Wall. Indeed, every other north face in the Alps had fallen. Now climbers fixed their attention on the Eigerwand. To many, it was a compulsion. It must be conquered.

* * *

The Wall does not merely wait. It lurks. Concealed within its dark, shattering concavities are the fiercest, most diverse assortment of barriers, of every form and description, to be found on a mountain of such size. Danger does not simply exist—it stalks the climber. Artillery bombardments, fired with swooping rapidity, rain down bursts of ice, rock, and snow from the countless cracks and corridors that stitch its face. Steep icefields and rock buttresses fly up at horrifying angles, leaving scant margin for error. Ropes are frayed on the hard yet constantly crumbling surface. And then there is the weather. If all hell is not breaking loose, it surely will do so soon.

There is, in brief, nothing likable about the Wall. But it is the ultimate challenge in the Alps. Its tale is dipped in blood, for at least forty men have been killed on it, including eight of the first ten who made the attempt.

Unfortunately, in the turbulence of the 1930s the Wall became a symbol—of Nazi and Fascist ambitions, of Teutonic superiority. Although this circumstance may have been overworked at the time, to climb for the glory of one's country became, if not the prime motive of the serious climber, at least the clamor of the unknowing public, and the incentive for the brash and the inexperienced. In this frenzied atmosphere, the Munich school of climbing became identified with bold attempts on the most difficult peaks—mostly the north faces.

From the Kleine Scheidegg, one can readily detect the circuitous approaches up the Eigerwand. In time, the distinctive names given the various points and barriers became virtual household words in the Alps. If a party reached the Death Bivouac or the Traverse of the Gods, any climber knew exactly what was meant.

From the bottom, the usual route, as it developed, carried up through the First Pillar, the Shattered Pillar, the Difficult Crack, the Hinterstoisser Traverse, the Swallow's Nest, the Ice Hose, the First Icefield, the Second Icefield, the Flatiron, the Death Bivouac, the Third Icefield, the Ramp, the Traverse of the Gods, the Spider, the Exit

The Eigerwand

Cracks, and the Summit Icefield. These were only labels. But each offered a peculiar, often vicious gauntlet, and each was pregnant with meaning for anyone who took it up.

On August 21, 1935, two seasoned Munich climbers, Max Sedlmayer and Karl Mehringer, formed the first rope to come to grips with the Eigerwand. They fought their way up the lower snow slopes and rock sentinels, and quickly moved above the windows of the Eigerwand station where they settled into their first bivouac. The second night they attained the upper segment of the First Icefield. From below, spectators gathered, peering endlessly through the telescopes at Kleine Scheidegg, to watch what was sure to be history in the making.

With a suddenness that only the Eiger knows, a violent, prolonged storm broke over the Wall. Mist, hail, and snow hid the climbers from view. Two more days passed. On the fifth day, both were spotted inching up to the Flatiron, now well more than halfway up. But their situation was desperate, and most knowledgeable mountaineers grimly felt that it was only a matter of time. How long could they, in their drastically weakened condition, hold out?

A month later one of the bodies, frozen and half-kneeling in the snow, was spotted from the air by Colonel Ernest Udet, a German World War I ace, and Fritz Steuri, a guide, as they flew past the face. Sedlmayer and Mehringer had died in a stand-up bivouac, now known as the Death Bivouac, at the upper tier of the Third Icefield. The Wall had claimed its first victims.

Only a year later came the cruelest calamity ever to haunt the Eiger. Here again the party was a strong one with high hopes—two Bavarians, Anderl Hinterstoisser and Toni Kurz, and two Austrians, Edi Rainer and Willi Angerer. Each was an able, well-honed climber.

"We must have the Wall or it must have us!" they cockily declared, encouraged by eager newsmen.

Around noon on July 21, 1936, Albert von Allmen, an elderly guard on the Jungfrau railway, was standing at the gallery entrance that opens onto the face, shouting into the wind. The party had been climbing for four days and was above the Death Bivouac. They had cleverly solved one of the most vexing barriers—access to the First Icefield. Banging in pitons at will, Hinterstoisser nailed a ropeway across an otherwise impossible 100-foot traverse, which lay at a scary 70-degree angle. Then, having crossed what became known as the Hinterstoisser Traverse, fatally, unthinkingly, the party drew in the rope. Unbeknownst to them, retreat was now cut off. The descent could not be made unless the rope was left in place. They had, inadvertently, sealed their own death warrants.

Up they went. Suddenly Angerer was hit and injured by a falling stone. They bivouacked overnight, and the next day Angerer's

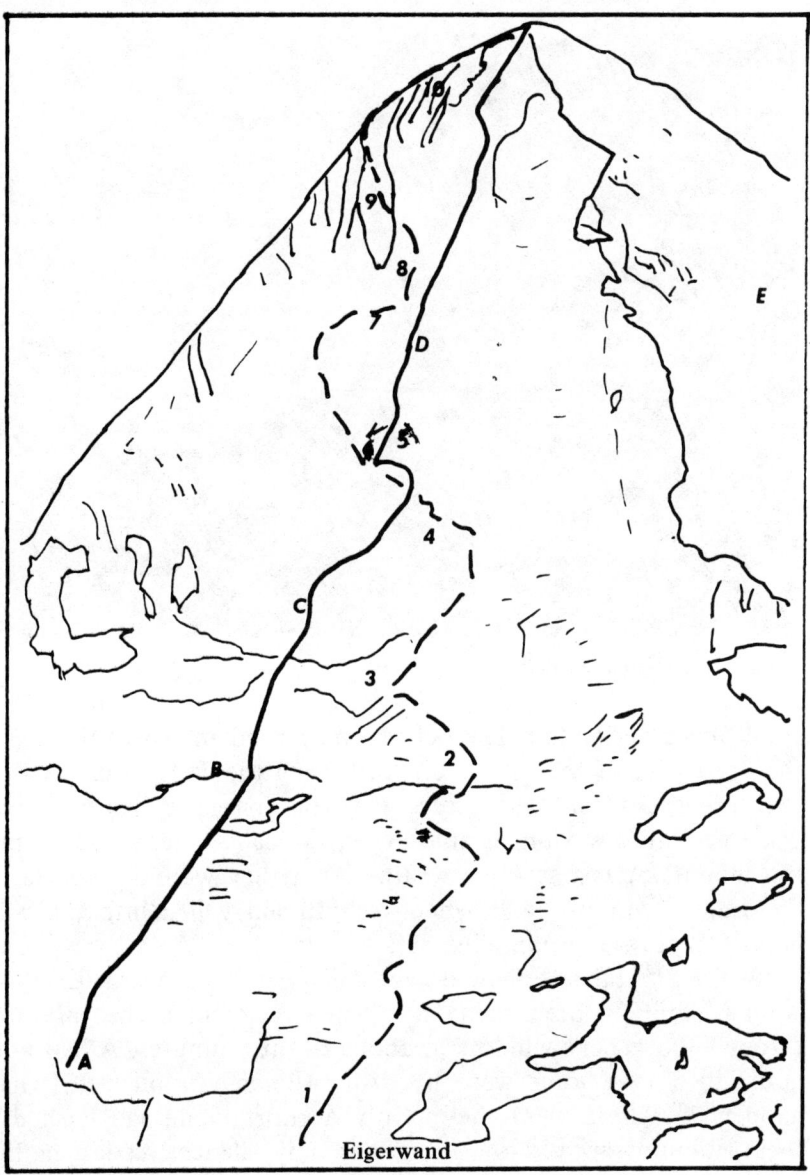

Dotted line: original 1938 route
Solid line: *Direttissima*.
1 — First Pillar
2 — Hinterstoisser Traverse
3 — First Icefield
4 — Second Icefield
5 — Death Bivouac
6 — Third Icefield
7 — Traverse of the Gods
8 — Spider
9 — Exit Cracks
10 — Summit Icefield
A — Foot of Fixed Ropes
B — First Band
C — Second Band
D — Where Rope with Harlin Broke
E — West Flank of Eiger

The north face of the Eiger

condition deteriorated. They chose to descend and spent the night near the upper rim of the First Icefield. During the early hours of the next morning they tried to recross the Hinterstoisser Traverse—only to discover that it was impassable. Now, typically, another storm plagued the mountain. It was Eiger weather. Yet they were not too far above the gallery window, and when von Allmen yelled into the cold air, hoping to draw a response, he did.

"We're climbing straight down. All's well," he heard. Excited, von Allmen went to brew some hot tea. He expected the party to pop through the gallery window in about twenty minutes. A half-hour, an hour, then two hours went by. Von Allmen was puzzled. What had happened? Where were they? Only a short while ago he had heard them, minutes away. Now there was only silence. At last he heard a desperate cry.

"Help! Help! The others are all dead. I am the only one alive." It was the urgent voice of handsome, twenty-three-year-old Toni Kurz.

Immediately the guard rang up the Grindelwald guides. When they arrived they learned what had occurred. Hinterstoisser had slipped and fallen the length of the face. Rainer, jammed up against a snaplink, had frozen to death. Angerer had fallen and, enmeshed in a rope, was killed by strangulation. Only Kurz was left, dangling in a rope sling.

The guides tried to reach him from below. Desperately Kurz shouted that such a route was impossible—that salvation lay only in ascending an ice crack and reaching him from above. By now it was getting late and the guides despaired. The ice crack looked inaccessible. Could Kurz stick it out for another night?

"No! No!" he exclaimed in panic and exhaustion. His hand and arm were frozen stiff. The guides sadly turned away. They felt they had no choice; they would return in the morning.

Another frigid night passed on the Eiger. Dawn broke, and the guides again approached Kurz. Remarkably, he was still alive.

They were now about 130 feet below him, but their view was blocked by an intervening overhang. An effort to fire a rope up to him by rocket proved futile. They suggested that Kurz drop down, retrieve the rope from Angerer's body, unravel it, piece it together to make it three times its original length, and lower it to them so they could attach a good rope and other items to it.

His body wracked with agony, Kurz climbed down; his left arm and hand were a purplish color, having become completely paralyzed. Bravely, he cut the rope away. Glued to the wall by the ice, Angerer's corpse sickeningly hung free. For five painstaking, unbearable hours the courageous Kurz worked with his teeth and his right hand to unravel the strands. Now the line was ready and he dropped it down. A rope, pitons, snaplinks, and a hammer were passed up to him.

At last Kurz was prepared. Roping up, he carefully began to descend. Down he came 120 feet. Only a few feet—represented by the overhang—separated him from his rescuers. His feet could be seen dangling over it. The guides strained and could almost—but not quite—touch him. One of them stood on another's shoulders, but still fell short.

Kurz wriggled anxiously, but his descent was blocked by a splicing knot that had become stuck in the snaplink. If it only could be forced through, Kurz would be safe. Shouts of encouragement came from below. There was a lull and then the guides heard a terrible moan.

"I'm finished," said Toni Kurz. His head drooped. The sling stopped swinging. He was dead.

"It was the saddest moment of my life," said Arnold Glatthard, one of the guides. Arnold Lunn called it equal to the most heroic instance of endurance in the annals of mountain climbing.

After that cruel twist of fate, the Swiss government proclaimed a ban on climbing the north face, but later withdrew it as unenforceable. Then, in 1937, it announced there would be no further rescue operations undertaken there; climbers would have to proceed at their own peril.

Criticism was widespread. The president of the Alpine Club wrote: "The Eiger north wall, still unscaled, continues to be an obsession for the mentally deranged of almost every nation. He who first succeeds may rest assured that he has accomplished the most imbecile variant since mountaineering first began."[6]

But the climbers still came, undeterred.

The first ascent of the Eigerwand was finally achieved by two German and Austrian ropes in a valiant climb made in 1938—just before the outbreak of World War II.

Anderl Heckmair, 32, was a landscape gardener by trade, but already acknowledged to be one of the best Alpinists around. He was plucky, a veteran, with an infallible sense of knowing when a mountain was ripe to be taken. For a big climb, he said, one had to be both fanatical and a fatalist. His partner, known as the Bivvy King for his talent for making cozy bivouacs even in the most trying conditions, was Ludwig Vörg, also experienced, who the previous year, with Hias Rebitsch, had spent

The notorious Eigerwand (13,026 ft.) seen from Kleine Scheidegg. *Courtesy Swiss National Tourist Office.*

112 hours on the Wall, reaching all the way up to the Ramp, the highest point yet achieved. Heckmair and Vörg were both strong north face climbers.

While the two Germans bivouacked in a cave on the lower part of the peak, a separate rope, manned by Fritz Kasparek of Vienna and Heinrich Harrer, a student who had just completed examinations at the University of Gratz, started up. Harrer later went on a Nanga Parbat expedition in the Karakoram Range and, when war broke out, was imprisoned by the British in India. He escaped twice and, in a miraculous journey across the Himalayan massif into Tibet, reached Lhasa and became a friend of the Dalai Lama, escaping when the Chinese Communists invaded Tibet in 1951. His daring adventures formed the basis for a best seller, *Seven Years in Tibet*.[7] But now Harrer was merely an ambitious though capable climber who had motorcycled to Grindelwald and hooked up with his friend, the able Kasparek, ready for the climb of his young life.

The two Austrians had studied the mountain carefully and concluded—erroneously—that, with Kasparek in the lead, Harrer would be better off without crampons, so he wore only nail boots. When still another Austrian team appeared on the scene, Heckmair and Vörg said that they would not climb, since the weather outlook did not look promising. In fact, Heckmair probably thought that it was getting too crowded on the great face. Now Kasparek and Harrer proceeded up, but, after while, the other Austrians, one of whom had been injured, were forced to retire. Kasparek and Harrer suddenly had the Eigerwand to themselves.

They climbed up beneath the towering Rote Fluh, and made the Swallow's Nest. After an easy bivouac, they resumed at dawn. On attaining a band of rocks that bisects the Second and Third Icefields, they espied Heckmair and Vörg rushing up from below. When the other Austrian pair had descended, Heckmair and Vörg did an about-face, running, not climbing up, as Harrer said, at express speed.

Heckmair immediately took the lead. Although they climbed as two separate ropes, basically they were a team. At one point, on the Ramp leading to the Traverse of the Gods, Kasparek fell sixty feet cleanly through space; luckily, he was uninjured.

The night was passed on the Ramp, 4,000 feet above the base. Vörg prepared some tea, coffee, and cocoa for all. The next day they were baffled by an ugly ice overhang, but Heckmair, agile as a cat, fought with it and finally squirmed over. Harrer called it a "toe-dance above a perpendicular drop."[8]

Shortly thereafter they were confronted with another imposing ice cliff—this one a thirty-foot hump, one of the most fearful pitches any of them had ever seen. Heckmair wrestled with it, fell off, went at it again. They now made the long rock crossing to the Spider. Every ascent of the Eigerwand necessarily passes through this section.

"The 'Spider' on the Eiger's face is white," Harrer observed. "Its body consists of ice and eternal snow. Its legs and its predatory arms, all hundreds of feet long, are white, too. From that perpetual, fearfully steep field of frozen snow nothing but ice emerges to fill gullies, cracks and crevices. Up and down. To left, to right. In every direction, at every angle of steepness. And there the 'Spider' waits."⁹

The first ropes ever to attain that height, they bivouacked low on the Spider. Two heavy avalanches came bolting down on top of their heads. Harrer used his rucksack as a shield to protect himself, holding onto the rope with his other hand. Kasparek grasped tightly onto a

Famous routes on the north face of the Eiger. *Courtesy Swiss National Tourist Office.*

piton, injuring himself. Heckmair grabbed his ice ax with one hand, Vörg by the collar with the other.

Slowly, said Heckmair, it grew lighter and the pressure eased.

"Wiggerl," he cried. "They're still on." (Heckmair often referred to Vörg as "Wiggerl.")

It was, he said, impossible, an outright miracle. "An indescribable joy swept over us. One only discovers how strong a thing team-spirit can be when one sees the friends again whom one has counted for dead."[10]

They climbed until about ten o'clock that night, bivouacking at 12,300 feet. It was the third bivouac for the Austrians, the second for the Germans.

The next day, nursing their way through the top of the Spider into the Exit Cracks, they linked together as a single rope. Heckmair again was faced with a monstrous-looking overhang of holdless, bulging ice. It was snowing hard. Wrote Heckmair:

> On the overhang itself I could only cross my crampons, because there was only a narrow strip of old ice in the gully and the new ice overlaying the rock was too hard, smooth and thin. The point of the ice-piton on to which I was clinging for dear life only went a little way in and so did the pick of my ice-axe. Suddenly the piton came out, and at the same moment my axe gave way. If I could only have straddled, I could have kept my balance. But with my legs crossed, there wasn't a hope.
>
> I shouted, "Look out, Wiggerl!"
>
> Then I came off.
>
> Wiggerl was looking out all right. He took in as much rope as he could, but I bore straight down on him—not through thin air, for the gully was inclined, but in a lightning-swift slide. Just as I fell, I turned face outwards so as not to go head over heels.
>
> Wiggerl let the rope drop and caught me in his hands, and one of the points of my crampons went through his palm. I did turn head over heels, but in a split second I grabbed the rope-piton, which gave me such a jerk that I came up feet first again. I dug all twelve points of my irons into the ice—and found myself standing.[11]

Now the party heard shouts from above. Knowing these came from rescuers, the climbers refused to answer, feeling that any reply might be misconstrued as a plea for help.

By noon they had reached the summit icefield. Harrer, in his old-fashioned boots, had a wretched time. The hours passed interminably. Then, almost ludicrously, in the fog and spindrift, Heckmair kept right on going until they saw dark spots far below. In the heavy mist, they had not only climbed the Eigerwand—but almost fatally stumbled over a sharp cornice clinging to the south face on the opposite side. It was 3:30 P.M., July 24, 1938.

"Joy, relief, tumultuous triumph?" wrote Harrer. "Not a bit of it. Our release had come too suddenly, our minds and nerves too dulled, our bodies too utterly weary to permit any violent emotion."[12]

A fierce storm engulfed the mountain, and the descent was hectic. As they reached the bottom a boy came running up to them.

"Have you come off the face?" he asked timidly.

"Yes," they said, "off the face."

The boy ran ahead, screaming at the top of his lungs.

Everyone below—rescuers, friends, journalists, onlookers—had given them up for dead.

Heckmair and Vörg were honored with a victory parade in Berlin, where they were introduced to Hitler. At the time, Heckmair was quoted as saying, "We the sons of the Older Reich united with our companions from the Eastern border to march together to victory." After the war, Heckmair denied having ever made the statement.

"Politics," he said, "just didn't come into it," and he decried as "nonsense" the accusation that only climbers from the Fascist countries were interested in the attempt, for reasons of national prestige. Harrer also later went to considerable lengths to play down the political aspects of the climb, and the hysteria that enveloped it.[13]

Of the four, only Heckmair and Harrer now survive. Vörg perished in the war, and Kasparek was killed while climbing in Peru.

The second ascent of the Eigerwand was achieved in 1947 by the memorable French team, Lionel Terray and Louis Lachenal, both now deceased.

Commenting on his reactions after having reached the summit, Terray stated:

"I felt no violent emotion, neither pride nor joy. Up in the clouds on this lonely ridge I was just a tired and hungry animal, and my only satisfaction was the animal one of having saved my skin."[14]

In 1952 the Wall was the scene of a sterling triumph by nine climbers from three nations, Austria, France, and Germany, who happened to converge on the mountain at the same time. What made it most interesting was the presence of two of the greatest Alpinists of the generation, Hermann Buhl and Gaston Rébuffat. The Austrian, Buhl, climbed with a strong second, Sepp Jöchler, while there were four Frenchmen besides Rébuffat, namely, Guido Magnone, Paul Habran, Pierre Leroux, and Jean Bruneau. Then there were two young German brothers, Otto and Sepp Magg, who did not even bother to bring a tent sack with them.

Buhl was a legend in his own lifetime. His amazing feat of reaching the 26,660-foot summit of Nanga Parbat alone ranks as one of the most

Aerial view of the Eigerwand. In the rear is the Finsteraarhorn (14,022 ft.), highest peak in the Bernese Alps. *Courtesy Swiss National Tourist Office.*

stirring epics in mountaineering lore. He also climbed another Karakoram giant, 26,400-foot Broad Peak, and did a sole winter ascent of the east face of the Watzmann in Bavaria, along with a host of other equally imposing climbs. He later plunged to his death on the Chogolisa in the Karakoram when a cornice collapsed from under him in a dim mist. Rébuffat was on the 1950 French Annapurna expedition and scaled every major north face in the Alps—from the Matterhorn to the Grandes Jorasses.

In some of the most wicked conditions ever experienced there, Buhl was the principal lead in the assault on the Eiger. Indeed, the Spider ground the members of the party through one of the worst ordeals they—or anyone else—ever encountered.

Buhl described it as the riskiest climbing he'd ever met. "There was no escaping it," he stated. "It was no longer a question of achieving a successful climb; it had become a fight for very life itself."

Wrote Rébuffat, in his *Starlight and Storm:*

> Just at that moment the elements were particularly savage; avalanches were falling at an unbelievable rate. When he [Otto] had reached a rather less exposed spot, he secured me in turn. In this fashion we traversed towards the middle of the ice slope of the Spider, which was less swept than its flanks, since it was slightly convex. But what a void yawned a hundred and fifty feet below! Slowly the tiny human forms moved upward, while from time to time an avalanche came spouting down from the couloirs above. Then the whole line of us at long intervals crouched against the glassy surface; each fought silently with all his strength to avoid being dragged off.
>
> It took hours to make six rope-lengths of height. Three hundred feet above me was Buhl, three hundred feet below was Bruneau. It

The Eiger, Mönch, and Jungfrau *(left to right)* as seen from a terrace on the Schilthorn above Mürren. *Courtesy Swiss National Tourist Office*

was a fearful battle, a struggle both personal and collective. Each one of us, and so the whole rope, advanced almost imperceptibly.[15]

The ensuing morning, on the last leg of the face, another supreme challenge was met. Tenaciously, almost inhumanly, Buhl fought for four hours on an overhanging ice gully, falling off several times, often leaving himself hanging fragilely by a single piton. In an act of sheer will and desperation, he finally prevailed.

"I have no words with which to assess Buhl's performance on that pitch," said Jöchler. "Anyone who saw him working his way up those 70 feet, ever and again coming off the ice glazed rock and being brought up sharp on the rope, would have shaken his head and refused to believe his eyes. And Buhl battled on, stretched to the utmost, for four hours, in spite of his lowered bodily and spiritual condition. I shall remain eternally grateful to Hermann; it was he who built a bridge for us all and gave us hope of survival."[16]

The greatest and most elaborate rescue ever effectuated on the Eigerwand, and one of the most controversial of all climbs, occurred over a ten-day period in August of 1957. By then the Wall had been scaled thirteen times—but not by an Italian.

Claudio Corti, a truck driver from the tiny village of Olginate near Lake Como, was a powerful, rough-hewn individual, unsophisticated, confident, compulsive, and, in the last analysis, less than cautious. He was willing to gamble his life to be the first Italian to defeat the Eigerwand.

Bad luck hounded Corti in the mountains. One ropemate was killed in a fall on the Piz Badille in 1952; two years later a similar fatality occurred. It seemed that those who climbed with him courted danger.

Corti persuaded forty-four-year-old Stefano Longhi, a factory worker from Lecco, to join him on the Eigerwand. The oldest man ever to make the attempt, Longhi had never climbed higher than 10,000 feet and was unfamiliar with ice slopes. Their preparations were casual; they even neglected to obtain a map showing the route.

Near the Hinterstoisser Traverse they encountered two Germans, Günther Nothdurft, a twenty-two-year-old demon of a climber who had scaled the northeast face of the Piz Badille in the Bregaglia in three hours, and Franz Mayer.

The climb seemed jinxed from the start. Nothdurft, the best of the lot, took feverishly sick; he and Mayer lost much of their food supply when a sack fell off during a bivouac; Longhi got frostbite and became seriously fatigued. Those who watched from the plains below noted that the four men were moving with unusual slowness, even in spots where rapid progress might normally be expected.

Then it happened. As they cautiously approached the Traverse of the Gods, Longhi, dead tired, came off, screaming loudly, "I'm going!" He dropped ninety feet before the rope drew him up; swinging helplessly, he was a small weight on the end of a string. Although his hands were frozen, Longhi worked his way down to a ledge.

Corti and the two Germans tried to pull him up but found it impossible. Three hours passed. Corti despaired; he told his friend that he would finish the climb quickly, seek help, and return tomorrow.

So Longhi was abandoned to his fate, tied to a precarious nook on the Eigerwand. That same afternoon another blow fell. Corti was struck by a rock in the Exit Cracks and tumbled sixty feet. Nothdurft and Mayer were able to haul him up, but Corti was in no shape to continue. The German pair left him a red bivouac tent and started up to fetch assistance. He never saw them again.

About fifty rescuers had now been assembled—although the local guides refused to take part. Among the volunteers were Lionel Terray, Ludwig Gramminger, Max Eiselin, who organized and led the Swiss conquest of Dhaulagiri, and the great Italian climbers Ricardo Cassin and Carlo Mauri; Cassin had made the initial ascent of the Grandes Jorasses's Walker Spur and, like Mauri, knew both Longhi and Corti. As they ascended the west ridge to reach the top, from which rescue operations were to be conducted, they heard cries of desperation echoing off the face.

"Stefano! We have come to save you!" called Cassin.

"Hungry! Cold!" yelled Longhi over and over.[17]

A cable and winch were hauled up—the first use of such a contraption on the Eiger. Now a daring German, Alfred Hellepart, was lowered down the face some 1,200 feet. After more than an hour, he found Corti, weak and almost incoherent, sitting on a ledge. Hellepart fitted him into a harness, then enjoined the Italian to crawl up on his shoulders and back. Hellepart gave the "up" signal. But the winch was incapable of pulling the weight of both men, so the rescuers resorted to manpower. Thirty men began hauling by hand, at about 20 feet to a stroke. Though in serious condition, Corti, clutching tightly to Hellepart, was slowly pulled over a breach in the Exit Cracks to safety. Yet some of the volunteers were perturbed. They noted that the delirious man asked nothing about the fate of his companions. Corti only seemed to be interested in whether he would be recognized as the first Italian to "scale the Wall."

Terray now volunteered to try to fetch Longhi. More than two hours went by when he heard a feeble voice call from below, "Come!" But it was getting late and Eiger weather had arrived. Terray was yanked back to the top.

Corti was now almost unconscious and, at Terray's stout insistence, was brought down the west ridge in a sled. As the party descended, Cassin shouted out over the Wall to Longhi, "Courage!" He told him to keep his hopes up; help would return in the morning.

A fierce storm now lashed the Eigerwand with an unbridled intensity. During a clearing of the clouds the following dawn, the telescope below fixed on the Wall as it had done so many times before. The ledge Longhi had occupied was vacant. Some fifteen feet below, caught in a stranglehold of ropes, standing upright, his head twisted and caked with ice, Longhi was seen. A plane took off to confirm what everyone knew: Longhi, after ten days and nine nights on the Eigerwand, had been knocked from the cliff by the storm and had succumbed; his stretched-out body was pinioned to the Wall.

Corti had been saved in the most daring rescue operation ever attempted in the Bernese. Climbers from six nations had shared in it. But now a storm of a different sort broke over the Italian. Nothdurft and Mayer had not been found. Corti's conduct—the apparently thin preparations, his having induced Longhi to go, then leaving his friend on the face—was seriously questioned. He was accused of possibly having committed a crime on the mountain, and of covering up. His statements were hopelessly beset by contradictions. The respected Cassin branded him a liar and a faker.

"If Longhi is up there and dead, it's your fault!" Cassin said. "You wanted him up there."[18]

Hideously, for almost two years, Longhi's torn corpse remained draped against the Wall, for all to see. At last, after much bickering a fund was raised and a group of twenty-four Swiss guides, led by Werner Stäger, retrieved it.

But what about Nothdurft and Mayer? They had disappeared completely. It was not until four years later, in September of 1961, that the riddle was solved. Their bodies were found a bit off the usual route on the west ridge. The Germans had finished the climb. Then, despite the heavy storm, they endeavored to descend to the Eigergletscher station for help. They had not gone far when an avalanche buried them.

That same year—1961—the Wall was climbed for the first time in winter. The assault team, which took six and a half days, was composed of Toni Hiebeler, a sporting-goods store owner from Munich; Anderl Mannhardt, a sawmill operator; Toni Kinshofer, a carpenter; and Walter Almberger, a miner. Each was solid, knowledgeable. Almberger had scaled the north face of the Matterhorn, Hiebeler the Walker Spur. They prepared meticulously for a year, and left nothing to chance. Hiebeler's theory was that while conditions on the Eigerwand were much more frigid in winter, such exposure would be more than counterbalanced by the favorable fact that the main objective danger—avalanches—would be minimized; the rocks and snow would be plastered to the face by the cold, and the fearful shellings that had taken so many lives would be avoided. The theory was correct.

The ascent was questioned on one ground: the party had, at first, failed to reveal that it had climbed up to the level of the gallery exit, dumped some supplies, then retreated in a storm—after which, rather than starting from the bottom again, it simply walked up the Jungfrau tunnel to the exit and resumed the climb at a point 1,443 feet above the base.

Two years later a young Swiss guide, Michel Darbellay, made the first solo ascent in 18 hours.

One last great problem remained. The north face of every noted mountain in the Alps had now been scaled—even in winter. A new breed of climbers was looking for other fields to conquer. They found it in the "direttissima." Rather than following a natural, organic route, using the mountain to one's advantage, they sought to climb via a predetermined line, straight up, no matter how difficult, or how much technical hardware had to be employed. Such an achievement on the Wall became the ambition of a bold young American, John Harlin, a Stanford University graduate, ex-football player, and talented U.S. Air Force pilot.

The Mönch, Tschuggen, and Jungfrau (*left to right*) from Männlichen. *Courtesy Swiss National Tourist Office.*

Harlin formulated his plan of attack with infinite care. He assembled a strong rope: Dougal Haston, a Scottish climber who later scaled Annapurna and the southwest face of Everest, and Layton Kor, a lanky, rock-climbing expert from Colorado. Harlin and Haston already had separately climbed the Eigerwand—but not by the direct route; the former also had the Aiguille du Fou and the second winter ascent of the Mönch's north face to his credit, and was the founder of a mountaineering school at Leysin. Like Hiebeler, Harlin elected to make the assault in winter, to avoid slides and icefalls. He reconnoitered the face by air. To train, the team carried snowballs around in their bare hands and skied without gloves.

When the Harlin party started up, it was surprised to meet a well-financed and organized eight-man German group that even had its own team manager—plus the same aspiration, the Eiger direct. They intended to tackle the peak in stages, moving up in the manner of a Himalayan expedition.

The attempt was immediately beset with ragged weather, forcing a succession of discouraging delays. At one juncture the Harlin group spent five days in a snowhole at the Death Bivouac. Haston eventually spent a total of twenty-one days on the face.

At 3:15 P.M. on March 22, 1966, in the midst of preparations for the final strike, Peter Gillman, a newspaperman with the London *Daily Telegraph,* was watching the climbers through a telescope from Kleine Scheidegg. Casually he swung it up to the Spider, where the two teams were now poised. Victory seemed to be near. Suddenly, chillingly, a red form plummeted across the eye of the lens, tumbling over, laying out, falling helplessly. Gillman fervently hoped that some equipment had merely fallen, but in his heart he knew better. A fixed rope, frayed by the friction of an unyielding boulder, had broken. John Harlin, thirty years old, had dropped to his death.

From conception through execution, the "direttissima" had been Harlin's personal enterprise. Stunned, the men left on the Wall thought of abandoning the attempt. Those who were stationed below the fixed ropes, many of which were now found to be damaged, had to retreat, including Kor. As for the others, higher up, it settled on them that Harlin would have wanted them to finish his masterwork and, in his honor, they did. On March 25, 1966, Haston and four Germans, Jörg Lehne, Günther Strobel, Roland Votteler, and Sigi Hupfauer, emerged from a swirling snowstorm and completed the "direttissima." They did not escape unscathed; two of the Germans suffered serious frostbite and the amputation of all of their toes.

But the conquest of the Wall was complete.

In due course the Eiger's towering face seemed much tamed. The redoubtable Reinhold Messner and Peter Habeler scrambled up it in a record ten-hour burst in 1974. They used the experience as a warmup for a successful two-man assault on 26,463-foot-high Hidden Peak in the Himalayas a year later. Both were incredible feats.

* * *

Alfred, Roberto, and I spent about twenty to thirty minutes huddled on the windy summit of the Mönch, taking in the splendiferous view. The descent was fairly uneventful. After a while we rejoined Don, who for almost two hours had been sitting quietly on a boulder, staring into the valley of ice and snow that trailed off from the arête. His self-assurance shaken, suffering from vertigo, he wove his way down with cautious slowness, panting and straining on pitches that, when he was in good form on the first part of the ascent, were a snap. I had seen the phenomenon before: once panic and fatigue set in, even the simplest steps, especially when the exposure is marked, become a struggle; coordination deteriorates; breathing is labored; fear replaces confidence—none of it logical, but all quite real. Looking at that deep valley for a long time no doubt accentuated the problem. Alfred nursed Don down on a tether much of the way—an absurd situation considering he was not an incompetent climber. It was just a form of mountain sickness, not rare at all—akin to seeing a prize fighter inexplicably develop a glass jaw in the middle of a bout.

The next day, with four pert girls vacationing from New York City, I crossed the valley to the picturesque village of Mürren, and rode the tram to the top of the 9,748-foot Schilthorn. This presents the most impressive of all views of the Jungfrau-Mönch-Eiger triad. (The Schilthorn was overpopulated, and even the men's room was a gathering spot since it had a "007" painted on it, a reminder that a James Bond movie had been filmed there.) We stood on the outside platform at length, literally soaking in the magnificence, transfixed. Every few minutes a tram departed for the valley. But the day was too fine to be shortened.

We walked down some rocks below the Schilthorn, and slowly, laughingly wended and romped along the two-and-one-half-hour path that led through delightful cow pastures and potato fields to Mürren. The Bernese trinity stood before us like gargantuan stage props. A critic would indeed call them good theater. The Mönch wore its usual pale white covering. The Jungfrau looked as seductive, and the Eiger as ominous, as ever. The plunging gray-black walls of the Wetterhorn sparkled in the sun. The hours drifted by. We passed through tidy farm gates, vaulted rustic fences, traversed haystacks, and conducted our own series of mock corridas, red bandannas and all, with every lame bull in sight. After many such wayside frolics, we randomly made our way back to Wengen.

4

On the Edge of Everest

Have we vanquished an enemy? None but ourselves. Have we gained success? That word means nothing here. Have we won a kingdom? No ... and yes. We have achieved an ultimate satisfaction ... fulfilled a destiny.... To struggle and to understand—never this last without the other; such is the law.... We've only been obeying an old law then? Ah! but it's the law ... and we understand—a little more. So ancient, wise and terrible—and yet we see them; with steps for children's feet.

—George Mallory

Everest is a harsh and hostile immensity. Whoever challenges it declares war. He must mount his assault with the skill and ruthlessness of a military operation. And when the battle ends, the mountain remains unvanquished. There are no true victors, only survivors.

—Barry C. Bishop, in Hornbein's *Everest—The West Ridge*

George H. Leigh Mallory was a schoolmaster, writer, wartime artillery officer, would-be actor, accomplished oarsman, and, without doubt, one of the finest mountaineers of his or any era. Destiny was to make him as closely identified with Mount Everest as was Whymper with the Matterhorn.

Born on June 18, 1886, at Mobberly, Cheshire, in England, the son of a parish rector, Mallory spent his formative years at Winchester School. In 1905 he enrolled in Magdalene College at Cambridge University on a history scholarship. His interests there flourished. He was a bright, fanciful youth of rangy and supple build, dashing and well liked, with a neat waffle of tawny hair turned back over an open-featured face. Yet, although George Mallory even then had a special quality about him, it is unlikely that his teachers or classmates foresaw the mark he would leave on the world.

One prominent and fashionable lady, a climber herself, met Mallory at a hotel in Zermatt when he was only twenty-three. She described him as he read a book, seated "in a sort of oblivion, never looking up, only sometimes raising a hand to push back the shock of brown hair which fell constantly over his forehead." She found him "picturesque and untidy," but the things that chiefly aroused attention were "his good looks and his complexion . . . his skin was clear and fair as a girl's." He was "charming, happy, equal, generously admiring. He was very intolerant of the potterers and gossip-mongers, very modest about his own performances; he did not mind, in fact rather enjoyed, confessing with a half-shamefaced, half-whimsical amusement to some of his more desperate escapades."[1]

Early in his life Mallory made friends with R. L. Graham Irving, his tutor at Winchester, and the noted climber Geoffrey Winthrop Young. Quickly he became an ardent and able mountaineer. While still at Winchester he notched his first major ascents—the Grand Combin, Mont Blanc, and Monte Rosa—during a holiday with Irving. Mallory climbed often in Wales and was captivated by the Alps, eventually scaling Mont Blanc three times. Young regarded him as being deerlike in grace and having power of movement; he was said to be self-reliant, self-effacing, and radiantly independent.

After his graduation from Magdalene College, Mallory published a book on James Boswell's life, which he had prepared in the form of an essay while a student. He then took up a career in teaching at Charterhouse, where one of his pupils was Robert Graves, the poet. But his abiding interest was in the mountains, and his lyrical articles, some published in the *Alpine Journal,* showed it. For him the mountains represented far more than an athletic challenge. He sought to probe and understand the mood, spirit, and inner feelings that mountains evoked. His descriptions of his climbs were seldom merely technical; they reflected Mallory's exploration of self as much as the cracks and gullies with which he grappled.

"A day well spent in the Alps is like some great symphony," he wrote.[2]

When, in response to a question as to why he climbed, Mallory said "Because it is there," he may have been facetious, as some believe; but the more likely explanation is that, in that enigmatic but illuminating phrase, Mallory caught the essence of his own being and his lifelong spiritual embrace with the world of high places.

It was not until 1852 that the world's tallest mountain was identified. Until that time, Everest bore a simple designation, Peak XV, the result of a survey undertaken by Sir George Everest, surveyor general of India.

Then one day, at least according to legend, a young computer clerk named Hennessey rushed into the office of Andrew Waugh, who had succeeded Everest, and excitedly blurted, "Sir! I have discovered the highest mountain in the world." Waugh named it after his predecessor. Its height was originally set at 29,002 feet; today it is acknowledged to be 29,028 feet.

Almost three-quarters of a century were to pass before the British formulated an organized expedition. In the interim the mountain was scarcely approached by outsiders. Two early trailblazers, Dr. A. M. Kellas and Captain John B. Noel, probably came nearest. In 1913 Noel, disguised as a Moslem, traveled by foot to within forty miles of it, the closest of any Westerner up to that time.

In 1921, sparked by the urgings of Noel, Brigadier General C. G. Bruce, and the combined efforts of the Alpine Club and Royal Geographical Society, which formed the Mount Everest Committee, a reconnaissance party was organized. Led by Lieutenant Colonel C. K. Howard-Bury, it obtained permission to enter Tibet from the Dalai Lama, a by-product of a treaty concluded by Francis Younghusband in 1903. Mallory, thirty-three, already had made his mark and was an obvious choice of the Alpine Club as a lead climber.

Mallory left a less-than-idealized impression on Younghusband, then the first chairman of the Mount Everest Committee. "There was nothing remarkable in his appearance," said Younghusband.

> He was of the ordinary type of young man that you see in thousands every day. He was not like [Brig. Gen.] Bruce was at the same age, a giant of strength and bursting with physical energy. Nor was he of the wiry, vivid, alert type we see among Frenchmen and Italians. He certainly was good looking, with a sensitive, cultivated air. And now and then he would speak in a sudden, perhaps rather jerky impatient way, showing that there was more going on within him than met the eye. But no one who had not seen him on a mountain would have remarked anything very special in him. And if the man in the street had had the selection of the climbers he would have chosen robust, more vigorous looking men than Mallory.[3]

When the invitation to join the expedition was extended to Mallory, he accepted it without visible emotion. "He had the self-confidence of assured position as a climber," said Younghusband. "He had neither exaggerated modesty nor pushful self-assertiveness. He was conscious of his own powers and of the position he had won by his own exertions; and he had, in consequence, a not obtrusive but quite perceptible and quite justifiable pride in himself as a mountaineer."[4]

When asked whether he objected to sharing a tent with another climber who was thought to have an irritating personality, Mallory snapped that he "didn't care who I sleep with as long as we get to the top." To Younghusband, if the confident young man was not boisterously enthusiastic, he was "keen enough at bottom—keener than the most boisterous."

Noel, who went on two expeditions with him, thought Mallory was high strung, restless, and often ill at ease; the desire to reach the top of Everest permeated every fiber of his being.

The reconnaissance party made its approach through Darjeeling, India, from which point it marched 300 miles in a circular arc, via Phari and Kampa Dzong, to the north or Tibetan side of Everest. The southern part, situated in Nepal, was barred to foreigners. Dr. Kellas, who had taken the first photographs ever made of the mountain, died of a heart attack en route.

After a month-long trek, the party reached the Rongbuk monastery and camped at 16,500 feet. The dark ridges of Everest were now only sixteen miles away.

When Mallory spotted the mountain, the first thing he noticed was that it was built on big and simple lines.

"At the end of the valley and above the glacier Everest rises not so much as a peak as a prodigious mountain-mass," he stated. "There is no complication for the eye.

> Considered as a structure Mount Everest is seen from the Rongbuk Valley to achieve height with amazing simplicity. . . . We do not see jagged crests and a multitude of pinnacles, and beautiful as such ornament may be we do not miss it. The outline is comparatively smooth because the stratification is horizontal, a circumstance which seems to give strength, emphasizing the broad foundations. And yet Everest is a rugged giant. It has not the smooth undulations of a snow mountain with white snow cap and glaciated flanks. It is rather a great rock mass, coated often with a thin layer of white powder which is blown about its sides, and bearing perennial snow only on the gentler ledges and on several wide faces less steep than the rest. The summit lies back so far along the immense arêtes that big as it always appears one required a distant view to realize its height.[5]

Mount Everest, felt Mallory, had the most stupendous ridges and

Mount Everest (29,028 ft.) peeks over the guardian ramparts of Nuptse, as seen from the monastic village of Tengboche.

appalling precipices he had ever seen. All talk of an easy snow slope was now a myth.

Almost six months were spent in the region. The prime task—to find a feasible route to the summit of the "Mother Goddess of the World," or *Chomolungma,* as the natives call it—was undertaken by Mallory and G. H. Bullock. They scouted the west face, which was found to be too steep. Mounting a col to the northwest of Everest, they looked down into the Western Cwm and the Khumbu glacier, and saw Pumori and Cho Oyu. It was decided that the twisted icefalls and cataracts of the cwm offered no hope, although Mallory found the sight to be "fantastically beautiful." From the head of the glacier Mallory earlier had seen a long saddle linking the north face of Everest with what is now called Changtse, or North Peak. This saddle was the key to the riddle, and became known as the North Col. Mallory was now committed; the route up Everest would lie via this col, up its steep but feasible face to the northeast ridge, which tilted gently to the summit. Every subsequent attempt until World War II used this line.

The next problem was reaching the North Col. Mallory had passed the ice stream of the East Rongbuk glacier, but thought it was too small to have emanated from Everest. In fact, it led directly to the base of the col. Misled, Mallory and Bullock ascended Lhakpa La, a 22,350-foot pass, which dropped down into the East Rongbuk basin from the east. With three porters, Mallory, Bullock, and E. O. Wheeler briskly tackled the 2,000-foot-high ice cliff, which was dangerously stitched with large crevasses, and finally reached the saddle, at 23,000 feet. Fearsome blasts of wind discouraged them from proceeding higher. Carefully Mallory studied the long face and ridge that rose before them. He was confident that an ascent was feasible. A route to the summit of Mount Everest surely had been found.

In 1922 Mallory and the British returned—this time to climb. Now they were led by Brigadier General Bruce, a strapping, take-charge genius of a man, who was at once a first-rate organizer and yet was well known and respected by the Gurkas. There were four main climbers: Mallory; Howard Somervell, a generous, affable surgeon who possessed unflinching endurance and who was so moved by the appalling living conditions in India that he became a medical missionary there; Major E. F. Norton, a methodical artillery officer who spoke Hindustani; and Captain George Finch.

This time the approach was made up the East Rongbuk glacier. Conditions were vastly changed from the previous year. Beaten back by raging winds and blizzards, and surrounded by gaping chasms that promised death with one misstep, the party realized that the ascent to the North Col would be the most hazardous part of the entire climb. Three camps were pitched on the glacier, a fourth atop the col, and the last, at 25,000 feet, on the northeast ridge.

Norton, Somervell, and Mallory now launched the first attempt ever on Everest. (H. T. Morshead fell ill and remained at Camp 5; Finch, also sick, was compelled temporarily to stay below.) Without oxygen bottles, drawing five breaths to the step, progressing at the rate of 400 feet per hour, they managed to attain 26,985 feet by 2:30 in the afternoon, at which point they stopped, aware that at such a pace they could never hope to reach the summit and safely return. On the descent the entire party was almost killed. One of them slipped and was carrying the others with him toward a crevasse; Mallory's quick reflexes in driving his ice ax deep into the granular surface averted disaster. When they finally reached the North Col at 11:30 P.M., starved, frostbitten, their senses numbed, they found to their dismay that the porters had evacuated it, taking all the cooking utensils with them. The upshot was that, with Norton's culinary talents, they feasted on a concoction of strawberry jam, milk, and snow.

A few days later supplementary oxygen was employed for the first time on an Everest assault. Finch and Bruce pressed up to 27,235 feet, the highest point thus far attained.

The expedition was, however, fated to end in disaster. After the initial setbacks, the lama of the Rongbuk monastery sent a message, warning of danger. It was, of course, disregarded.

On June 6, 1922, having regrouped its forces on the glacier, the party prepared to take the offensive once more, hopefully before the monsoon struck. Climbs on Everest are invariably governed by the monsoon season, which normally stretches from early June through September. (*Monsoon* is derived from the Arabic word for season, and is formed by a southwest wind, laden with moisture, which blows across India from the Indian Ocean.) Now Somervell, Mallory, and another climber, C. G. Crawford, led the way up the ice wall of the North Col, joined by fourteen porters, forming a total of four ropes. It was a day splashed in sunshine, and the large party gingerly inched its way up to within a few hundred feet of the col. The danger of a snowslide was, they were sure, behind them. The climbers heard what was described as "an ominous sound, sharp, arresting, violent and yet somehow soft like an explosion of untamped gun powder."[6] Mallory was thrown off his feet as a mound of snow broke over the party; swimming desperately, half suffocated, he was able to fight his way to the top. He yanked on the rope; the porter who had been climbing behind him scrambled to his feet. Looking around, Mallory spotted Somervell and Crawford crawling out of the white dust. What of the others? Far below four porters were frantically pointing toward a forty-foot crevasse into which the avalanche had spilled. Seven Sherpas had been swept to their deaths; two of their bodies were never found. The 1922 assault was abandoned.

Undaunted, the British returned again in 1924. At the outset Brigadier General Bruce came down with malaria, and had to be replaced as the leader by Norton. The party received the customary blessing of the lama at the Rongbuk monastery. This had little effect upon the weather Gods. The climbers encountered some of the most violent storms ever experienced on Everest. Two porters eventually died from the effects of a blizzard. For a while it seemed the attempt would be thwarted before it got underway. Supplies that had been carefully packed and labeled in England were dropped at a dump site short of Camp 3 and indiscriminately opened—leading to almost insurmountable turmoil. In a tempest the party retreated to base camp at the head of the glacier, and reassembled. The porters were in a bad state, physically and emotionally, and Norton chose to recharge their spirits by repairing to the monastery to seek the good wishes of the lama.

Now the party moved to the attack again, and, with Mallory in the lead, ice steps were laboriously hacked through a large and menacing chimney that cut across the ice wall of the North Col. Mallory's performance on this perilous stretch, which enabled the party to entrench itself on the col, left its impression on Norton, who wrote: "Confronted with a formidable climbing obstacle, Mallory's behavior was always characteristic; you could positively see his nerves tighten up like fiddle strings. Metaphorically he girt up his loins, and his first instinct was to jump into the lead. Up the wall and chimney he led there, climbing carefully, neatly, in that beautiful style that was all his own."[7]

Now a new calamity hit, one that was to have serious repercussions. On one of the carries to the col, four of the porters, no doubt fearful of the first 200 feet of the descent, which were the most risky, insisted on remaining behind. Another storm broke, the temperature dropped sharply, and they became trapped alone on the col. Norton was faced with a grim decision: should he attempt to conserve the strength of his best climbers, or use them to mount a rescue? He felt that he had no choice. On May 24, 1924, the snowing ceased, and Mallory, Somervell, and Norton set off for the col again. Wading through the drifts, Mallory assessed the odds at ten to one against making the rescue. After a monumental effort the porters were safely brought down—a feat made all the more exasperating when, in reply to Norton's shouted question as to whether they were fit to walk, one of the porters, unaware of the mischief they had caused, answered, "Up or down?" "Down, you fool!" exclaimed Norton.[8]

The porters received a safe conduct back to the basin of the glacier, but the climbers paid a high price. The effort put forth in the rescue was a strenuous one, and in all probability it cost Norton, Somervell, and Mallory whatever chance they had of making the ascent. Noel, for one, keenly felt that Mallory's strength had been sapped, and that he was a spent man, before he made his last fatal assault on the mountain.

Nonetheless, the group girded for this, their third assault. On June 4, 1924, Norton and Somervell, after having camped at 26,800 feet, flung themselves at the northeast ridge, climbing without oxygen equipment. The first 700 feet went easily, and then, suddenly, the shortage of oxygen was felt hard. They began drawing 7 to 10 breaths a step, and never were able to move more than 20 to 30 yards without pausing for a couple of minutes. Rather than following the ridge, they broke out over the face, moving laterally as much as vertically, but more closely approaching the plumb line of the summit. At around 28,000 feet Somervell suffered a severe constriction and soreness of the throat. He stopped, leaned on the rocks, and waved to Norton to go on alone. Norton traversed a yellow band of limestone to a large, open couloir that led directly to the summit ridge. The footing there was perilously slippery and laden with snow. Norton clung to small nodules of rock at some points, was hip deep in snow at others; he moved cautiously, aware that one mistake would surely be fatal, for the gully was tilted at a keen angle and deposited its refuse onto a glacier thousands of feet below.

Exhausted, suffering from snow blindness, Norton reached his limit at 1:00 P.M., having attained 28,126 feet. Considering that he was moving alone, without supplementary oxygen, it was an unparalleled feat of high-altitude climbing.

Below, Mallory waited with Andrew Irvine, a bullish twenty-two-year-old Oxford student, ready for his try. Up to Camp 6 they went, with geologist N. E. Odell in support. Question has been raised as to why the youthful Irvine, and not Odell, who was far more experienced and now better acclimatized, was chosen by Mallory as his partner. No doubt it was due to the fact that Irvine was highly skilled in handling and repairing the oxygen equipment. Also, Odell had been slow in acclimatizing, but later it was seen that he was in a more fit condition than anybody else in the party, the more so because, unlike Mallory, Norton, and Somervell, his strength had not been depleted by the Herculean effort needed to retrieve the four porters from the North Col. Norton, now temporarily blind, thought Odell should go, but decided not to say anything to avoid interfering with Mallory's preparations.

George Mallory and E. F. Norton approaching high point of 26,985 feet on Mount Everest on May 21, 1922. *By permission of the Royal Geographical Society.*

From Camp 6 Mallory scribbled a note that one of the Sherpas took back to Odell. It read:

> We're awfully sorry to have left things in such a mess—our Una cooker rolled down the slope at the last moment. Be sure of getting back to IV tomorrow in time to evacuate before dark, as I hope to. In the tent I must have left a compass—for the Lord's sake rescue it: we are without. To be here on 90 atmospheres for two days—so we'll probably go on two cylinders—but it's a bloody load of climbing. Perfect weather for the job.
>
> Yours ever,
G. Mallory.[9]

Dawn of June 8, 1924, broke calm but misty. Mallory and Irvine left Camp 6, at what hour is unknown, while Odell climbed up from Camp 5 to watch them and lend support upon their return.

The two climbers disappeared into the haze and were never heard from again.

At 12:50 P.M. Odell, about halfway to Camp 6, reached a rock buttress and looked up to the two steps that led to the summit. For an instant the mist parted. His report: "I noticed far away on a snowslope leading up to what seemed to me to be the last step but one from the base of the final pyramid, a tiny object moving and approaching the rock step. A second object followed, and then the first climbed to the top of the step. As I stood intently watching this dramatic appearance, the scene became enveloped in a cloud once more, and I could not actually be certain that I saw the second figure join the first."[10]

Odell reached Camp 6, bringing the compass that had been requested and which he placed in the middle of the tent. At 4:30, seeing no sign of the climbers, he returned to the col. The next morning Odell once more, without oxygen equipment, ascended to the high camp, squinting at the topmost shoulder of Everest for some trace of Mallory or Irvine. There was none. The compass lay in the tent where he had left it. For two hours in the face of a gale he scrambled above the camp, well over 27,000 feet, but his efforts were futile. Looking at those heights, Odell was dazzled, almost inexorably drawn to go higher, to try for the top. He wondered whether Mallory had felt the same impulse. Then he came down.

What happened to Mallory and Irvine—the eleventh and twelfth victims to perish on Everest? Nine years later, in 1933 on the next expedition, L. R. Wager and Wyn Harris found an untarnished ice ax lying bare on the rocks about 250 yards east of the first step. It bore the label "Willisch of Tasch"—a brand used by Mallory and Irvine. This led to endless speculation. Were the climbers swept off the mountain at that point? Did they attain the summit and falter there on their return?

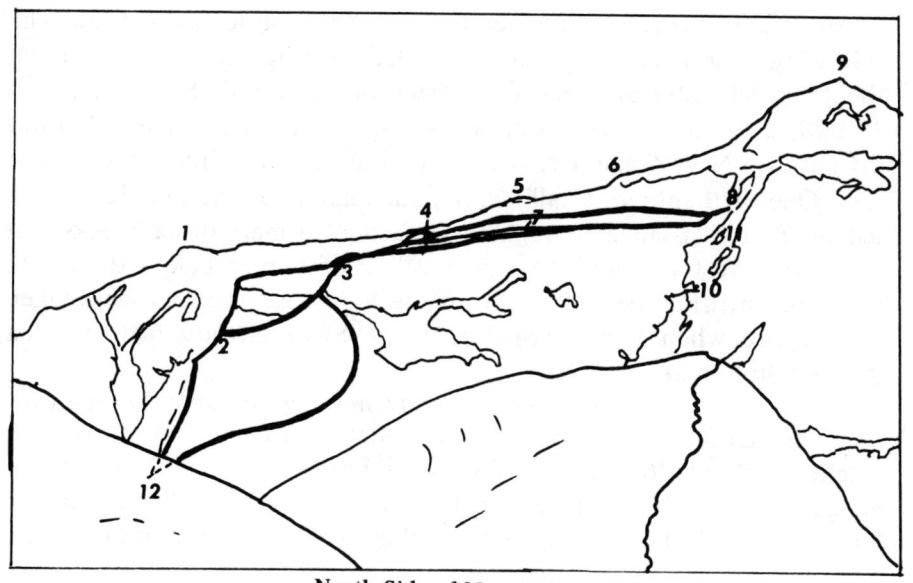

North Side of Mount Everest

1 — Northeast Ridge
2 — Camp 6 (1924)
3 — Camp 6 (1933)
4 — Mallory or Irvine Ice Ax Found in 1933
5 — First Step
6 — Second Step
7 — Shipton's Highest Point
8 — Highest Point Reached in 1924 and 1933
9 — Summit (29,028 feet)
10 — Great Couloir
11 — Subsidiary Couloir
12 — Camp 5

Was the ax dropped so that it fell to that height? Or was it merely left there on the way up—an unlikely practice for a mountaineer. Odell thought it was probable that the men had been forced to bivouac on the mountain. The likeliest explanation is that Mallory or Irvine slipped and fell the length of the north face to the firn below. The full and true story lies entombed within the icy crusts and glacial wastes of Everest.

In the 1930s four attempts were made on the northeast ridge by successive expeditions led by Hugh Ruttledge (twice), Eric Shipton, and H.W. Tilman. Hounded by bitterly foul weather, none came close to victory, although the Wager-Harris and Shipton-Frank Smythe ropes exceeded 28,000 feet in 1933. In 1934 Maurice Wilson made an unusual pilgrimage through Tibet to the Rongbuk glacier, intent on scaling Everest alone. He froze to death below the North Col.

After the turmoil of World War II receded, attention returned to Everest in 1950 and again in 1951—thirty years after Mallory's original reconnaissance. Nepal opened its borders just as the Chinese Communists were assuming control over Tibet, sealing it off from outsiders. Now it would be seen whether a southerly route could be found up Everest from the Nepal side.

An Anglo-American group scouted the Khumbu icefall in 1950. The following year a reconnaissance party led by Shipton trekked through the Solu Khumbu and Namche Bazar up to Gorak Shep, at about 17,000 feet, where a lake camp was set up. At the last moment Shipton invited two New Zealanders who had climbed in the Himalayas to join him. One of them was a tall, sinewy man named Edmund Hillary, who led the reconnaissance through the treacherous maze of ice blocks that guard the Western Cwm, the great valley of silence below the South Col. The British expected to return the following year and were taken by surprise when they learned that the Swiss already had received permission to make the attempt.

In 1952 the Swiss, led by Dr. Gabriel Chevalley, became the first ever to attain the South Col, the snow-neck that joins Everest to Lhotse at a height of about 26,000 feet. Raymond Lambert and Sherpa Tenzing Norgay spent a frigid night in a tent, without sleeping bags, stove or liquids, at 27,550 feet. The next day they reached their limit at 28,215 feet, the highest point yet attained.

Now the British were again to have their chance at the prize. Two years of planning went into the 1953 attempt, headed by Colonel John Hunt. The party assembled in Bhadgaon, near Katmandu. From there

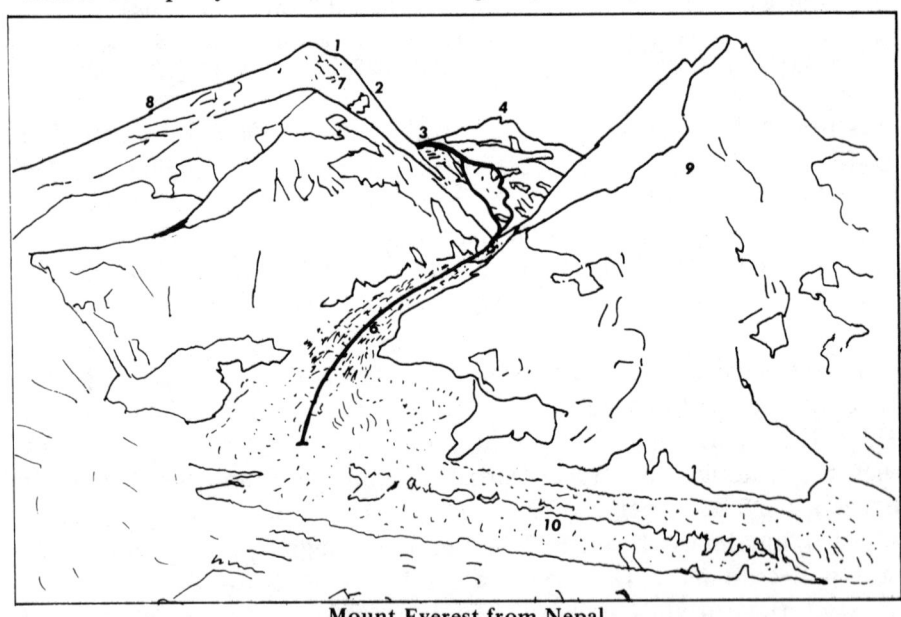

Mount Everest from Nepal
Solid line: Usual route from base camp to South Col.

1 — South Summit	4 — Lhotse	8 — Northeast Ridge
2 — Southeast Ridge	5 — Western Cwm	9 — Nuptse
3 — South Col	6 — Khumbu Icefall	10 — Khumbu Glacier
	7 — Rock Band (Southwest Face)	

20 Sherpas and 350 coolies carried some 473 items of baggage, weighing seven and one-half tons, over a 17-day route via Those, Junbesi, Jubing, and Namche Bazar to Tengboche, which, at 12,715 feet, harbors the chief Buddhist shrine in the Khumbu. The party went on several stiff training climbs and then directed its attention to the tricky business of threading a route for the Sherpas through the menacing blocks of the Khumbu icefall.

Two assaults were planned. The first would emanate from the South Col camp at 26,200 feet, the second from a bivouac higher up on the southeast ridge. On May 26, 1953, Charles Evans and Tom Bourdillon set off about 7:30 A.M. from the col, having been delayed by a defect in their oxygen equipment. They climbed steadily and surmounted a steep rise that tilted at a sharp angle below the South Summit. By one o'clock they had breached this lower summit, at 28,700 feet. The 300-foot ridge that separated them from the top looked imposing, and, at their rate of climbing, they figured they would not be able to reach the crest and return to the South Summit before 6:00 P.M., after which another 3,000-foot descent would have to be covered without supplemental oxygen. Tired, pressed for time, fighting difficulties with their oxygen sets, they turned back, content in the knowledge that they had reached a higher point on Everest than anyone before them.

Now Hillary and Tenzing—the same Sherpa who had come so close to success in the valiant 1952 Swiss attempt—were to have their chance. They bivouacked well above the col, on a tilting ledge, at 27,900 feet. They spent a difficult night, sleeping only intermittently, and periodically resorting to oxygen bottles. Hillary was half propped up, trying to hold the sides of the tent so it would not be blown over, and Tenzing clutched an air mattress that was on the brink of rolling over the steep ledge. After a breakfast of sardines, crackers, and lemon juice, they set out at 6:30 A.M.. The day sparkled; more important, it was windless. They moved rapidly. In two and one-half hours they were able to crampon onto the South Summit. Now the final challenge rose before them. Hillary studied the virgin slope carefully. He wrote:

> At first glance it was certainly impressive and even rather frightening. On the right, great contorted cornices, overhanging masses of snow and ice, stuck out like twisted fingers over the 10,000-foot drop of the Kangshung Face. Any move onto these cornices could only bring disaster. From the cornices the ridge dropped steeply to the left until the snow merged with the great rock face sweeping up from the Western Cwm. Only one encouraging feature was apparent. The steep slope between the cornices and the rock precipices seemed to be composed of hard, firm, snow.[11]

Hillary chopped steps in the crystalline whiteness, and the two men moved up steadily, where no man ever before had trod. An hour later they encountered a forty-foot rock obstacle, the most imposing problem on the entire ridge. The climbers had noticed this large step in photographs and had studied it through binoculars from Tengboche. Hillary found a narrow gap between the rock buttress and the adjoining snow cornice on the east side. He jammed into the crack, braced his back against the snow, and cramponed backwards up the pitch. Tenzing cautiously crawled up and joined him. They now turned for the last lap. Slowly they pressed forward and upward along the narrow blade that twists to the north, the fragile snow cornices teetering over the huge face to their right, the sloping wall of rocks falling away beneath them on their left. Repeatedly they cut steps to the top of one cornice, only to be confronted by others still higher.

Hillary, with the ax, had scarcely raised his head when he realized that the ridge in front of him, instead of monotonously rising, dropped away. Far in the distance could be seen the North Col and the Rongbuk Glacier. A few more whacks of the ice ax and the great task pioneered by Mallory and others thirty-two years before was concluded.

At 11:30 A.M. on May 29, 1953, after five hours of steady climbing, Hillary and Tenzing reached the top of the world.

Exegi monumentum aere perennius, as Horace said in his *Odes.* Their achievement stands as a monument more enduring than bronze.

Who was this Sherpa named Tenzing who, with the New Zealand beekeeper Hillary, in one fine, shining hour, became a universal hero?

Tenzing was born in a small village called Tsa-chu, near Makalu, in (as he believes) 1914. His first expedition came at age twenty-one when Eric Shipton selected him to join the 1935 reconnaissance party to Mount Everest. A year later he was back again, with Hugh Ruttledge, but the effort was stymied by violent weather. Later he became a member of a group that surveyed and mapped the Nanda Devi region.

In 1938 Tenzing undertook his third trip to Everest as part of the H. W. Tilman expedition. He performed well, helping establish Camp 6 at 27,200 feet, but again the "sahibs" were turned back. A decade later, after the flames of war had subsided, he accompanied Earl Denman on a solitary and adventuresome visit via Tibet to the base of the North Col.

Tenzing next journeyed to Lhasa where he met the Dalai Lama. His hardest climb came in 1951 when, searching for two lost Frenchmen, he and Louis Dubost reached the top of Nanda Devi East, at 24,400 feet. The ensuing year found him on Everest twice again—in the spring and autumn—with the Swiss.

Thus when victory—and the fulfillment of a lifelong dream—came in 1953, Tenzing was making his seventh attempt on the world's highest peak. He was thirty-eight years old at the time; Hillary was thirty-three.

In 1963 an American team placed six men on the summit and achieved the maiden ascent of the west ridge. Jim Whittaker, sharing a rope with Sherpa Nawang Gombu, became the first American to reach the top via the South Col, on May 1, 1963. Three weeks later Barry Bishop and Lute Jerstad attained the summit from the col, while Tom Hornbein and Willi Unsoeld accomplished the first traverse, ascending the west ridge and coming down the south side. On the hairy descent, the two parties met up with each other about 10 P.M. and, utterly exhausted, spent the night huddled against the cold rocks at an altitude of about 28,000 feet—a harrowing experience then thought likely to be beyond the limit of human endurance. Only a miracle—Everest was becalmed that night—enabled them to survive.

The Hornbein-Unsoeld traverse ranks among the most magnificent of all Himalayan mountaineering achievements. It represented a climb so ambitious in conception, and courageous in execution, that there have been few attempts at a similar feat to this day.

As for the original North Col route, the Chinese Communists claim to have reached the top from Tibet in 1960. In 1975 nine members of a Chinese-led party are known to have made the ascent from the north, including a woman, Phanthog. All nine were on the summit at the same time. Earlier in the same season, on May 16, 1975, a Japanese housewife, Junko Tabei, accompanied by Sherpa guide Ang Tshering, became the first female to complete the climb.

The climactic ascent of the most difficult route yet fashioned on Everest came in 1975 when the towering southwest face was scaled by a British expedition led by Chris Bonington. Like the Eigerwand in the Alps, the southwest face for years loomed as a lingering challenge, the principal obstacle being the sheer, 1,000-foot Rock Band that stretches high across the summit block; it requires the use of extreme rock climbing techniques at a dizzy height of 27,000 feet.

Snow chutes at the left and right ends of the Band provided the most obvious weaknesses in the line. After a reconnaissance in 1969, members of a powerful Japanese team reached 26,400 feet, just beneath the left-hand gully, before being thwarted the following season. However, four of its climbers did attain the summit via the traditional South Col route. Successive attempts by international, European, British, and Japanese expeditions similarly foundered in the right-hand fork; the Rock Band remained inviolate.

Bonington's post-monsoon 1975 party now elected to try the leftmost gully, and it proved to be more forgiving than suspected. With a daring lead, Nick Estcourt and Paul Braithwaite forced a ramp that led out of the chute to the top of the Band and the upper snowfield beyond. This runout paved the way for Dougal Haston and Doug Scott to attain the south and main summits on September 23, 1975; they survived a bivouac in a snow cave at 28,700 feet without oxygen sets. Two days later a second ascent was made by Peter Boardman and the Sherpa, Pertemba. Mick Burke, scrambling up alone, passed them just as they were descending in rapidly deteriorating weather; he was never seen again.

Spring of 1978 proved to be an exceptional season. Reinhold Messner and Peter Habeler established another first by attaining the summit without the aid of supplementary oxygen. Messner thus became the initial climber ever to scale four 8,000-meter peaks—Nanga Parbat, Manaslu, Hidden Peak, and Everest. Franz Oppurg then made the ascent solo from a camp pitched at 27,200 feet. During its series of assaults the Austrian team placed nine men on top of the peak. Then Messner, in 1980, made the entire climb solo, without oxygen equipment, from the Tibetan flank.

As of mid-1979, Mount Everest had been surmounted by a total of 84 persons. Sherpa Nawang Gombu was the first to achieve the feat twice. These mountaineers came from 16 expeditions representing Great Britain (twice), Switzerland, United States (twice), India, Japan (thrice), Italy, China, joint British-Nepal, South Korea, Austria, France-Germany, and Yugoslavia. Later two Poles completed the initial winter ascent. Some 50 climbers and porters are said to have perished in attempts over the years. As the world's highest pinnacle, Everest still stands as an awesome and eternal challenge.

The exploration of the remote regions of the planet Earth now has been largely accomplished. In 1522, after rounding Patagonia, Ferdinand Magellan's *Victoria* completed the circumnavigation of the globe. Henry Stanley crisscrossed Africa and helped trace the source of the Nile. Francisco de Orellana probed the Amazon, Charles Lindbergh soloed the Atlantic, and Auguste Piccard's bathyscaphe *Trieste* later dived 35,800 feet into the Mariana Trench. Under assaults by Robert Peary and Roald Amundsen, the North and South Poles had yielded to man. So, too, had the last great prize—the summit of Mount Everest.

* * *

For two and one-half hours, from Katmandu to Lamosangu by the Sun Kosi, we rode along the tumbling countryside, over lush hills of corn, barley, and millet that plunged hurriedly into deep river gorges, and abruptly reemerged on the other side. Immaculately kept terraced farms blanketed the slopes. The Kodari highway, built by the Chinese to link Nepal with Tibet, led us to within thirty miles of the northerly border.

A commotion erupted as soon as our three-car caravan halted. Loads were dumped unceremoniously on the ground—and a tangle of porters scrambled about madly dividing them up, pulling at our duffle bags and tent poles, fighting over whether a carry exceeded the sixty-five-pound average, hauling in a small scale to buttress their contentions, and, in the main, having much good-natured, brawling fun. In a flash all was settled, and before I could sort out my own rucksack, the entire train of men, women, and children had disappeared across a cable-suspension bridge and set upon a steep, rock-hewn trail.

We were embarked on a five-week trek through the Eastern Himalayas—to the Khumbu glacier and Everest base camp, and down the Arun River Valley south to Dharan, toward India, a distance of some 325 miles.

There were six trekkers in our party, plus myself: our guide, Stan Armington, a mountain climbing instructor from Portland, long legged, laconic, his tousled hair covering his face like windshield wipers, possessed of a keen business mind that yet much preferred a trail to a desk; Graham Wallis, from Victoria, British Columbia, a steady, soft-spoken engineer, observant and whimsical, a photography addict, and my tentmate throughout the trip (we became known as the "odd couple"); Walbridge "Bo" Powell, a teacher from Seattle, likable, wide-eyed, as big as a panda, a ceaseless plodder and self-anointed trek wit; his wife, Kathy, tall, gracefully self-propelled, pragmatic, never complaining; Tom Broderson, a public school administrator from Portland, a weathered, easy-going, clocklike hiker and climber who had resigned from his job to join up; and, Claire Lavoie, from Quebec, a smart-looking young girl of the outdoors who ran river boats during the

The rolling, well-manicured foothills en route to the Solu Khumbu

131

summer for Lute Jerstad, the Everest climber who organized the trip.

Our mini-expedition was stoutly abetted by eight Sherpas and eighteen porters. The entire party thus consisted of a stream of thirty-three persons, although the exact number varied frequently along the way.

From here I will let excerpts and adaptations from my 1972 diary pick up most of the story:

October 26 (1st day): We arrived in Lamosangu amid complete chaos. Our porters were arm-wrestling with the loads and each other. Some brought their little boys along to help. Our equipment and baggage seemed to be in an endless hodgepodge: foodstuffs, canned goods, pots and pans, utensils, sleeping bags, ice axes, tents, parkas, pants, egg crates, ropes, and an infinite number of other trail items were scattered aimlessly. Suddenly everyone—and everything—disappeared. We were on the trail.

Lamosangu is only about 4,000 feet up, and we must traverse six major ridges, proceeding west to east, before reaching the heart of the Solu Khumbu.

The Sherpas with us were: our pleasant sirdar (or straw boss), Dawa Sindar, intelligent, smiling, whose smooth duck-walk stride quietly but rapidly absorbed the trail; three orderlies, Agelu, Ang Tsering, and Ang Dawa, lean boned, eager, and surprisingly efficient; our chef, Ang Chatter; his helper; the Sherpa cook; and Ongchu, our delightful messboy.

The hills rose sharply from the river and we ached from the start. First surprise: in a clearing, with all of us pooped after only a two-hour pull, seven cups and a hot teapot materialized, spread neatly on a large burlap canvas by Ongchu. Each of us was supposed to be in good condition. The Powells had followed a steady training program, capped by driving to the High Sierra and scaling Mount Whitney. Tom Broderson went on a series of conditioning hikes and ascended Mount Hood. Graham had climbed around Vancouver. Claire had not ceased hiking since early summer. Stan already had two East Himalayan excursions to his credit. And there we sat already at a standstill. The Sherpas and porters were not bothered. How they managed those loads was incredible.

Some loud drums and flutes, and a stream of banners, came winding over the hill. A Buddhist funeral, said our sirdar.

"Much noise! Very dumb!" exclaimed Agelu, my personal orderly, happy at a chance to display his repertoire of English. Once or twice a day Agelu's dark rounded face would contort, and he would point a finger at his head and whirl his hand in circles, meanwhile bouncing up and down in place, chattering away excitedly in a polyglot of Nepali,

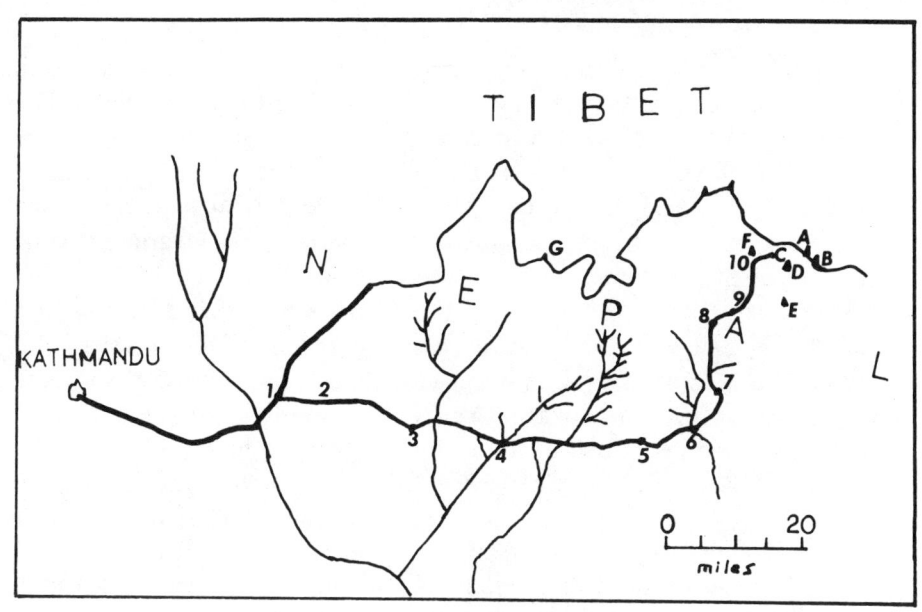

Trekking Route to
Mount Everest Base Camp

1 – Lamosangu
2 – Pakhar
3 – Kirantichap
4 – Those
5 – Junbesi

6 – Takshindu
7 – Puiyan
8 – Namche Bazar
9 – Tengboche
10 – Lobuje

A – Mount Everest
B – Lhotse
C – Base Camp
D – Nuptse

E – Ama Dablam
F – Pumori
G – Gauri Sankar

Sherpa, and broken English. This meant that he thought someone, or something, was crazy. Alert and supportive, Agelu fast became indispensable.

The villages we threaded through were small, simple, and dirty in a subdued way. Just a handful of inhabitants, and a couple of mudhuts, made up a place that appeared on the map. The villages might be fifteen minutes to two hours walking distance apart. Nepal is sparsely but continuously populated; there is practically no wilderness area.

The Western influence was evident. Tin cans and trashy campsites abounded. There seemed to be almost as many Westerners on the trail as Nepalese. Going to the "lavatory" was a continual problem. The Sherpas and porters dressed in frayed, overworn garments, but were modest about their personal habits. The scrub forest provided a good cover, and one rarely saw them using an outdoor bathroom. Yet, when one of us tried to sneak into the forest, native girls invariably came along, discreetly glancing the other way.

The most striking qualities of the Sherpas are their sincerity and friendliness. They are a loose and happy people, full of spirit and humor, spare, hard, proud, and yet childlike. (I never noticed an obese Sherpa the entire time I was in Nepal.) If they don't understand you, they simply smile. Most of them speak two languages: Nepali, the official language of the country, and Sherpa, a spoken but not written variant of Tibetan. Several knew a smattering of English as well as German or French, picked up from prior treks and expeditions.

We met two Canadian students who had been traveling through Africa, India, and Nepal since May. They had no food, having expected to buy it on the trail; so far no luck. We gave them some rice, cookies, and tea. Food we had aplenty.

Pemba, age nine, the son of one of the porters, became the immediate camp favorite. He carried Tom Broderson's thirty-four-pound fire-engine-red bag, which was wider than, and as tall as, Pemba. His black eyes fairly danced with gaiety, his stocky body bobbing along awkwardly but unsparingly; finding out to whom the bag belonged, he attached himself to Tom like flypaper.

We camped at a lovely site near Pakhar, about 6,500 feet. Before we arrived, the four tents were staked out, our duffle bags neatly placed inside and opened, the sleeping bags aired, the canvas was on the ground, and Ongchu was approaching us, teapot in hand. After four hours, we had reached our limit.

October 27 (2nd day): Up at 5:30 A.M.; on the trail an hour later. We trekked until 3:30 P.M., with time out for fried noodles and a ham roll that tasted like dogmeat.

We ascended to the top of a 9,000-foot ridge, past Mudi to Nigale, down a thin forest on the other side, then on to Serobesi near the Charenge River.

Here we encountered one of Nepal's hallmarks—a wooden Ferris wheel of the type inscribed on the country's paper currency, and a tall, four-legged wooden swing; also a cornmeal "factory," which derived its power from the rapids that spurt through the village.

Claire referred to Nepal as a land of "plain living and high thinking," while the United States, we concluded, represented "plain thinking and high living." Already we were grumbling about when we were supposed to reach "The Hill" (meaning Mount Everest).

Tom Broderson became the first victim: stomach cold or flu. But he kept pushing on. His free-swinging orderly, Ang Tsering, who seemed to have a girl friend in every village, took his rucksack from him, and stashed it atop a whole assortment of baggage that he carried as though it were a paperweight. It drizzled most of the day. I could not get used to the huge terraced plottages. How did they keep them so trim and manicured? Nothing was wasted.

The price structure in Nepal was revealing. Our sirdar was being paid twenty rupees per day, plus food. (Since one rupee equalled ten cents U.S., this amounted to two dollars.) The other seven supervising Sherpas received fifteen rupees a day, and food. The porters got only twelve rupees, without food; they must buy or forage on their own. If they didn't plan to remain throughout the whole trek, they would receive three rupees per day for their return journey, during which they would be entirely on their own. The Sherpas and porters ate, slept, and worked apart, akin to a self-imposed caste system.

October 28 (3rd day): Very hot. By now we are getting used to the Himalayan trot: up-up-up, down-down-down. There were only hills and ridges underfoot, no flat space. The big rivers flow south out of the mountains, whereas our route crosses them to the east. Hence, we invariably were climbing up the flank of one ridge, and down its far side, to reach the intervening waterways.

By an intense exercise of intelligence, it dawned on us that for every river or stream there are at least two slopes—the mathematical inevitability of which was enough to give everybody mental calluses. We were following thin mountain paths that actually constituted the principal trade routes in the area.

Major fact number one emerged: outside of human porterage, and a few scattered landing fields for small aircraft, there are no means of transport or communication into rural Nepal. No roads, cars, or buses are to be found—just coolie labor, hauling their wares and grain from village to village. Until recently, Nepalese paper currency often was unacceptable here, and the Everest expeditions used to carry large boxes of coins to buy rice and potatoes en route. Now the local teahouses, where a tourist can pass the night stretched out on a wooden box, honor paper bills, probably because this corner of Nepal has become a popular route of travel as a result of the Everest influence.

We moved through rice paddies and tiny villages populated by Chetris and Brahmins, both Hindu, the Buddhist Tamangs, and a few Newars.

A sturdy, load-carrying Sherpa encountered on the trail

At length we encountered a young Australian couple, very bedraggled. They had gone to Junbesi, then turned back. The girl looked as though she were going to strangle her husband (or boyfriend) for getting her into such a fix.

"This must be their honeymoon," chirped Bo. "Her hubby promised her the trip of a lifetime among the enchanting streams and valleys of pastoral Nepal—forgetting to inform her that she would have to march every lick of the way."

We lunched on curried potatoes, cheese, mutton, and turnip greens at a shady, tree-lined stop bearing the charming name of Kirantichap. Afterward we pushed up a steep incline, descended through pine trees and a dense forest to the Tamba Kosi (river), at 3,000 feet, and then ploughed back up a tiring slope through Busti to Namdu, which we reached by 4:00 P.M. We were making good time.

It was getting dark now about 6:00 P. M., and we bedded down promptly. Dinner consisted of turnip greens, chicken soup, rice, fried chicken (prepared by Ang Tsering, who had more culinary skill than our appointed chef, who had none), honey spread, oranges, tea—and more turnip greens. The fare was good, but we were unaware at the time that the diet would never change. Nepalese oranges are only about two inches in diameter, green colored but extraordinarily juicy.

We spotted the Himalayan range for the first time, but were unable to identify the peaks. The river, we noted, was a sickly green, probably due to glacial silt.

As we sat around the fire at night, chatting and playing cards, we found four of us agreeing that in each case our interest in the Himalayas and mountaineering in general was originally stimulated by Maurice Herzog's *Annapurna,* published in the early 1950s, an epic account of the first ascent of a peak 8,000 meters or more in height.

October 29 (4th day): A moderate monsoon teased us just as we broke camp. We forded a small stream and followed a twisting path through a scrub forest to Yarsa, a village inhabited by a Buddhist sect known as the Jirels. Each small village that turns up unannounced has its own distinctive ethnic group, although to the transient the way of life appears unchanging: truly they cultivate a living out of the earth. Farming, yak breeding, and small trade, much of it by the barter system, make up their existence.

Suddenly the rain came down in torrents, and we stopped at a teahouse around noon. The Sherpas were undaunted and quickly set up the tents in a rice field (or mud paddy). Our ponchos were soaked and we passed the afternoon huddled together on the porch of a teahouse. It was simply furnished: an open hearth in the corner; a rough, cold mud and brick floor; a wooden roof held down by stones; a few pots and utensils; boards and mats to sleep on; the fire always stoked, heating up a bowl of water for *cheea* (tea). In a dark corner lay a small, quiet child.

The weather was miserable. The host forced some *rakshi* down our throats; it's a fermented drink, distilled from rice or corn, remindful of Japanese sake, and tastes horrible. But Dawa Sindar gleefully reminded us that it was an insult not to drink it. Agelu bounced up and down again.

Life in the hill country, one noted, is shaped entirely by the environment. The complete absence of mechanized transport, and the insular existence, means that the land controls the destiny of the populace—the reverse of the West. Despite the grinding poverty, the people are cheerful, amiable, and generous to a fault. Small boned and light (most of them probably don't weigh more than 130 pounds), the Nepalese are blessed with unbelievable strength and hardihood; many of the porters are barefooted, but they seem not to notice the sharp rocks on the trail as they trudge along, stopping every half hour or so for a *churot* (cigarette), laughing, sipping *cheea,* swapping stories, mingling with the villagers, then saddling up again, the long bands holding their loads wrapped tightly around their foreheads, their torsos arched forward as they move up another slope.

One day seems like all the rest in this expanse of hills and horizons. The people live a simple, pastoral life. The only variations are the seasonal aspects of raising and rotating crops, and the weather. Amazingly, tiny villages abound everywhere, at every altitude. Often a dozen occupants live in a single room. Occasional surprise: some of the kids speak a bit of English, which is one of the two languages (Nepali being the other) taught in the schools. Since the populace is so thinly spread, and the distances are so great, it is a logistical problem just getting the children to school. Many solve this by staying with relatives near a school site. And everybody has relatives at every stop.

October 30 (5th day): We awoke to gorgeous sunshine. Faint mists stretched out at our feet. Multiple ridges bobbed away in the distance, like reflections off a mirror. Since all of our gear was drenched by yesterday's rain, we tied most of our clothes loosely onto our packs, hoping that they would dry on the trail, looking like an army of ungovernable ragamuffins. We never gave up on this inspired device and were forever dragging our wet laundry along outboard style—even though it never helped. The Sherpas were highly amused by the quaint sight, and always looked forward to wash day when the bedraggled sahibs could be depended on to make an ornate show of their best and soggiest finery.

The bright day was hardened by a steep pass that shoots right up above Yarsa. We crossed our second major ridge, dividing the Tamba Kosi and Khimti, at 8,200 feet. Bo had brought an altimeter, and our daily litany was composed of a numbers game that went something like: "2,500 up to 9,000 for lunch; 1,500 down to 7,500 to camp" (meaning we would do 4,000 feet vertical that day).

As we crested the ridge, beyond a teastop at Chisapani, a beaming tier of the Eastern Himalayas loomed up: far to our left, the stunning ice spire of 23,440-foot Gauri Sankar; directly in front, the Menlungtse ice block, 23,560 feet; and additionally, Numbur, 22,817 feet, and Choba Bhamare, 19,550 feet. All in one soaring vista of ice pinnacles and snow. After five days we were seeing 20,000-footers. Gauri Sankar, someone remarked, once was mistaken for Everest and thought to be the world's highest peak.

We hustled down the long descent to Sikri, skirted the riverbank, marched up a spur, then back down to the Khimti River Valley and on to Those, the largest settlement between our starting point and Namche Bazar in the Khumbu. Ample supplies of soap, fruit, candy, cigarettes, candles, sweaters, cloth, curious native-made metallic locks (which appeared to be completely inoperative), and other miscellany lined the shelves of the small, one-room shops that bordered the cobblestone streets. I think we were the only customers. But the local people seemed to be bright and prosperous.

Because of the storm, we lost a couple of porters here. The sirdar had no trouble replacing them. Every able-bodied man, woman, and child—and some who are not—is a candidate.

A shaky cable bridge caused some uneasiness at Those. Nepal is famous for its falling bridges. (Our map bears the following warning: "In Nepal all paths and bridges are liable to disappear or change at no notice due to monsoons, Acts of God, etc.") A couple of girl porters had to be helped across. I sympathized. Despite the cables, the contraption appeared to be held together by putty and glue. The wires linking the heavy cables to the trough of the bridge were rusted and frequently unattached. Where, I asked, is Nepal's head of transport? Stan said it probably never occurred to the government to have one. In fact, Nepal does have a department of roads, but the casual observer would think that its jurisdiction ends on the outskirts of Katmandu. The Nepalese use a bridge until it simply collapses; then they build a

A typical bridge crossing

139

new one—sooner or later. Repairing a bridge to give it a longer life is not considered cricket.

The dampness brought out the local leeches. Kathy got nicked by a couple of the filthy, blind little vampires; ditto Claire. They covered the foliage by the thousands, rearing up on their tails, itching to bite into every white-fleshed sahib that came through. The Sherpas and porters got their share too. Stan warned that the proper way to force them out is with a lighted cigarette. If you pull them out bodily, they may leave an infection or scar.

Every one of the group—we called ourselves the "Scraggly Seven"— now seemed fit. Coming from Los Angeles, however, I complained that my lungs could not stand the fresh air.

October 31 (6th day): Today we traversed our third major ridge, bisecting the Khimti and Likhu rivers, at 8,900 feet. At the crest we encountered a series of "mani" walls bearing the eternal Tibetan Buddhist inscription *om mani padme hum* ("Hail, jewel of the lotus flower"). We were now entering the region dominated by the Tibetan culture of the Sherpas. We descended to the first Sherpa village we've seen, Changma (or Bhandar), with its prominent Buddhist chortens and "gompas" (temples).

Ethnically, the Sherpas are of Tibetan stock, and the name, which means "Easterner," is applied to those who migrated from Eastern Tibet and settled in the Solu and Khumbu regions, which form a major watershed of the Himalayas. As high altitude climbers, or "tigers," the Sherpas have of course acquired a special reputation for hardiness and endurance in the vast, dizzying reaches of their land. Some of our porters were ethnically Sherpas, others were Tamangs or Chetris.

The Sherpa family unit is intriguing. Polygamy is prevalent; likewise polyandry. A wife having two husbands, usually brothers, is looked upon with favor, especially among the rich, because it promotes fraternal solidarity and discourages the breakup of family-held property. Both premarital sex and adultery are common. In the latter case, the husband may demand token satisfaction from the offender (often one of his best friends), consisting of a beer or payment of a small fine, called *phijal,* or he may consider that the *sönam,* or moral merit, of the offender has been diminished, which is punishment enough since it will impede his progress toward higher fulfillment in the Buddhist order. After this private ritual, all parties will resume their amiable ways as though nothing has happened. If a husband dies, his younger brother often steps forward to wed the surviving widow.

Dissolution of marital ties is accomplished with equal informality, usually by mutual consent. In this case, the husband will invite all of his

Thatch homes in the Khumbu

in-laws to his house, serve *rakshi* and *chang* (a kind of Nepalese beer), and a thread, grasped by the husband and one of his wife's relatives, will be severed, symbolizing that the marriage is at an end. If the divorce is not by agreement, then the spouse seeking it will simply pay his partner a fixed number of rupees; this remittance, called *phorjal*, releases the two from any further marital obligations. All in all, a neat system—certainly superior to paying exorbitant legal fees!

November 1 (7th day): Changma sits on a long gentle plain, and countless serrations of green and rusty hills flow up and down into the distance. No high mountains were in sight, just ridges—except later in the day Numbur came into view again. We hiked down to another cable bridge, then up again to Sete, at 8,400 feet, where we spent the night. One of the elderly porters severely sprained his foot, so a confederate toted him on his back for several days until the injured man, who must have weighed at least 125 pounds, safely reached his home at Chaunrikharka. Thus far the days and nights were hot and warm, respectively. It would change soon.

Mani walls intersected every path. One must pass them on the left; the theory is that, by repeating the ritual on the return, one will encircle the wall and the offerings to the Gods will be complete. These stone-slab tributes to Buddha represent marvelous feats of craftsmanship and they abound everywhere, by the hundreds—a sure sign that one is in Sherpaland. It obviously took a great many years, and much painstaking workmanship, to chisle and lay them. Occasionally the tribute is carved out of a huge boulder, at an inaccessible place or elevation that leaves the beholder to wonder whether the artist accomplished his task by an act of divine levitation.

November 2 (8th day): Off again at the break of dawn. We gradually climbed to the tip of the 11,580-foot Lamjura ridge via a moss-covered forest of rhododendrons, firs, and spruce trees. The rhododendrons form a cavelike pocket through which the trail winds. This is the highest point on the way to Namche Bazar. We "lunched" at 9:00 A.M. (after a breakfast at 6 o'clock), because our sirdar said that no water would be available for a long distance. (This happened several times, and I slowly realized it wasn't lack of water, but merely the fact the Sherpas had been up most of the night singing and drinking *rakshi* and *chang* that led to these premature halts. Indeed, on entering their home regions, Sherpas would call upon almost any excuse not to push a full day—they were tired, a wife or relative was ailing, a party was planned, or a smile would gush forth that instinctively told one to accept the situation and not argue or examine too closely into the reasons given. If the men would not march forward with our food, sleeping bags, and tents, that settled the matter. Our dependence on our Sherpas and porters was absolute.)

We eventually plunged down the ridge to Junbesi, tucked away at 8,800 feet, where we passed the night. It is a delightful Solu settlement,

Buddhist flags at the top of a mountain pass

featuring a red-trimmed, tin-roofed schoolhouse with English-speaking teachers who handle classes six days a week. Most of the students were boys; the girls were busy in the fields. The kids were engaged in a fast game of volleyball when we arrived; naturally, they halted to inspect the curious apparitions that had descended upon them.

Junbesi lies in the shadow of Rauje and, typically, is divided by charming but hazardous rapids. The Sherpas value their elbow room, for the huts were spaciously stretched far up the hillside, so that each had sizable plottage for gardening and growing rice. We noted that prices were going up: tea costs fifty paisas or five cents, double the tariff we have paid until now.

Five porters left us here. Since they broke their agreement to go further, they were paid at the rate of ten instead of twelve rupees a day. They were immediately replaced, three of them by women.

As usual, clouds and mists sank into the valleys at about 2:00 to 2:30 P.M. each day, cutting off all views.

November 3 (9th day): A marvelous day! We left Junbesi late, around 7:15 A.M., and wended around a long series of wooded slopes for a couple of hours. Then the trees receded, and on rounding a bend the inimitable magnificence of the Eastern Himalayas swiflty burst into focus. It was a startling sight. The chalky, forbidding snow steeples literally scratched at the heavens: Thamserku, Kangtega, Karyolung,

From the ridge above Junbesi, the first sight of the High Himalayas

and Chamlang, all well over 20,000 feet, each as dazzling and overpowering as the next.

Then to our left, about thirty-six miles away on a straight line, its south side protruding like a solitary black tooth behind the great Nuptse-Lhotse wall, reposed the summit pyramid of Mount Everest— menacing, lonely, too high, dark, and stately. We shouted with exaltation. After nine days on foot, our goal was at last in sight. Nor did it disappoint. The slanting, pointed crown was distinctively set off from its neighbors. Everest is a monarch surrounded and protected by its satellites. We spent an hour there, intoxicated by the sight.

To Mallory, Everest was a "prodigious white fang—an excrescence from the jaw of the world." When Jerstad first glimpsed the peak as a member of the 1963 Everest expedition, he described it as a "great white monster" that, with its gigantic plume of snow at the summit, buffeted by fierce winds, presents an "incredible sight." To the Sherpas, Everest simply is "The Mountain That Is So High No Bird Can Fly Over It." Each invokes his own vision.

We were fortunate that the weather was clear. Stan said that on his two previous treks clouds had obscured the grand view from above Junbesi.

Slowly we strolled down to a small village, crossed the Solu River, then trudged to the top of another pass, the Takshindu, at 10,500 feet. Here we descended an unending ridge, through thick tropical rain forests past a noted monastery, to Manidingma, at 7,600 feet. My blazing feet groaned all the way.

For once we had soft, straight ground to sleep on. Usually it was a lumpy yak pasture, a cornfield, or a turnip patch, each about as comfortable as a bed of ratchets.

Supper was the usual. I noted that our plates and silverware were always carefully washed in boiling water, and dried on each occasion with the same filth-laden greasecloth—a prized possession that our singleminded cook used religiously for five straight weeks.

It was getting chillier, so most of the group were pulling on their down pants and parkas.

November 4 (10th day): The descent continued across the Dudh Kosi (Milk River) up to Jubing for a lunch of fried eggs and chapatis; then up again, steeply, to Khari Khola, at 6,800 feet, a dirty, chaotic settlement where one of our Sherpas lived. Jubing is occupied by the Rais, who are of Mongoloid extraction and who have evolved their own distinctive religion that, strictly speaking, is neither Buddhist nor Hindu.

Claire and I continued to be consumed by fleas. To remedy the crisis, we borrowed flea powder from the Powells and made a large production of sprinkling it all over.

Agelu, my man Friday, was a jewel. But I noted that while he often offered to help me, he does not do the same for the women. For instance, today he asked to do my laundry (which he beats expertly on the rocks); I refused (for the first and last time). Although Claire was nearby, scrubbing her clothes, he did not extend her the same offer. It's simply that women are expected to fend for themselves. Similarly, if a female porter is having difficulty, the men usually do not assist. Yet the women carry loads as heavy as the men do.

November 5 (11th day): Another perfect day. We had been fortunate—only one inclement day thus far. We started up a mean-looking ridge to Kharte, at 9,300 feet, and followed through a thick scrub forest to the summit of Bupsa ridge, another thousand feet higher. After pausing there at the teahouse, we dropped easily down to Puiyan for the night.

The Bupsa ridge offered a spectacular view: Karyolung, 21,920 feet;

A wayside inn on Bupsa Pass.

Numbur, 22,817 feet; Kwangde, 20,320 feet; and Khumbila, 19,297 feet—all encircling Namche Bazar, which lies at the head of a long valley. We had ceased our eastward swing, and now turned north towards Everest.

Bo took it upon himself to award the Order of the Burned Out Boot to Tom Broderson for expertise in hiking. There also was the Order of the Flaming Blister, which I was given by acclamation.

We philosophized that trekking in Nepal requires a sense of low comedy, wobble-proof knees, and a liking for nosebleeds. Also, one should not think beyond the next meal stop, which usually consisted of burnt potatoes and turnip greens—except on days when Ang Chatter tried something wildly creative, like unburnt turnip greens and potatoes.

November 6 (12th day): We were supposed to go through Surke and Chaunrikharka to Phakding—but one of the porters resided in Surke and Dawa Sindar in Chaunrikharka, so although we reached the latter early, at 2:00 P.M., our baggage train came to a halt and would go no farther.

At Surke we lunched on dark buffalo meat, noodles, and *chang*— again at 9:30 in the morning. *Chang* is potent stuff at any hour. A murky brew, it is derived from rice or corn, and can be heavy or thin, but in either case it smells exactly like peppered vomit and stokes the searing fires of hell within one's digestive tract. To refuse to drink it is the ultimate discourtesy, and some of the Scraggly Seven, such as Graham and Stan, insisted they loved it, and showed it by getting stiff as boards.

We constantly ran into other trekkers, who were inbound or outbound, and who had been having various interesting experiences of their own. Peace Corps volunteers, World Health Organization officers, medical doctors, and anthropologists often sprang up out of the woods; they were undertaking surveys for a rural water-supply system, studying at a monastery, checking on cholera or tuberculosis, analyzing the population patterns, and inspecting sites for a Hillary school—so named after Edmund Hillary, who, since scaling Everest, has diligently collected funds and built schools, hospitals, and bridges throughout the region, and is revered by the natives for this reason.

The view up the valley toward the peaks that dwarf Namche Bazar was overwhelming. Now the trail became busier; to avoid about two weeks' hike, many fly into the tiny airstrip at Lukla and then proceed up the valley. There is a major disadvantage to this shortcut, as we later learned: the lack of conditioning and acclimatization is very noticeable once one seeks to go beyond Namche Bazar or Tengboche. Of the trekkers we met, all who made it up to the Khumbu glacier and Gorak Shep had taken the long way, from Lamosangu; the others, who flew in to Lukla, typically came down with fatigue or altitude sickness, which forced them back. Despite the fast-growing popularity of the trek, Mount Everest still has a few defenses. Good conditioning is the main recipe for reaching base camp.

Dawa Sindar invited us into his home for an evening of *chang*, singing, and folk dancing. The dance has a simple, steady beat—a repetitious shuffle that increases to a lusty tempo as the Sherpas, linked arm in arm, form a semicircle, voicing a low, soulful lament. As the rhythm builds, the dancers, still interlocked, commence making a slow, then slightly faster, hissing sound, tapping their feet alternately, swaying back and forth, until a kind of euphoric frenzy is reached. Here the routine abruptly stops, there is a brief pause, and the entire cycle begins anew. This dance is cherished by the Sherpas who, with *chang* in hand, stick to it without variation for hours on end.

By midnight the dancing and howling were going full blast and still there was ample *chang* left. The Sherpas produce *chang* as though it spurts from a gusher in the Dudh Kosi.

To celebrate the safe arrival of the elderly porter who sprained his ankle, his wife was guest of honor at the party, and Dawa Sindar bedecked her with the traditional present of the Sherpas—long, white cheesecloth scarves, called *katas*. I personally felt these also should have been conferred on the poor, spunky porter who carried his ailing cohort all the way.

Dawa Sindar's home was well kept and neat. He was relatively well-to-do, and the walls were lined with many large dishes and baskets, some of them expensive. Goats occupied the cellar, below the house, to help provide warmth. Typically, the place had stone walls, plastered and whitewashed, with a roof of wooden slats weighed down with rocks. There was no chimney, and thus ventilation was limited—a common circumstance that contributes to the ever-present health problem.

November 7 (13th day): After the late-night *chang* party, the Sherpas and porters scarcely were able to drag themselves out of the sack. Likewise the sahibs. This was slated to be our day for the big arrival in Namche Bazar. We didn't come close.

Five times we crossed the Dudh Kosi via quaint log bridges that look ready to disappear down the rapids any moment. We christened them "hurry bridges" (rather than Hillary bridges). As a rule, no more than one or two persons mounted these ramshackle devices at a crack.

Ang Chatter bought a goat, took out his trusty khukri knife, and beheaded, skinned, and cooked the animal for supper. Observing the bloody ritual, we left most of the mutton on our plates. Real outdoorsmen, observed Graham. The Sherpas use the khukri for virtually everything: cutting trees; killing animals; plucking hairs from their faces (most of them are beardless); trimming fingernails and hair; fixing supper; or repairing the house.

Sherpa traders returning from market at Namche Bazar

We camped at the base of the long slope that leads up to Namche Bazar, just past Jorsale. Above us ranged Thamserku, 21,730 feet of extraordinary elegance. A couple of parties coming down the trail assured us it was extremely cold beyond Tengboche, and that deep snow made hiking up Kala Pattar a chore.

The U.S. presidential election was held today. We had no idea who won.

November 8 (14th day): Two quick hours of hiking up a 2,000-foot incline brought us to Namche Bazar, the chief trading center in the Khumbu. It was a notable moment for us; we had been pointing for it for two weeks, and humorously assigned it all kinds of outrageous names, "Nancy's Brassiere" being the favorite. From the first step we constantly intoned in Nepalese: *"Kun bato Namche Bazar jancha?"* ("Which trail goes to Namche Bazar?").

At 11,300 feet, Namche Bazar is a thriving community that, unlike the other villages en route, has streets and flocks of small shops, plus approximately one hundred houses tightly compacted in a natural amphitheater. Saturday is market day, and the surrounding populace carries foods and wares many miles to participate, often starting out a couple of days in advance.

Namche Bazar also is a government control point. Passports and trekking permits are cleared here; one is not allowed to go on a trek in Nepal without a special permit that spells out one's destination. Understandably, the Nepalese do not relish having hundreds of foreigners scrambling all over their mountains without knowing who or where they are.

We were now in the heart of the Himalayas. To the west were the hulking masses of Kwangde and Karyolung. Hovering directly over the town was the sacred peak Khumbila, while immediately to the east towered the imposing white buttresses of Thamserku, 21,730 feet, and Kangtega, 22,340 feet. Thamserku was one of the most flamboyant peaks I had seen. Shaped on top like an open fan, its two intersecting blades teed-in to each other, looking incredibly steep, and the whole airy edifice was bottomed out by a heavy outpouring of glacial ice and séracs.

After lunch we left for Tengboche. Now the lovely sculptured ice palace of Ama Dablam, 22,494 feet, rose into view. (*Ama Dablam* means "mother's watchcharm"; a *dablam* is an elaborate necklace emblem worn by the Sherpanis.) Here indeed is one of the world's most stunningly impressive peaks. It has been climbed in winter, although it looks extraordinarily steep.

In the near distance, now about fourteen miles away, appeared our

Thamserku and Kangtega peaks, on the way to Everest

objective: Lhotse, at 27,890 feet the world's fourth highest, poking its neck above the cloud cover for the first time; Nuptse, 25,850 feet, a bulwark standing athwart Everest; and behind it, the sovereign itself, 29,028 feet, remote, impenetrable, as Mallory said, a prodigious mass.

The tents went up on the bank of the Imja Khola, at 10,900 feet. Here we encountered large, perpetually spinning prayer wheels, turned by the force of the stream running through them. We noted small boys packing wood up the slope, far from home. Local councils decide what part of the forest may be cut. Trees near a village thus may remain untouched. A violator can be forced to pay a fine, which may consist of a keg of *chang* or several rupees.

That night we repacked all of our gear, changing into heavy boots and eliminating all items that would not be needed above the snow line. In this way seven duffle bags were reduced to four. Many of the porters were not equipped for the cold weather ahead, so their number was cut to eight.

The sun was now disappearing at about 5:45 P.M.

November 9 (15th day): Bill Tilman called Tengboche the most beautiful place in the world. Surrounded by the high arching walls of the mountains, the site of the most important lamasery in Sherpa country, it is, at 12,700 feet, the gateway to Mount Everest and the garden spot of the Himalayas.

Spectacular 22,494-foot tower of Ama Dablam rises above the Tengboche monastery near Everest.

From the river we sprinted up the hillside, through wrinkled firs and rhododendrons, in less than two hours. Tengboche is a busy place; it has a hotel with menu and is the crossroads for every traveler who is headed toward the Khumbu glacier, or returning. It is enveloped by 20,000-footers. Kangtega ("Saddle") looks like an overpiled ice-cream cone from here; beside it lurk the shining ice-heads of Thamserku, and ahead, irresistibly dominating the multifaced valley, is the omnipotent Ama Dablam. A striking aspect of the Eastern Himalayas is their individuality; each peak has its own distinctive shape and personality, and thus is easy to identify.

Tengboche was founded about fifty years ago by Lama Gulu. Its central temple was destroyed in 1933 by an earthquake but has since been restored.

Much of the talk centered on the British expedition, which was then attempting to climb the southwest face of Everest. The world's tallest had never been scaled in this, the postmonsoon season. The British hoped to strike for the top within the next ten days or so.

By 1:30 P.M. we were in Pangboche, which, at 13,170 feet and with some sixty houses, is the highest year-round village in the region. The porters went on their usual mid-day strike, but with the noble help of little Ongchu, who pushed ahead and dared anyone not to follow, we were able to continue to Orsho, where the tents were struck in a rocky, now all-too-familiar *yersa* or yak pasture.

The ridge up Pumori—directly across from Everest

November 10 (16th day): Today we passed along the lengthy earth-slash of the Imja basin, beneath Taweche, 21,463 feet, and Tsolatse, 21,129 feet, all the way to Lobuje. (To give it a name is somewhat pompous; Lobuje is an unpopulated 16,175-foot-high yak pasture, a marking spot along the trail that spins up to the Khumbu glacier.)

The day broke unbearably cold. Ongchu, who had regularly warmed our mornings with oatmeal thus far, served up seven bowls of frigid cornflakes. We trekked all day, from 13,300 feet to 16,175 feet—almost a 2,900-foot gain.

At Phalong Karpo, we met a French expedition whose eight-man team had scaled 23,442-foot Pumori, which sits directly across the Khumbu glacier from Everest. At the same time we witnessed a near-fatal case of pulmonary edema. A French-born airlines employee living in Nepal happened to be a friend of the climbers. When he learned of their fine success—it was only the second time the peak had been climbed—he flew into Lukla and, with his wife and some friends, immediately set out to greet them. A youthful, robust man, he had gone to this altitude before, but not recently. Below Lobuje he began experiencing a dry cough, abnormally severe fatigue, and discoloration in the fingers, all symptomatic of pulmonary edema. With the onset of this malady, one has no choice but to instantly retreat to a lower altitude to regain oxygen. Otherwise the consequences can be severe or fatal. The Frenchman insisted on proceeding, hoping his body would adjust. Shortly thereafter, he collapsed. His whole party was now in a state of panic. The sick man could not walk and scarcely could breathe. They placed him on a canvas and endeavored to drag it down the long slopes. His friends were exhausted and progress was halted. Now they grabbed him under the shoulders on each side, and were able to carry him along slowly.

Fortunately, they chanced to meet the French climbers who were, of course, in splendid condition, and with the latter's assistance they were able to carry the victim to Phalong Karpo, at 14,249 feet. Here he was treated by the expedition doctor, whose medical supplies were limited since most of them already had been carried down. Help was summoned by dispatching a Sherpa runner to Namche Bazar, which radioed the British expedition at Everest base camp, the latter in turn radioing Katmandu for help.

The doctor was supervising the construction of a stretcher out of wooden planks when a helicopter flew in just after we arrived. Its appearance was a great relief to all, not excluding the doctor, who felt the sick man might not survive. Later we were able to verify that he was hospitalized and recovered.

Twice, now, friends had trekked up to greet the French climbers—only to collapse at their feet. They expressed the hope that everyone would wait until their return to Katmandu, so they could celebrate

Hiking into Imja basin, which leads to Mount Everest

properly; as it was, they were rushing most of their welcomers to the nearest hospital.

It was a close call, and the severity of it had a sobering affect on us all. We hiked more slowly and became more conscious of any physical ailments. Indeed, it seemed that we became a collection of overwrought hypochondriacs.

The French had taken six weeks to ascend Pumori by its south ridge. They had advanced to within 650 feet of the summit, after having set up three camps, when a severe blizzard struck, forcing a full-scale retreat to the bottom, after which the assault was launched again. They were especially pleased that every climber in the group eventually made the top. As for the British, it was felt that they were in good position on Everest, but the southwest face was said to be cold almost beyond belief. The thought struck me that here we were, comfortably sipping wine together, with only a long, gentle plateau before us—all at an altitude almost the height of the Matterhorn.

The valley we now followed was remindful of a capacious tundra. Enveloped on all sides by startling uplifts, its tentacles stretched for miles. We reached Duglha (one emergency hut, unoccupied) and swung sharply upward, into the mouth of a crusty, boulder-strewn moraine. It took about one hour and forty-five minutes to hike through it.

Now we stepped onto the Khumbu glacier, and one by one the great peaks of Pumori, Lingtren, 21,972 feet, Khumbutse, 21,785 feet, and

Sprawling Khumbu Glacier and the needle spire of Ama Dablam

Changtse, 24,780 feet, broke forth. Well formed, like a brilliant crescent moon that flashes up without warning, Pumori looks as though it might be easily ascended, but it is in fact quite challenging. The British recognized its unique charm when they first spotted it in 1921. We could not yet see Everest, for it was blocked by the enormous south and west walls of Nuptse, behind which rose the misty figure of Lhotse. To the south a circle of white layered giants punched holes in the sky.

Until 2:30 in the afternoon the weather was almost tropical. We hiked in light sweaters. But the Himalayas are an arena of extremes. Lobuje that night was like the Antarctic. All of us donned every stitch we had—down pants and parka, sweaters, heavy windpants, two or three woolen caps, gloves, and liners—after which we slid into our heavy sleeping bags and zipped them shut. At the wooden hut our Sherpas were huddled together, singing bravely, trying to stay warm.

We read by candlelight until 7:00 P.M., then lights out. We were camping at 16,175 feet—the highest any of us had been (except Stan, of course)—indeed, higher than Mont Blanc.

November 11 (17th day): I awoke to find my boots frozen as hard as concrete, and spent a half-hour beating and warming them over a fire. It was a mistake not to have kept them in a sleeping bag.

From Lobuje to Gorak Shep required about three and one-half hours. Gorak Shep is, again, a dot on a map, near a small glacier lake, slightly over 17,000 feet and about fifteen miles from Namche Bazar. It was employed as a base camp by the Swiss in their 1952 Everest effort.

Chris Brasher, a former Olympic gold medalist and now a sportswriter for the London *Observer,* was headed down the trail to Kunde for an interview with Hillary. Brasher had been following the Everest assault and predicted a final attempt within a week. If the weather held, he said, prospects looked good. Although the British sponsored the successful 1953 expedition and pioneered the entire Everest region going back to the 1920s, it is a curious but undeniable fact that no Britisher had at the time ever set foot atop Everest. (This omission was, of course, remedied in 1975 when the southwest face was finally scaled.)

We reached Gorak Shep about 12:30 P.M. A half-hour later I coaxed my faithful, intrepid Agelu to press on to Kala Pattar. A little Sherpa boy, Nagoud, joined us.

We encountered a blanket of snow, and the climb to the top, which took two hours, was a fine example of spasmophilia on a mountain. Kala Pattar is littered with boulders, and, with the snow cover, it was hard to tell whether one was stepping onto flat ground or large rocks. The result was that I slipped and slid most of the way up the gentle hill, falling over backwards and forwards, acting like a one-winged duck in a

Above: Stunning pinnacles of Pumori (23,442 ft.), Lingtren (21,972 ft.) and Khumbutse (21,785 ft.), left to right, encircle Khumbu Glacier
Below: Taking a break near Phalong Karpo while en route to Lobuje and Gorak Shep (left); Nuptse's precipitous walls (right)
Facing page: The grand concourse of the Khumbu Glacier leading to Mount Everest (top and center); gigantic bulwarks of 25,850-ft. Nuptse (bottom)

whirlpool. Agelu responded to my tribulations with suppressed mirth and a profusion of apologies. Every time I stumbled to the canvas he would turn and announce, quite diffidently, "Much sorry," as though he were personally responsible for having created my inelegant plight. He axed out steps from halfway up, and without him I might not have made it, despite the easy incline of the slope. I fairly sagged up to the summit, and Agelu, who is quite strong, became winded himself as we neared the top—a fact that afforded me some small solace. We could tell by where the tracks left off about 300 feet below the cairn on top that few if any persons had completed the climb since a heavy blizzard had struck about three weeks before.

Kala Pattar sits at 18,192 feet, and although it is set off as a separate knoll on maps of the region, it is actually a spur on the southeasterly ridge of Pumori. Its sole function, which it serves well, is to provide a marvelous closeup of Everest and the whole of the Khumbu valley. And

Elderly Buddhist monk in the Solu Khumbu

Ama Dablam from a distance

what a view! Words are so feeble an instrument to describe it.

To my right, turning south, extruded many of nature's haughtiest sculptures—Ama Dablam, Thamserku, Kangtega, Tsolatse, Taweche, and, behind them, the splendid Hongu-basin peaks. The full spread of the Khumbu glacier could be seen spiraling its broad ribbon toward the jaws of the Everest icefall and the Western Cwm, embroidered by a stream of pointed, wind-formed séracs and a heavy moraine. This highway of moving ice and snow led up to the Lho La, the pass into Tibet, where it swung sharply right and upward to the South Col. Behind me was the perfectly formed Pumori, which Mallory described as being "unrivalled anywhere in the district for the elegant beauty of its cornices and towers." And finally, directly across, reposed the grand and solid colossus of Everest, now fully revealed, bulging over the precipitous ice walls of Nuptse and Lhotse. In some strange way I felt detached; lofty and yet so near, Everest still held to its frustrating remoteness; unless one climbs it, perhaps one inevitably is made to feel like a stranger, and not a part of it.

When Agelu, Nagoud, and I made our way back to Gorak Shep, Jimmy Roberts, a retired British army officer who has led, participated in, and supplied Sherpas for many Himalayan expeditions, including the 1953 British success, and who was a deputy leader on the current attempt on the southwest face, had completed his twice-a-day radio contact with Everest base camp.

Mount Everest—with the South Col, South Summit, and Southwest Face (including Rock Band) visible. Photo taken from atop Kala Pattar.

Summit block of Mount Everest as viewed from the air. To right is Lhotse (27,890 ft.)

"This weather won't hold forever—they're taking too long," he muttered. Prophetic words, it turned out.

We ate a supper of rice and potatoes in Stan's tent and retired early. The weather at Gorak Shep seemed less severe than at Lobuje.

I had not washed for three days, nor changed a stitch of clothing since below Tengboche; still didn't know who was president.

November 12 (18th day): Another brilliant dawn. At nine o'clock I departed with Stan, Tom Broderson, Dawa Sindar, and Ang Tsering for base camp. This involved a sprightly two-and-one-half-hour waltz through the glistening militialike séracs of the Khumbu glacier, a veritable museum of ice. The glacier was bordered by patches of moraine, and dotted with fascinating ice formations of all shapes, sizes, and hues. The séracs are formed by a unique combination of wind, cold, and heat, and grow out of the glacial carpet like tall spikes. The glacier flows beneath the awesome ice cornices of Nuptse; it is relatively slow moving and not large, since the area, protected by the mountain axis to the south, receives little rainfall and is mainly fed by avalanches. The Himalayas themselves are a young range, supposedly first formed

Nuptse peak

Trekking party traverses Khumbu Glacier

Sérac on Khumbu Glacier

some 70 million years ago as a consequence of the tectonic clashing of the India and Asiatic plates. At one time a great sea covered the area, and, before the ultimate dispersion of nature's forces thrust Everest to its present height some 500,000 to 800,000 years ago, the Numbur-Karyolung-Kangtega group was higher. To a nongeologist traversing the glacier, these considerations are obscure and unreal. The gigantic scope of the valley, and the frightful surge of snow walls and hanging glaciers that peel down from those nearby heights, grip the imagination, excluding all else.

Base camp, at 17,800 feet, the nerve center of the latest attempt on the southwest face, lay immediately below the icefall. In the caressing sunshine, a mood of quiet optimism prevailed among the climbers. Camp 6 had been established at 27,000 feet.

David Bathgate, who helped lead the way to the high camp, explained that, due to the frustrating delays, several weeks' time had been lost and the aim now was to place just one team on top. That was to be composed of Dougal Haston (the now deceased conqueror of the Eiger and later this very southwest face) and Hamish MacInnes, who planned to string a rope across the prominent Rock Band that seams the face—about 1,000 feet wide and roughly the same distance below the summit. The Rock Band had been partly climbed the previous year by a morale-troubled International Expedition, with Haston and Don Whillens in the lead, but the climb was abandoned when the support gave

Khumbu Glacier and the outpouring of the great icefall that lies between Everest and Nuptse

The tumultuous Khumbu icefall as seen from Everest base camp

out. Hence no one knew what lay above it. Now the British had endured three blizzards, and temperatures had dropped to forty degrees below zero. Still, most of them felt that if the present weather held, nothing could stop them. Resting in camp were two Sherpas, Pertemba and Jangbo, who, without bottled oxygen, had ferried loads up to Camp 6. Probably they had gone as high as had any Sherpa unaided by supplementary oxygen. Each planned to take one more load the next day. (Three years later Pertemba also finally scaled the southwest face, and ultimately he became the first man to make the ascent by two different routes.)

The camp was strewn about with numerous tents—triangular, semicircular, and boxshaped—and stacks of oxygen cylinders lay in the snow. I had brought along a recent issue of a news magazine, given to me to take up by an Australian couple, and this was received with undisguised joy. Except for the radio, all contact with the outside world was cut off; still, it remained for an expedition nurse, a wife of

Crossing the Khumbu Glacier

one of the climbers, to advise me that Oakland and Nixon had captured the world series and presidency, in that order.

Every so often the conversation was interrupted by atomic-type blasts, as the sheer walls avalanched, throwing up mushrooms of snow, leaving the black and brown rock skin bare; echoes from these rumbles seemed to last half a minute.

For our Dawa Sindar, base camp was a familiar place; already he had been to the South Col. One of the orderlies, Ang Dawa, served on the 1953 British encampment.

Behind base camp, in twisting, chaotic steps, rose the Khumbu icefall and the Western Cwm. (The summit cannot be seen from base camp.) The icefall is the most hazardous section of the Everest ascent, and the British had installed dozens of ladders and bridges in threading a path through it. Indeed, it has accounted for most of the tragedies on the mountain. This time proved to be no different. When the British were pulling out, an Australian friend of the climbers, who volunteered to help, was crushed when a building-sized ice slab toppled over onto him. This enormous ice stream, which drops over a 2,000-foot course and is a half-mile wide, is pinched between the flanks of Everest and Nuptse, contains blocks that weigh 50 tons, and its condition changes daily. There are a continual creaking and groaning of the stress points, and thunderous cracks as the glacier periodically splits and buckles. Yet for many years this maze was the only path by which Everest had been climbed.

The broad sweep of the Khumbu Glacier (from Kala Pattar)

By 5:00 P.M. we were back in Lobuje, and the next day we returned to Tengboche below the snow line. Behind us, the Everest-Nuptse-Pumori triumvirate acquired a ghostly aspect in the fading twilight. In their transcendental splendor they evoked thoughts of all that has gone before, over a period encompassing more than fifty years. It seemed too easy, in this modern day, to set out with Sherpas and porters, and travel across those ridges and gorges that ultimately led us to the base of the great icefall and to Kala Pattar, from where the forbidding slopes of Everest could be so conveniently studied. The trails are well occupied now, and many tourists come to this high and remote domain. One may even land by plane at a modern Japanese-built hotel above Namche Bazar and partake of the Himalayas, and of Everest, without drawing a deep breath.

To Mallory and his fellow climbers, these would seem to be strange doings indeed.

Wending through the Khumbu Glacier

Pumori (23,442 ft.) by twilight. Mallory regarded this as perhaps the most **singularly** beautiful peak in the Everest region.

Exiting through the Imja Valley

The last two weeks of our trek led us across the Inukhu Kosi to the lush Rai settlements of Bung and Gudel, over the thickly wooded 11,000-foot Salpa Pass, along the tropical sandbars of the Arun River, through the swirling towns of Hile and Dhankuta, down to Dharan and then by jeep to Biratnagar, near the Indian border.

At Pangu a New Zealand medical team was collecting specimens for research on one of the Khumbu's most serious problems, goiter disease, which is caused by lack of iodine in the diet. Down the hill to join them came a swarthy, long-striding individual who was making his regular pilgrimage among the schools and hospitals of the Sherpa region. Edmund Hillary looked like he could still take the measure of Everest. But he brought the news that 140-mile-per-hour winds, plus sub-zero temperatures, had aborted that season's British attempt on the southwest face.

Bung and Gudel, straddling the Hongu River, are cheerful, prosper-

Our Sherpas surmount a long, steep pass

ous villages whose spacious hills are decorated with neat thatch huts and boundless strips of rice, wheat, maize, papaya, sugar cane, and millet. Though no prettier, the girls there wore more ornaments, beads, and necklaces than our Sherpanis, and dressed in bright red sashes as opposed to the browns and purples we were used to seeing. At Phedi, Ang Dawa revealed his engagement to one of the quiet, attractive Sherpanis—prompting another party.

The rolling hills that turned southward were dotted with green tropical brush, plus, we noted, lines of coolies portering their baskets to nearby villages. Each carried a T-stick, which was used both for walking and sitting, and they moved in short bursts, stopping repeatedly, wearing amiable but unchanging blank looks. We figured that each time one of them halted, the trail must back up for miles.

The warm climate also brought out night crawlers of all sorts. Bo kept a stiff upper lip among these alien creatures. Gazing at the tea

From Bung to Gudel—heading south toward India

Fording a typical stream

A precarious river crossing—with thrashing rapids below

Our party treks through beautiful grain fields toward the winding Arun River, one of the few waterways that bisect the Himalayan uplift.

Stupendous south face of Annapurna I (26,504 ft.) presides over Annapurna Sanctuary.

brought to us one evening by the punctual Ongchu, he announced sotto voce, "There's sugar in our ants." Such sage pronouncements helped considerably during the long, dry pull ahead.

On the last day we mounted the 4,000-foot crest of Dandapani in the Siwalik range. On one side of us, framed among the gangling vines, appeared Makalu, 27,709 feet, Jannu, 25,296 feet, and the extraordinary bulk of the 28,145-foot Kangchenjunga, the world's third highest peak. To the south lay Dharan and the dusty, carpet-flat Terai that stretches rawly into India. There was a titter among the Sherpas. Some of them never before had ventured outside their native Khumbu. In thirty-five days we had traveled much of the length and girth of the Eastern Himalayas, from Lamosangu to Mount Everest at the Tibetan border, then south to the frontier of India. Ang Tsering and Ongchu were awash in *chang*. Agelu and the porters were boisterously singing. We followed Dawa Sindar down the last long ridge and left the great Himalayas behind.

Seasons later, in a 24-day journey made in 1979, I tracked around the Annapurna range, via Manang Valley and 17,771-foot Thorong La, then plodded through thick bamboo forests to explore the towering splendors of the Annapurna Sanctuary. Truly Nepal is a mountain lover's nirvana.

5
A Pilgrimage on Fujisan

> *Lo! There towers the lofty peak of Fuji*
> *From between Kai and wave-washed Suruga.*
> *The clouds of heaven dare not cross it,*
> *Nor the birds of the air soar above it.*
> *The snows quench the burning fires,*
> *The fires consume the falling snow.*
> *It baffles the tongue, it cannot be named,*
> *It is a god mysterious.*
> *The lake called Sé is embosomed in it,*
> *The river we cross, the Fuji, is its torrent.*
> *In the land of Yamato, the Land of the Rising Sun*
> *It is our treasure, our tutelary god.*
> *It never tires our eyes to look up*
> *To the lofty peak of Fuji!*
>
> —*The Manyōshū,* The Mushimaro collection

A golden gauze hung lightly over the dew as I stepped into the bus whose sign proclaimed in two languages that it was bound from Gotemba to Yoshida. For a few precious seconds a thickening outline shone tentatively through the mist, and the shimmering, conical hulk of 12,389-foot Fujisan—the Fire Goddess—stood in bleak silhouette, as symmetrical as a wigwam. In a twinkling the vision dissolved and secluded itself among a toiling bank of vapors and clouds. Vaguely I wondered whether I would ever see its exquisite fullness again.

It was early October. Pleats of diaphanous ice and snow draped down from the tapering spire, covering the upper quarter of the mountain. The prime climbing season lasts from the beginning of July to the end of August. Once the snows arrive in September, the upper stations are sealed. Still, at least 100,000 persons—some estimates are thrice that—succeed in making the ascent each summer, many proceeding by dark to escape the heat and also enjoy the earliest and most glorious sunrise that can be seen in the Japanese archipelago.

To its countless faithful, Fujisan presents an ever-varying perspective —reflected most typically in Hokusai's and Hiroshige's 100 views and even better-known 36 views in impressionistic woodcut prints. "The weather of Fuji changes seven times in an hour," goes one saying. Above all, Fuji—the sacred mountain of the Shintoists—symbolizes eternal beauty. It is truly a park as much as a mountain, and for pilgrims more than mountaineers. It is there to inspire and be embraced.

My brief glimpse of the striking form brought to mind a well-known verse by the eighth-century poet Yamabe Akahito:

> As slow I pace on Tago's shore
> Fair Fuji I descry;
> Her peerless peak aloft doth soar,
> Snow-crowned against the sky.

According to another of Japan's numberless proverbs, "There are two kinds of fools—the man who has never climbed Fuji and the one who climbs it a second time." Yet there are members of the Fujiko—organized groups of pilgrims to whom the ascent is a sacred act of piety—who reputedly have scaled it more than 200 times.

The bus rattled along the flat highway circling the mountain. A couple of hours later I checked into a *ryokan* in Yoshida. Reports about conditions varied. One native warned that the climb was not feasible since snow storms already had swept in from Siberia weeks before; another said it would be more difficult now, but certainly not impossible. All huts above the fifth station were shut, but this seemed to be of slight moment since I hoped to make the climb in one day anyhow.

The next morning I hustled around Yoshida, gathering some food and a sweatshirt. Yoshida was a cuspidor of mud puddles and loosely linked streets, neglected and unkempt now that the tourist season had ended. It drizzled steadily and I knew it must be snowing on the upper slopes. Looking through the heavy fogbanks in the direction of Fuji, one could even doubt that it was there.

Fuji rises in splendid isolation to the east of the Japanese Alps, some fifty-five miles from Tokyo. Its cylindrical proportions are almost flawless. The base circumference is 65 miles, set around an axis that at various points measures from 21.7 to 24.8 miles. The swooping upside-down-hourglass figure tapers from a gentle 3 degrees at the foot, to about 30 to 35 degrees at the midsection, and tops out at a precipitous 60 degrees.

Despite its impressive size, Fuji is blessed with an astonishingly ephemeral quality. In its magical, blinking mutations—fading from tawny bronze to a fiery, streaking crimson or purple, and to intermediate shades and hues the eyes cannot grasp—it occasionally seems to be more of a mirage than a mountain. In one instant it is brilliantly garbed in the crisp, trim splash of the gaudy sun, its cascading lines set boldly forth in every concave nuance and detail. Then, at the turn of the head, a veil descends, the scene is transformed, and another dramatic interplay unfolds: a dimly seen configuration, striated with an apricot or hazel complexion, dour and moody, a phantom half lost, half seen, sturdy yet elusive. In a wisp or a glare, swiftly or with a creeping evanescence, before the senses can adjust, a porous curtain blocks Fuji from view, and it is mysteriously swallowed up, all at once, yet somehow not at all. Wraithlike, it quivers and struggles, debouching as a hard, earthy presence, then, ever so serenely, with the passing of the wind, apotheosizing into a trembling shadow and, now again, prepossessingly, into a celestial throne that stretches high above a perennial plumage of blossoms and thistles.

In the words of one early observer:

> If you look a thousand times
> a thousand wonders are presented
> in the ever-changing beauty of
> cloud and wind about Mount Fuji.
> The autumn clouds
> paint Mount Fuji in ever-changing ways.[1]

At 4:30 A.M. a soft hand stirred me. The charming, black-tressed girl in a striped kimono brought in a tray of boiling tea. A glance outside showed the dark, clear sky to be ablaze with stars. A bus was scheduled to leave at 7:00 A.M. for Umagaeshi (which means "horse send back place"), but I thought it better to push on right away. The manager handed me a rough, indecipherable map and a walking stick. Eagerly, he tried to point the way to the Sengen shrine by which I would find the path to the base. I felt no more comforted than if Moses had cryptically waved to the east to show where the Red Sea would surely part.

The mystical, ephemeral figure of Fujisan (12,389 ft.). *Courtesy Japan National Tourist Organization.*

The morning air was damply brisk as my pilgrimage began. I was traveling lightly, with only a handful of edibles stuffed in my pocket and a thin jacket folded inside a bicycle pannier that I used as a rucksack. The glistening dawn augured a bright, cloudless day. *Ame futte ji katamura,* say the natives; "after rain comes fair weather."

I walked at a rapid clip and within twenty minutes found the Sengen shrine or *Fujitake-jinsha,* which guards the bottom part of the trail; its counterpart is constructed on the summit. *Sengen* means "God of the Mountain." Other shrines appear at the second, third, and fifth stations. The *Omuro-Sengen,* at the second station, is the oldest temple on Fuji. But the true diety of Fuji is *Konahana Sakuya-hime-nomikoto* ("The Princess who makes the Blossoms of the Trees Flower"), grandchild of the sun-goddess *Amaterasu* (who, according to Shinto mythology, was a direct ancestor of the first Japanese emperor, Jimmu Tenno, a ruler in 660 B.C.—thus laying the foundation for the doctrine of imperial divinity that survived in Japan until the end of World War II). Typically, the shrine consists of a simple, unpainted wooden structure before which stands a detached portal, or *torii.* Inside, where the *kami,* or dieties, dwell, there are votive offerings, seals, charms, and woodblocks. Annually, on August 26, Yoshida holds a fire festival, celebrating the closing of another season. Bonfires and torches mark the trail to the fifth station, and a lacquered portable shrine, shaped like the mountain, is paraded through the streets. According to tradition, Fuji invariably used to erupt on the northeast side, causing the townspeople to pray for calmness and peace, and leading to the festivities that are now observed.

Several times I stopped at farmhouses and murmured to their sleepy occupants, *"Ohayo!* Fuji?"—which was answered amid a hassle of confusion and, at last, a finger pointing the way. By 7:00 A.M., exactly two hours after setting out, I had, much to my surprise, threaded through the thick forest to the first station. Despite the size of the monolith that palely squatted before me, finding the correct route to the base was no easy matter. Thus far the path had been largely flat; now it began to incline. At the third station two men and a woman were seated around a small fire in one of the huts and hospitably bade me join them. I was anxious to proceed so I waved goodbye and, in a shower of *sayonaras,* crunched on. Remnants of rape-blossom stems and lichen lined the path, which now consisted mostly of volcanic sand. Nearby I passed a stone inscribed with a poem by Shoku Sanjin:

> Oh Fujisan
> Take off that dress of *kiri* [mist]
> That I may see thee in thy lovely nakedness.

The snowy flanks of Fuji seen from Lake Yamanaka. *Courtesy Japan National Tourist Organization.*

The upper snow mantle of Fuji twinkled brightly in the fresh ambience, and the craggy slopes surged upward in a splay of creases, beckoning its supplicant. By 8:45 A.M. I was at the fifth station where today—but not then— a modern toll road conveniently leads one to an altitude of about 7,900 feet. One of the stone shelters there looked lived-in, but its inhabitant was absent. Now a regal view of Yoshida and the surrounding lakes of Yamanaka, Kawaguchi, Sai, Shoji, and Motosu could be seen. A vast oasis fanned out below, in off-black, damask, and sepia, baring spans of fields that, in season, shone radiantly of lilies, azaleas, and cherry blossoms. Underfoot I noticed slim traces of alders and white birches.

By now every step became an effort. "Go slow" is the supreme law of the trail. I had been violating that commandment by moving much too fast. From the start I noticed that the slopes were swept by an infernal sea of small pebbles and fist-sized chunks of cinders and black schists that perpetually shifted and broke underfoot. It was akin to being trapped on a treadmill. For every two steps forward I backtracked one to the rear. My legs began jiggling and stalling. Beautiful Fuji—known as the Peerless Peak—is a solid pile of porous scoriae and pumice, or as one frustrated critic said, "A fraud—a disgusting mass of humbug and ashes."

* * *

At 12,389 feet, Fujisan is the highest peak on the Japanese mainland.

According to legend, it is the product of a great natural convulsion that boiled up out of the sea in 285 or 286 B.C., simultaneously forming it and, in counterbalance, scouring out Lake Biwa, some 150 miles away. Scientists believe that the hull of the mountain originally was seated during the Glacial Age some 600,000 years ago, was reshaped into *Ko-Fuji* ("Old Fuji") about 50,000 to 60,000 years ago during the era of the Cro-Magnon Man and Neanderthal Man, and, after another expulsion of lava and ashes, attained its present shape as *Shin-Fuji* ("New Fuji") during the Alluvial Epoch only about 10,000 years ago. The constant work of erosion has glazed its sides so that its ridges fall in direct lines, like the fine ruffles of a skirt, from top to bottom.

Now dormant, Fuji is a stratified volcano of rock and gravel that has blown its top at least eighteen times over the centuries. The last major explosion occurred in 1707, raining hot debris on Edo (now Tokyo) and gouging out the Hoei crater, which sits on the southeast flank and forms the most noticeable blight on the peak's pyramidal perfection. Hoei is some 990 feet deep, almost half again the size of the summit bowl. Another major scar is the *Osawa* ("Big Valley"), a frothing slash that spins down from the summit rim, created by fierce winds that blow in from the west. Osawa is infrequently climbed and has been the site of numerous accidents and deaths.

Of the world's 457 volcanoes, 362 lie on the edge of the Pacific, and Japan alone has 186 situated along an elongated barrier that stretches from the Aleutians and Kuriles down the length of the Southeast Asian coast. The staggering earthquakes that shook Japan in 1891 (24,000 perished) and 1923 have been linked to Fuji and its 60 parasitic volcanoes. *Vulcanism,* so named after the Roman god of fire, involves the burning of incredibly hot (1,800 to 2,200 degrees Fahrenheit) steams and gases (some toxic, others containing carbon dioxide essential to plant life) that are locked within an orange-red molten ooze called *magma.* Upon eruption, the magma turns into lava, which solidifies into rock as it swims down the slopes. The intensity of the blow-off of lava and gases often shapes the steepness of the sides of the volcano. Hence, Fuji and such brethren as Etna, Vesuvius, and Popocatepetl, rise more sharply than Hawaii's squatty Mauna Loa.

When the Japanese first settled on Honshu, they encountered a primitive Caucasian race known as the *emishi* or *ebisu,* or Ainu, who have since retreated to the northerly outposts of Hokkaido and Sakhalin. Only about 17,000 of these once-fearless aborigines survive, but it was they who, despite their uncouth ways, are generally believed to have given the great mountain its name (as they did many other places on the Japanese Islands). In Ainu, *Fuji* (or *Huchi* or *Fuchi*) means the "fire goddess," or "smoking." But the origin of the word finds its most intriguing aspect in its written form, as analyzed by Dr.

The many views...

Frederick Starr in his worthy and loving book, *Fujiyama—The Sacred Mountain of Japan.* Oriental characters often convey both a sound and a pictorial image or idea; in the case of homophones, a single sound is pregnant with diverse meanings. Many characters produce the same two sounds, *Fu* and *ji* (*yama* means "mountain"; the Japanese prefer the ideogram *san*). In short, characters that create these sounds may be translated as "prosperous warrior" (or "rich samurai"); "not two" ("matchless" or "unrivaled"); "not death" (or "immortal"); "illimitable" or "rich scholar." In poetry, *Fuji-no-yama,* meaning "the mountain of Fuji," is preferred; the peasants call it simply *Ō Yama* ("honorable mountain"). Philologist Basil H. Chamberlain has theorized that, from the phonetic standpoint, Fuji's true derivation may be the Ainu word *push,* which means to "rise violently" and is the appellation originally given to the nearby river Fujisawa; in time the mutation from *push* to *Fuzi,* as it once was known, occurred.

Starr was a true "Fuji-phile." Once a teacher of anthropology at the University of Chicago, he visited Japan some sixteen times, and ascended Fuji five times, garbed in the usual white tunic and sunshade, and following all the prescribed rituals of Fujiko. After his death in Tokyo in 1933, a monument was erected to his memory at the start of the Subashiri trail. The slab quotes him: "Fuji bare and naked in a blaze

...of Japan's shrine-mountain. *Both photographs courtesy Japan National Tourist Organization.*

of sunshine is beautiful; Fuji with its summit wrapped in cloud and mist is more beautiful; Fuji blotted out by the fog until but a hint or line is left is most beautiful."

Another Westerner who became entranced by Fuji was Lafcadio Hearn. Born in the Ionian Islands in 1850, of Greek-Irish descent, he received his education in England, France, and Ireland before migrating to the United States in 1869. Colorful, restless, and sensitive, Hearn suffered from total blindness of the left eye, which failed to prevent him from developing into a prolific writer. After an impoverished youth, when he was forced to sleep in the streets, he became a newspaper reporter and took delight in writing about the strange and the grotesque. His early works included collections of Creole proverbs and Chinese folk tales. In 1890 he came to Japan where he found fulfillment, authoring twelve books, including the well-regarded *Japan —An Attempt at Interpretations,* before dying there in 1904. He adopted a Japanese name (Yakumo Koizuma) and citizenship, married a woman of high samurai station, and was given a chair in English literature at the Imperial University in Tokyo. Deeply interested in Buddhism, he sought to forge a link between the Oriental belief in reincarnation and the Darwinian doctrine of evolution that prevails in the Occident.

Hearn made the climb in 1897. He obviously had a difficult time, thought the slopes were steep ("an amazing angle. . . . That stupendous pitch gives me a sense of dizziness . . . appears unnatural, frightful . . ."), and mentions the "help of ladders." In *Exotics and Retrospectives* he wrote:

> The most beautiful sight in Japan, certainly one of the most beautiful in the world, is the distant apparition of Fuji on cloudless days,—more especially days of spring and autumn, when the greater part of the peak is covered with late or early snows. You can seldom distinguish the snowless base, which remains the same color as the sky: you perceive only the white cone seeming to hang in heaven; and the Japanese comparison of its shape to an inverted half-open fan is made wonderfully exact by the fine streaks that spread downward from the notched top, like shadows of fan-ribs. Even lighter than a fan the vision appears—rather the ghost or dream of a fan:—yet the material reality a hundred miles away is grandiose among the mountains of the world.[2]

(In a letter written to Professor Chamberlain in 1894, he took a different tack, vigorously complaining that there was no "sentiment" in the traditional comparison of Fuji to a white half-open inverted fan.)

The sight from the summit overwhelmed the romantic-minded Hearn:

> But the view—the view for a hundred leagues,—and the light of the far faint dreamy world,—and the fairy vapors of the morning,—and the marvellous wreathings of cloud: all this, and only this, consoles me for the labor and the pain. . . .Other pilgrims, earlier climbers,—poised upon the highest crag, with faces

turned to the tremendous East,—are clapping their hands in Shinto prayer, saluting the mighty Day....The immense poetry of the moment enters into me with a thrill. I know that the colossal vision before me has already become a memory ineffaceable,—a memory of which no luminous detail can fade till the hour when thought itself must fade, and the dust of these eyes be mingled with the dust of the myriad million eyes that also have looked, in ages forgotten before my birth, from the summit supreme of Fuji to the Rising of the Sun.[3]

The crater was less to his liking. "No spot in this world," he stated, "can be more horrible, more atrociously dismal, than the cindered tip of the Lotos as you stand upon it."

No mountain epitomizes the spiritual, cultural, and historical odyssey of a country as vividly as Fujisan. Its meaning is, indeed, outside the range of Western experience.

Although young Japanese often now regard Fuji cynically, as a faded symbol of triteness, for many it remains the abode of the gods and an object of infinite and ineffable beauty—a fateful linking of the mystical wonders of heaven with earthly realities. Fuji expresses the heritage of the country and its people, and, indeed, its own fortunes have been influenced by the political and social gyrations that have occurred over the years. Japan had virtually no recorded history until A.D. 400, when the Yamato clan assumed control over the central and western part, and established a seat of power near Kyoto. Thereafter Buddhism, with its attendant Chinese culture, was introduced and eventually became closely intertwined with Shintoism. The latter, based on worship of the marvels and forms of nature, developed primarily into a series of traditional rituals and customs, highlighted by pilgrimages to sacred shrines and the celebration of festivals. Reciting prayers, dancing, and food offerings are all essential to its practice.

During the Tokugawa era (1603-1867), when intercourse with foreigners was shut off, it is known that the climbing of the mountain was exceedingly common. After 700 years of military dictatorship, the country's feudal barons *(daimyo)* lapsed into debt and the samurai families became discontent. Japan thus was ripe for change when in 1853 Commodore Matthew C. Perry steamed into Tokyo Bay and in time forced a treaty opening the way to foreign commerce. The Meiji Restoration followed. Feudalism was abolished, the capital was moved to Tokyo, and Japan quickly began to adopt Western ideas and methodology. At the same time, nationalistic fervor became dominant and ancient myths of imperial worship and racial divinity were revived.

Inevitably, Fuji was formally Shintoized and vestiges of Buddhism were ordered removed. For the Buddhists, the crater was itself an inner temple. The bonze Matsudai erected the Dainichi Temple on the summit as early as 1149. Nichiren, the founder of a well-known Buddhist sect, made the climb in 1229.

Fuji worshippers are represented predominantly by the Fujiko, the religious cult that for centuries has conducted sacred pilgrimages on the mountain it idolizes. Its leaders possess an irrepressible (outsiders would say morbid) affinity for being buried inside Fuji, believing it to be a sure path to immortality. The sect was founded in 1558 by an eighteen-year-old youth named Takematsu, later called Kakugyo, who ascended Fuji 120 times and made the Chudo circuit around the waist of the mountain 33 times. (It must have been a healthy regimen for he lived to the age of 106.) From the time he became an ascetic he carried out his ritual on a square wooden block, from which he derived his name; *Kaku* means "square," and *gyo* means "religious discipline." A determined chap, he performed 2,000 days of *gyo* standing on that block. He died in a cave and left as his legacy a religious formula, or *ominuki,* which his followers invoke on the summit.

Another Fujiko ascetic, Ito Ibe (later known as Miroku), culminated his teachings from another vault carved in the mountain. He made the ascent annually, and, at sixty-three, chose to die there. He walked up the Yoshida trail to the seventh station, accompanied by his devoted follower Tanabe, where a hole, contoured to his specifications, was excavated; at his bidding, it was completely sealed, excepting only a space around his face. Snugly locked into position he fasted for thirty-one days, dispensing a different spiritual message each day; not too surprisingly, he then expired. Although despised during his lifetime, and given to loud diatribes, he became popular in death and developed a host of followers. His enemies broke open the tomb and scattered his remains. Faithfully, Tanabe gathered up many of them, hiding them in a place known only to his devotees. Miroku's "messages of the thirty-one days" are considered sacred among the Fujiko, and all of its major sects are now said to be descended from him.

Most of the white-garbed pilgrims who climb Fuji, led by guides or *gorikis,* are members of a Fujiko group. For them, the effort is no mere holiday or vacation, but the sacred denouement of a lifetime's preparation of soul and body. Some regions send representatives, and their faithful, in effect, climb by proxy. Others probably do not comprehend the invocations they are chanting. Still, the ascent is for them the supreme act of worship, and its crowning moment is to espy the sunrise from the summit, or *goraiko.* Normally the pilgrims come down the same route used for the ascent; they do not traverse or "crack" the mountain. In earlier times, they are said to have fasted a hundred days before making the attempt.

Mythology, legend, art, poetry, and proverbs—all are as much a part of the Japanese essence as the tea ceremony and the sun-spot flag.

"The breezes that blow down from the mountain-top are the breath of its guardian goddess," states one saying. "The rain that falls on it is her tears."

Another: "Fuji-no-yama is the origin of all other mountains, and its grandeur equals that of both sun and moon."

Wrote Basho:

>   On Kawaguchi's shore I muse
>   While Fuji through the changing mist
>   Presents all hundred views.

From the Sasakawa Tanero collection:

>   Though the winter is furious,
>   the clouds on Fuji's summit are not disturbed.
>   When one looks up to Mount Fuji's peak,
>   Anxiety and irritation about this
>   decadent world disappear.

Also:

>   From what primeval slime
>   springs the spotless lotus-blossom of Mount Fuji?
>
>   Amid the sea of sky and wave of cloud
>   the petaled mountain, Fuji's peak, floats.

The first reference to Fuji appears in the *Nihon-shoki* (*Chronicles of Japan*) which was written in A.D. 714. The *Manyōshū* (*The Collection of Myriad Leaves*), the country's most ancient and venerable anthology, contains eighth-century poems extolling its wonders.

Not surprisingly, one of the oldest of Japanese fairytales, called *Taketori Monogatari,* or the *Bamboo Cutter,* concerns Fuji. Written in the ninth or tenth century, it tells of a woodsman who finds a supernatural little girl three inches high inside a luminous piece of bamboo he has cut. Within three months she grows into a strikingly beautiful maiden and five young noblemen bid for her favor. She gives each an impossible task to test his desires, and none succeeds. Finally, the emperor proposes to her. When he touches her, she vanishes to the moon, but bequeaths to him an elixir of eternal life. Disconsolate over

The white vestments of Fuji. *Courtesy Japan National Tourist Organization.*

losing her, he decides he does not wish to live forever and takes the magic potion to the summit of Fuji where he burns it. Fuji thus has smoked ever since. One scholar claims that the name was itself derived from the phrase *fu-shi*, or "elixir of no-death."

Fuji has proven to be an irresistible attraction for Japanese artists. Of these, the eccentric, superstitious, and highly gifted Hokusai (1760-1849), a leader of the noted Ukiyo-ye School of Art, is the most acclaimed. He often is called the Rembrandt of his country. His 36 Views (in green, blue, yellow, and brown) and 100 Views of Fuji (in tints of black and red), the latter painted at the age of 76, are classics of their kind. Hokusai heartily believed in goblins, lived in abject squalor, ate just enough to survive, and cared about nothing except his artwork.

Hokusai's imaginative interpretations of Fuji pointed to the transitory nature of human existence, and, in their time, were daringly innovative. The variety of the depictions, with Fuji usually in backdrop, is impressive; the mountain forms a universal bond with the exigencies of daily Japanese living. The matchless peak appears behind umbrella tops set out to dry in their maker's yard; through the closely spaced stems of swaying bamboo; reflected in a sake cup grasped by a tippler; caught in the breaking curl of an oceanic wave; beyond hanging strips of cloth outside a dryer's place; behind a timber yard; from the Nihon Bridge; and as seen by wayfarers relaxing at a teahouse on the Tokaido road. One is called the *Three Lucky Things* (Fuji, falcon, and eggplant); another, the *Three Whites* (Fuji, snow, and crane).

Fuji also is the subject of the world's oldest known mountain-climbing painting, which hangs in a sanctuary in Fuji-no-miya.

No authoritative account remains of the initial ascent. However, a Buddhist monk, En-no-Shōkaku (also referred to as Ennogyoja), is said possibly to have been the pioneer Japanese to have attained the summit in A.D. 663. The oldest recorded climb is related in *Fujisan-Ki,* penned by Miyako-no-Yoshika in the 870s.

En-no-Shōkaku founded the Buddhist order of *Gyoja,* composed of religious pilgrims called *yamabushi,* who climb in white tunics, *kyahan* ("gaiters"), *waraji* ("straw sandals"), a *yuikesa* ("stole"), and, on their heads, a black cloth of twelve folds (representing the different stages of *Karma*). Carrying an octagonal *kongō-zuye* ("staff"), they call out the eternal incantations: *Rokkon Shojo* ("May our six senses be made pure") and *Oyama wa seiten* ("May the weather on the honorable mountain be good"). (The heart is the sixth sense.) En-no-Shōkaku, a

View of Fujiyama from the top of Mt. Shichiman. *Courtesy Japan National Tourist Organization.*

patron and originator of *Shungendō,* mountain-devotees of the Shingon and Tendai sects of Buddhism, came to a dismal end (as, it seems, do many Japanese heroes). Suspected of sorcery, the emperor had him imprisoned. When he broke out, his mother was taken as a hostage. According to one of the prevailing versions, both of them were exiled and sailed on a raft of sods toward China.

Sir Rutherford Alcock, the first British minister to Japan, became the initial foreigner to make the ascent on September 10, 1860, at the age of fifty-one. He encountered a series of obstacles from Japanese officialdom and for that very reason pressed the attempt, so as to test the validity of a treaty provision guaranteeing freedom of travel to foreign envoys. He described the climb in *The Capital of the Tycoon:*

> Various motives led me to plan an expedition through the interior to the far-famed sacred mountain; and various causes also delayed my departure until I had some reasons to fear the Japanese Ministers might prove right in their confident predictions, that it was too late to accomplish the ascent. August was already past and the first days of September were gliding on, while I was yet engaged in removing the obstacles raised by the Ministers themselves in the first instance, and admirably spread over time and space subsequently by their subordinates—with a fertility of invention and hardihood of persistence, which, if it did not secure them success, would in a better cause have entitled them to great praise.
>
> From my subsequent experience, I should judge the ascent to be well nigh impossible after any snow has fallen. But although they go in numbers, strangely enough it is only the poorer classes—to whom, one would suppose, both time and money must be the most difficult to command; while the absence of either would create insurmountable obstacles. But what will not faith and energy—even a Pagan's faith—accomplish? It appears, if I may believe the Ministers, that it is not considered consistent with the dignity of a Daimio, or even an officer of any rank, to make the pilgrimage—perhaps because too many of the greasy mob must unavoidably come in close contact with them. Be this as it may, it was one of the objections strongly urged by the Ministers: "It was not fitting in a person of the rank of a British Envoy to make the pilgrimage, limited by custom if not by law to the lower classes!"[4]

Alcock observed that "servants and followers of every denomination, under every imaginable pretext," attached themselves to the party, so that he ultimately found an entourage of 100 persons, and more than 30 horses, traveling along the road to the Hakone range. He described the actual climb, made via Murayama, as follows:

> In the winding ascent over the rubble and scoriae of the

mountain—which alone is seen after ascending about halfway—little huts or caves, as these resting-places are called, partly dug out and roofed over to give refuge to the pilgrims, appeared. There are, I think, eleven from *Hakimondo* to the summit, and they are generally about a couple of miles asunder. In one of these we took up our quarters for the night, and laid down our rugs, too tired to be very delicate. Nevertheless, the cold and the *occupants* we found former pilgrims had left, precluded much sleep. Daylight was rather a relief; and after a cup of hot coffee and a biscuit, we commenced the upper half....

The last half of the ascent is by far the most arduous, growing more steep as each station is passed. The first rays of the sun just touched, with a line of light, the broad waters of the Pacific as they wash the coast, when we made our start (after sleeping in a hut overnight). The first station seemed to be very near, and was reached within the hour, but each step now became more difficult. The path, if such the zig-zag may be called which our guides took, often led directly over fragments of out-jutting rocks, while the loose scoriae prevented firm footing, and added much to the fatigue. The air became more rarefied and perceptibly affected the breathing. At last the third station was passed, and a strong effort carried us to the fourth—the whole party by this time straggling at long intervals. This was now the last between us and the summit. It did not seem so far, until a few figures on the edge of the crater furnished a means of measurement, and they looked painfully diminutive. The last stage, more rough and precipitous than all the preceding, had this farther disadvantage, that it came after the fatigue of all the others. More than an hour's toil, with frequent stoppages for breath and rest to aching legs and spine, were needed; and more than one of our number felt very near the end of their strength before the last step placed the happy pilgrim on the topmost stone, and enabled him to look down the yawning crater.[5]

Alcock's ascent took twelve hours of actual climbing, eight on the second day.

The distinction of having been the first woman known to have made the climb belongs, curiously enough, to a European—Lady Parkes, wife of Sir Harry Parkes, the noted British minister who served in Japan from 1865 to 1883. She reached the top in 1867—five years before Fuji was formally opened to females in the wake of the Restoration. Women's libbers will be interested to know that, prior to that time, the fair sex was prohibited from going above the 5,000-foot line.

In season the climb is usually as safe as an Easter stroll. But out-of-season attempts, subject to the raging vagaries of Pacific storms, can be quite a different thing; one 1518 account tells of thirteen persons perishing in a summit tempest. Such efforts seem to offer a special attraction for foreigners. Dr. Frederick A. Cook, the polar explorer, accomplished it in November 1915. In May of both 1892 and 1893 the Rev. Walter Weston, a knowledgeable climber, piloted two successful attempts amid heavy snowdrifts. During the first effort, from Gotemba, his coolies warily sat on the roof of the sixth station and refused to go farther. A year later, proceeding via Murayama, his party weathered a storm and returned gleefully to learn that it had been honored by an obituary in a local newspaper.

Staring into the gaping crater after the difficult ascent, Weston observed in his *Playground of the Far East* (London: John Murray, 1918) that, "Here and there huge icicles hang blue against the dull deep red and purple of the rocks inside the crater lip. All is cold and still as a grave." His mood brightened: "It is soon a positive relief to turn from all this deathly whiteness to let the eye rest on the vast expanses of country clad in all the tender freshness and warmth of color of its young spring life."

Beginning in 1913, a competition was held to determine Fuji's fastest climber. The first winner, a student called Ito, made the 9,000-foot vertical ascent on the Gotemba trail in two hours and thirty-eight minutes, winning a prize of about three hundred dollars. In contrast, only two emperors are believed to have made it to the top.

Six main trails lead to the crater: Yoshida, Gotemba, Kawaguchiko, Subashiri, Funatsu, and Fuji-no-miya. On the Yoshida path, the winding ascent from the Sengen shrine measures about 12 miles. In season, a bus operates to the fifth station, taking one and three-quarter hours, after which the remaining 3.32 mile stretch can be hiked in some three hours and thirty minutes, and the return in two hours. Each of the trails is now neatly divided into ten sections (*go*), and varies in distance from 9 to 15 miles. In season, stone huts along the way offer hot food, wooden beds, and insufferable chaos; they usually are as crammed as the five o'clock Tokyo-Nara express.

Many aspirants start late in the afternoon, take the bus to the fifth station, hike all night, and reach the summit in time for the sunrise; this has the twin virtue of avoiding the fierce mid-summer heat and the necessity of camping overnight. The majority, however, start earlier in the day, attain one of the upper stations before dark, sleep in a hut, and complete the ascent the next morning. They circle the rim, and return by late afternoon of the second day.

* * *

Departing the fifth station, I slipped over ancient lavas and ashes, scarcely thinking of the ineluctable beauty and meaning of Fujisan, and began to move above the hemlocks, silver firs, and larches that ring its mighty frustum. I had started at the wrong time (5:00 A.M. instead of 5:00 P.M.), in the wrong season, and with the wrong equipment (no provision for the snow). Also, I lacked sleeping gear should the need arise. (I did sniff out latrines en route and found one, at the sixth or seventh level, which I felt could be discretely broken into if the weather deteriorated.) It took me only a few paces to realize, with chagrin, that I was the only one on the trail and, indeed, on the north side of the mountain. Having called my prudence into account, I further accentuated my distress when, to quote my diary: "I got dizzy, my legs completely gave out, and I stretched out in a virtual collapsed state right in mid-trail. I felt terribly exhausted and kept thinking I should turn back and forget about Fuji. Never before felt dizzy like that. After a twenty minute rest (and candy bar) while stretched out on the ground, continued climb, stopping for five-minute rests at almost every station—but feeling generally strong and good."

From the slopes below, the summit had shone clear and white. Now it was hidden and I seemed to dissolve among the lonely, columnar cosmos of slanting rocks, pulverized basalts, lava wastes, and relentless switchbacks. Occasionally, vestiges of shrubs, moss, and brush offered company, and flocks of birds could be seen heading toward distant waters. The mountain—the incarnation of pious charm and grace—seemed to undergo a change of mood. It became an uncompromising tormentor, hard and unsympathetic, ravaging and loathsome. It did not yield; it resisted—with the sharp ripostes of a searing sun, the ever-moving rocks underneath, and the long paths that wove slantwise and upward like rolls of yarn, without holding forth any promise of reward. Even my bag of extra clothing proved, at this point, a hindrance—although it was helpful on the breezy top. I thought, better a warm sun than a snowstorm—for which I was amply unprepared.

By making the voyage in the off season, I was, of course, eluding the oceans of humanity that pour up and down the slopes in summer time. Once one sets out during that intense period one is committed, irrevocably swept along by the passionate mob, a sand pebble washed ever upward on the beach. To stop and descend in mid-flight is akin to fighting a riptide. All this mad fun and jostle I missed. Mine was a mission as quiet as it was solitary.

At the eighth station the mountain asserted its last and most effective defense—a glossy altar of snow and ice. The outlying towns and lakes—Kawaguchi and Yamanaka—now were unrecognizable. A viscous film broke over Mt. Tenjo to the north. Except for excessive fatigue, I almost, but not quite, preferred these snowfields to the jerky, reverse-gear movements on the charred stones below. Reaching the ninth station, I could not discern whether I was five minutes—or well more than an hour—from the top. The latter was, perforce, correct. This

Across the Fujisan summit

Down the throat of Fuji's main crater

was the most grueling part, and helped explain why the postseason ascent of Fuji has never been the country's most popular pastime. The snow was piled up about ten feet high in places, and the well-worn trail simply disappeared beneath it. This itself was of no appreciable concern, for to follow it would have merely prolonged the time required. The steep, direct path up was harder but more efficient.

The real puzzle—one I had never considered before—was: how can steep snowfields be climbed when, at each step, one sinks in to the hips or waist? The simple answer: one does not "climb" at all (inspired discovery)—at least not with the feet; instead, one (meaning this one) desperately drops to all fours and, like a Pomeranian poodle, waddles, slides, and catapults oneself forward on elbows and knees—and the more scurry per thrust the better. Thus it was that in this blasphemously thrashing manner, I was able to haul myself over the long white apron that hangs like a painted shell from the beckoning summit. A more orthodox approach would have been to use snow shoes, which would have dealt the noble peak a mortal blow with a mere ruffling of a few ice crystals. However, such was the infinite imprecision of my scheme of attack that this stratagem did not faintly occur to me until I was back in the lowlands. Perhaps it is fair to say that little else can be expected of a visiting minion who casually glances out of his *ryokan* one chilly autumn morning and decides to start his day's pleasure by ploughing up the nearest mountaintop. Since members of the Fujiko spend the better part of their lives prepping for the task, it probably is not asking too much for others to give at least a full day's thoughtful allotment to the job.

Having contrived manual locomotion as a radically new and modern technique for snow climbing, I gradually pummeled my way upward and reached, not yet the summit, but the point of being utterly frazzled. (The Shintoists, I suspect, would somehow call it a state of grace.) In any event, in this condition of unholy exasperation or benign unction—choose as you wish—I spotted the *torii* of the Kusushi shrine and ambled up, surmising it must be another *gome* that would justify a rest stop.

Passing through the portal, I was relieved and surprised to find a crown of dark, scarred boulders piled, half-iced, half-bare, in the glint of the sunlight. The black, unforgiving walls of the *Nai-in,* or "Sanctuary," plunged sharply. Because of the incessant winds, the summit crags often remain snowless. A spring gurgled busily; I could not be sure whether it was the so-called Golden or Silver Sparkling Waters. The crater formed an enormous orifice, 726 feet deep and 1,650 feet wide, and was studded with eight surrounding peaks, called the *Yatsuda Fuyo* ("The eight petals of Fuji"). The topmost point,

The summit rim of Fuji

Kengamine, lies 250 feet above the huts on the rim. The crater looked deceptively shallow, yet harsh and inhospitable. Its sands were hot enough to bake eggs. It was 1:00 P.M. (October 8)—a fast eight hours since I had left Yoshida.

To the east, the bleak Pacific diligently tossed up frothy breakers against the coastal plain; much of the island, from Yokohama to Shizuaka, and the prominent Southern Alps, could be glimpsed amid blazing tints that danced tantalizingly on all horizons. From the cap of that graceful spire, it seemed here, indeed, was where West and East conjoin. Fuji is the centerpiece of a 122,300-acre park—a treasure house, in season, of cherry blossoms, sunny waterfalls, and deciduous broad-leaved trees, an incomparable arbor that houses 2,000 species of plants, 45 of mammals, and 179 of birds.

Poetry still is as much a part of Fuji as its fissures and ashes. On the summit one is given to such moods.

Said Kada-no-Azuma-Maro: "The mountain which I found higher to climb than I had heard, than I had thought, than I had seen,—was Fuji's peak"

From the collection by Sasakawa Tanero:

> By climbing Mount Fuji
> I found heaven and earth
> not so far apart.

For almost two hours I traipsed around the rim, traversing Kengamine, which took forty minutes to reach. Two men were standing on the lip opposite—the only people I spotted on the peak all day—but I was unable to determine whether they were climbers or manning the weather station. By 3:00 P.M. I was heading back down.

The upper part was akin to dancing in a sandpile; the soft snow crumbled so that the whole exercise took on the aspect of a bobsled ride. I reached the lower portion of the snowfield when I suddenly noticed that the sun was disappearing over my left shoulder at an oddly accelerating rate. I figured something must be amiss and, by the time I realized what had happened, it was too late, and too time consuming, to backtrack and change course. At the eighth station I inadvertently had taken the Subashiri route, which veers east, rather than the trail to Yoshida, which lies north. By reason of Fuji's girth, this slight error meant I was destined to wind up about 20 miles from my starting point. Consequently, when it turned dark, around 7:00 P.M., I was still wandering grumpily along a horse trail, lost and tired, when by all that is humane I should have been quaffing sake in Yoshida.

An hour later my status was still quo, and I started looking for a spot in which to pass the night. At this juncture the fates relented. Out of a clearing stepped an armed Japanese guard who, of all things, was standing watch over a munitions dump. He had a walkie-talkie, and, after some linguistic legerdemain, I was able to persuade the skeptical voice on the other end to dispatch a jeep. Following a bouncy forty-five-minute ride through the forest, I landed back in Yoshida about 9:00 P.M.

This modest episode formed the basis of two of the most forgettable articles ever to appear in the *Nippon Times* and *Mainichi,* in which I described the ascent. The opening theme of one piece was (incredibly):

> The legs were twanging like tuning forks, the old stomach was doing loop-the-loops, and I felt as if I were going to cry, like Johnnie Ray. Pretty soon I folded up and collapsed in a heap somewhere about the 6,000 ft. level like an accordion. Yes—climbing Fuji, I had been told, was a snap. Simply a snap. Just put on some hiking boots and walk along a vertically inclined plane for some two and half miles. I intend to give the lie to this piece of misinformation. . . . It was 1:40 P.M. when I finally scrambled up to that grayish marker on the peak. I don't know the artist who designed that thing, but it looks exactly like a fireplug. Now why would anyone want to put a fireplug at a place which at the present is probably the coldest, most fire-proof spot in all the Far East? Another case of mountain sickness. . . . By 9 P.M. I was back in Yoshida safe in the knowledge that: (1) Climbing Fuji is

like visiting never-never land; (2) The Dodgers, who had been scoring dozens of runs at 10,000 ft., had actually been going down while I'd been going up. They'd wound up in the dumps just like I had.

(The ascent occurred on the day of the last game of the World Series.)

So much for the *Nippon Times*. Mercifully, I shall spare the reader any further rendering of that less-than-epic account.

The manager (who spoke some English) and the young maiden (who did not) at the inn greeted me warmly; in view of the hour, they thought I would probably pass the night on the mountain. I do not know whether they truly were impressed, but at least they pretended to be. Bashfully the girl unlaced my boots, readied a scalding *ofuro* or bath (the Japanese know of no other kind), tucked me into bed on the *tatami* mat, and then—in a most unusual gesture—brought in a hot brew with two cups. Quietly we sipped it together, her face suffused with happiness. She seemed pleased that a foreigner had made a solo ascent through the drifts to the top of her shrine that is a mountain.

Outside a swatch of stars glimmered imperceptibly. The sacred peak stood in haunting dishabille against a murky, spotted sky. A spectral vapor spread through the forest and up those tenebrous slopes. Fujisan was, again, supremely alone.

A few weeks later I stood aboard an American-bound ship anchored in Yokohama Harbor. In tranquil splendor the sky-pagoda poked its ermine crest through the clouds. Slowly, enigmatically, it drifted away. Ishikawajozen said it best:

> A white fan
> Hangs upside down
> In the Tokaido bay.

6
Excursions in the High Sierra

Rising on the other side, cliff above cliff, precipice piled upon precipice, rock over rock, up against sky, towered the most gigantic mountain-wall in America, culminating in a noble pile of Gothic-finished granite and enamel-like snow. How grand and inviting looked its white form, its untrodden, unknown crest, so high and pure in the clear, strong blue! I looked upon it as one contemplating the purpose of his life.

—Clarence King (from Mount Brewer), *Mountaineering in the Sierra Nevada*

How glorious a greeting the sun gives the mountains! To behold this alone is worth the pains of any excursion a thousand times over. The highest peaks burned like islands in a sea of liquid shade. Then the lower peaks and spires caught the glow, and long lances of light streaming through many a notch and pass, fell thick on the frozen meadow.

—John Muir, *The Mountains of California*

The heart of the High Sierra remained remote, serene, and grandly untouched. The House was divided against itself; blood ran steadily in Vicksburg and the Shenandoah Valley. The railhead stopped at St. Joseph. To the west lay parched, dusty roads, where stage wagons, bearing the ragtag and the visionary, were lustily harassed by brigands and smugglers. Apache tribes and cattle rustlers still scoured the land. Echoes of vigilantes lingered ominously over the Barbary Coast. Gold prospectors, gaunt and indomitable, doggedly panned the deep-set veins of the Mother Lode.

The year was 1864. Judged by time and circumstance, such brassy tumult was scarcely conducive to the lonely, painstaking work of exploring the monstrous, snow-flecked sculptures—the Range of Light, as John Muir called them—that stretched 430 miles down the Central California Basin from Lassen Peak to the Tehachapis. Yet, a small party, riding out of Thomas's sawmill near Visalia and hacking pluckily through dense chaparral across the San Joaquin plains, aimed to accomplish just that.

The story of Josiah Dwight Whitney's California Geological Survey, founded in 1860 on a grant of a meager $20,000, is a familiar part of the lore of the Sierra Nevada; still, its impact warrants a brief retelling. There were William H. Brewer, Whitney's stalwart field leader, a graduate of Yale Sheffield Scientific School; mining specialist William Ashburner; topographer Charles F. Hoffman; paleontologist William M. Gabb; and engineer Chester Averill. In time came young Clarence King and his pal, James T. Gardiner.

It was King and the packer, Richard Cotter, who, having bidden farewell to Brewer, tackled the vast granite ridges to the east, scaling 14,018-foot Mount Tyndall and, in one grand stroke, unlocking the secret fastnesses of the High Sierra.

In many respects King was the Horace Bénédict de Saussure of his time. Born of aristocratic families, both were trained, dedicated scientists, possessed of fine literary talents, and politically influential. King's career was as closely bound up with Mount Whitney and the opening of the Sierra Nevada as was the erudite Genevan's with Mont Blanc. But a twin quirk of bad luck—stormy weather and a mapping error—deprived King of his deeply held ambition to become the first to stand upon the highest point in the land.

King was a man of remarkable and diverse gifts. He was, at once, learned, witty, disciplined, curious, and imaginative—a masterful writer and raconteur, geological theoretician, mining expert, connoisseur of art, mountaineer, and world traveler; despite a tendency to be snobbish, he also possessed a marvelous capacity for friendship. His probably was the first attempt at serious mountain climbing in the range.

Clarence Rivers King was born in Newport, Rhode Island, in 1842. One of his close friends was James Gardiner (earlier spelled Gardner), with whom he shared boyhood experiences at a Hartford, Connecticut high school. Only five feet six inches tall at full stretch, agile and stocky, King enrolled in a two-year course at the newly founded Yale Scientific School, a branch of learning then somewhat neglected by Ivy League institutions. He was an active student, boxing, serving as stroke on the crew, and playing an avid game of cricket.

Stirred by the poetic writings of John Ruskin, the scientific insights of John Tyndall, and the scholarly lectures of Harvard professor Louis

Agassiz, King resolved to make geology his life's work. Glaciologist Tyndall's *Hours of Exercise in the Alps,* with its absorbing accounts of attempts on the Matterhorn and the virgin ascent of the Weisshorn, undoubtedly fired his eager, impressionable mind with the excitement of high mountain adventuring.

One day a professor read King a letter from Brewer, vividly describing the latter's work, as a member of the Whitney party, in surveying 14,162-foot Mount Shasta, then considered to be the tallest peak in the country. King quickly decided to head west, and Gardiner, seeking an escape from his intensive law studies, joined him. In a riotous cross-country journey, they linked up with an emigrant family, traversed the Wasatch range to Carson City, visited the hectic diggings at the Comstock Lode, tangled with a wild bull, and hitched a wagon ride across the Sierra to Placerville. En route they lost all of their belongings in a fire and, according to King, who already was nurturing a flair for the melodramatic, were arrested for kidnapping runaway blacks. He also claimed to have been challenged to a duel in a bar, his life being saved only by a timely combination of bluff and spunk. Supposedly he jammed his fingers forward in his pocket, as though aiming a pistol, and snapped a toothpick, mimicking the sound of cocking the hammer. His tormentor retreated. At least it made for a colorful tale.

Chance now intervened to forever alter the course of Sierran history. While he was traveling to Sacramento on a paddlewheel steamer, Gardiner's attention was drawn to a bearded, thirty-five-year-old ill-dressed intellectual who, King was sure, must be Brewer. The pair introduced themselves, shortly thereafter met Whitney, and volunteered to join the survey without pay. The initial tasks involved studies of lava flows on Mount Lassen and the snowfields on Mount Shasta. King's career was now set on a firm and glittering course.

Thus it was that Brewer, Hoffman, Gardiner, Cotter, and King came together in May of 1864 to make the first organized probe of the "new Alps."

At the head of a valley near Roaring River, on the west side of the range, the party arrived at the base of a 13,557-foot pyramid that was initially climbed by Brewer and Hoffman and promptly named Mount Brewer. Their supposition had been that the snowy crests rising before them on the westerly side were the summits of the Sierra. Now their eyes were drawn to the huge wall that lay across a canyon to the east. "Hoffman showed us on his sketch-book the profile of this new range," stated King, "and I instantly recognized the peak which I had seen from Mariposa, whose great white pile had led me to believe them the highest points of California."[1]

King insisted on exploring this fresh discovery. It was a hazardous and gritty undertaking for the time, but Brewer was finally persuaded to give his consent, noting that "King is enthusiastic, is wonderfully tough, has the greatest endurance I have ever seen and is withal very muscular. He is a most perfect specimen of health."[2]

Recalled King: "It was a trying moment for Brewer when we found him and volunteered to attempt a campaign for the top of California, because he felt a certain fatherly responsibility over our youth, a natural desire that we should not deposit our triturated remains in some undiscoverable hole among the feldspathic granites; but, like a true disciple of wisdom, this was at least overbalanced by his intense desire to know more of the unexplored region. He freely confessed that he believed the plan madness, and Hoffman, too, told us we might as well attempt to get on a cloud as to try the peak."[3]

King's description of his and Cotter's first ascent of the dominating spire that towered across the divide was vividly related in his classic *Mountaineering in the Sierra Nevada*. To reach the base they had to carefully lasso each other down precipitous cliffs and cross the gaping Kings-Kern Divide. Stated King:

> The summit peaks to the north were piled in Titanic confusion, their ridges overhanging the eastern slope with terrible abruptness. Clustered upon the shelves and plateaus below were several frozen lakes, and in all directions swept magnificent fields of snow.... But if nature had intended to secure the summit from all assailants, she could not have planned her defences better; for the smooth granite wall which rose above the snow-slope continued, apparently, quite around the peak....It was all blank except in one spot; quite near us the snow bridged across the crevice and rose in a long point to the summit of the wall,—a great icicle column frozen in a niche of the bluff,—its base about ten feet wide, narrowing to two feet at the top....At last I reached the top, and, with the greatest caution, wormed my body over the brink, and, rolling out upon the smooth surface of the granite, looked over and watched Cotter make his climb.
>
> We now had an easy slope to the summit, and hurried up over rocks and ice, reaching the crest at exactly twelve o'clock. I rang my hammer upon the topmost rock; we grasped hands, and I reverently named the grand peak Mount Tyndall.[4]

This account, it should be noted, contrasts with the survey report, taken from King's own words, that the "summit was reached, without serious difficulty, after some risky climbing."

From atop the peak King and Cotter espied even taller pinnacles to the south. That which looked highest of all was a "cleanly cut helmet

California Geological Survey field party of 1864. James T. Gardiner, Richard Cotter, William H. Brewer, Clarence King. (l. to r.) *Courtesy, The Bancroft Library.*

of granite . . . fronting the desert with a bold, square bluff which rises to the crest of the peak, where a white fold of snow trims it gracefully . . . .Its summit looked glorious, but inaccessible."[5]

In such manner did King first portray 14,494-foot Mount Whitney, highest mountain in the forty-eight contiguous states.

After a hairy, tattered descent, King and Cotter rejoined Brewer, ending their five-day ordeal. King now redoubled his efforts to find and scale the newest prize. He approached Mount Whitney from the west along Hockett Trail and the South Fork of the Kaweah River. Within three days he attained the base, but a high wall thwarted him some 300 to 400 feet from the top. Describing the long ride back, King, exercising literary license, told of narrowly avoiding being waylaid by two Spanish-speaking thieves. It amounts to suspenseful reading, but does not precisely coincide with his report to Whitney: "Of the ride to Clark's ranch via Nillerton and Mariposa, I have nothing of interest."

When exiting through the Kearsarge Pass region during their three-month expedition, the Brewer party saw two grand peaks in the distance. They were christened Mount Clarence King and Mount Gardiner.

King, Gardiner, and Cotter later conducted a boundary survey of Yosemite, eventually scaling the solitary obelisk of Mount Clark in 1866. King and Gardiner also went to Prescott, Arizona, near which, according to King, they were captured by Indians, half stripped of their clothes, and about to be put to a torch when the U.S. cavalry happily intervened.

The Sierra remained the centerpiece of King's interests. He scrambled around the beautiful Minarets, giving them their name, and was driven off 13,157-foot Mount Ritter by a storm, leaving this notable jewel to be claimed by the venerable John Muir ten years later.

King was still a young man, and the broad and colorful pages of his variegated life were just unfolding. He devised a plan to conduct an extensive geologic, petrologic, and topographical survey of territory 100 miles on either side of the 40th parallel, along the rail route that would extend from the Rocky Mountains to California. The tracking, identification, and evaluation of the enormous mineral resources of the Western Cordilleras would constitute a great public undertaking. After a fight for the program in Washington, enabling legislation was enacted, and King, age twenty-five, was placed in charge of the Geological Exploration of the Fortieth Parallel, reporting directly to the Army's chief of engineers. Four major generals were passed over to award him the post.

This landmark project consumed several prime years of King's life, resulting in the publication in 1878 of an 800-page treatise, *Systematic Geology,* the crowning product of the 40th-parallel reports and of his career. He was now firmly entrenched as one of the West's most eminent geologists. Two years before he had been elected to the National Academy of Sciences, the youngest person to be so honored in his lifetime.

On one outing King waggishly wrote:

> Mappin' up wat's called out West
> Bustin' rocks fer Uncle Sam
> Tearin' holes in pants and vest
> Eatin' semi-fossil ham—
> That's wat fell ter this child's lot.[6]

It was during this period that King personally exposed the infamous Emma Mines scandal, adding luster to his reputation both in the United States and abroad. Rumors were rampant about the discovery of an extremely rich diamond bonanza, and the San Francisco and New York Mining and Commercial Company, backed by bankers, generals, and other business leaders, was formed to sell stock in the venture. The exact place of the find was a tightly kept secret, but King was intrigued by its description and confirmation of the claim given by a minerals analyst whom he respected. Speculation centered on Arizona as the locale. King, however, divined that it could only be situated right within the boundaries of his own 40th parallel survey. He traced the leads to Diamond Mesa in Colorado, where he found that the field had been deliberately salted with diamonds and rubies. The jewels appeared mainly near the surface in a manner that only clever hands, not nature, would ordinarily deposit them.

According to legend, one member of the group, finding a half-cut stone, said, "Look here, Mr. King. This is the bulliest diamond field as ever was. It not only produces diamonds, but cuts them moreover also."[7]

On confirming the fraud, King rushed back to San Francisco and, convinced that the mining barons themselves had been deceived, confronted them with his evidence. It developed that two swindlers named Philip Arnold and John Slack had brought the gems from Amsterdam and London, and planted them in the field.

The resulting exposé, which killed the proposed sale of public stock and saved investors millions of dollars, made King the paragon of the season.

In 1871, seven years after his initial attempt on Mount Whitney, King took a stagecoach to Lone Pine, California, still burning to be the first to claim the grand prize. With a local man, Paul Pinson, he approached its sheer eastern side via a southern outlet.

They made rapid progress. "When within a hundred feet of the top," wrote King theatrically, "I suddenly fell through, but, supporting myself by my arms, looked down into a grotto of rock and ice, and out through a sort of window, over the western bluffs, and down thousands of feet to the far-away valley of the Kern."[8]

Soon he and Pinson had surmounted the last blocks and "Mount Whitney was under our feet."

He then described a "small mound of rock" piled upon the peak, and "solidly built into it an Indian arrow-shaft, pointing due west." Did this necessarily mean, as King assumed, that Indians had preceded them? Or was it another dramatic tidbit? Perhaps. More to the point, King stated that "dense, impenetrable clouds had closed us in."

Then: "Sombre storm-clouds and their even gloomier shadows darkened the northern sea of peaks. Only a few slant bars of sudden

**Mount Whitney
(from east)**

1 — Summit (14,494 feet)
2 — Day and Keeler needles
3 — Mountaineer's route
4 — East face

light flashed in upon purple granite and fields of ice. The rocky tower of Mount Tyndall, thrust up through rolling billows, caught for a moment the full light, and then sank into darkness and mist."[9]

What King and Pinson had seen from the summit was not, of course, Mount Tyndall. They were standing on Sheep's Rock, later called "False Mount Whitney" or Old Whitney, then Mount Corcoran, and now Mount Langley, 14,027 feet high. The "rocky tower" to the north was the very Mount Whitney on whose summit they mistakenly believed themselves to be perched. The peak measured 400 feet lower than expected, but King felt the variance was caused by the bad weather.

For two years King lived in the contentment that his had been the first ascent of the country's highest mountain. On August 4, 1873, at a meeting of the California Academy of Sciences, presided over by Whitney, W. A. Goodyear convincingly proved that King and Pinson had scaled the wrong peak. Reported Goodyear:

> On the 27th day of July, 1873, Mr. M. W. Belshaw, of Cerro Gordo, and myself, rode our mules to the highest crest of the peak southwest of Lone Pine, which, for over three years now had been known by the name of Mount Whitney, and which was measured and ascended as such by Mr. Clarence King, in the summer of 1871.
>
> I know this peak well, and cannot be mistaken as to its identity. As seen from Lone Pine, it appears perhaps the most prominent peak in the whole Sierra. . . . Moreover, since Mr. King's ascent of it in 1871, the half dollar which he left at the summit has been found there, with his name inscribed upon it. . . .
>
> It is by no means the highest among the grand cluster of peaks which form this culminating portion of the Sierra Nevada; nor is it the peak which was discovered by Prof. W. H. Brewer and party, in 1864, and then originally named by them Mount Whitney. . . .
>
> Certain it is, however, that the peak which for over three years has borne the name of Whitney, has done so only by mistake, and that a new name must be found for it; while the name of Whitney must now go back to the peak to which it was originally given in 1864. . . .
>
> Whether the peak is utterly inaccessible or not is still a question. I am disposed to think that it can be climbed; but it will certainly involve a great deal of hard, and very possibly, some dangerous work for anybody who shall attempt to reach its gigantic crest.[10]

In his detailed account, Goodyear went on to demonstrate that by measurement, shape, location, description, and accessibility, King and Pinson could not have climbed the summit of the Sierra, but instead had been on a peak five or six miles to the south.

This crushing news reached King while he was traveling in the east. He hastened to California to scale the true Mount Whitney, a task accomplished on September 19, 1873. There he found a cairn and records of two previous parties.

How had King misgauged his previous ascent of what turned out to be the Mount Langley of today?

"My little granite island was incessantly beaten by breakers of vague, impenetrable cloud, and never once did the true Mount Whitney unveil its crest to my eager eyes." But, he continued with tongue well in cheek (or even elsewhere), that occurrence would have left nothing for Goodyear, "whose paper shows such evident relish in my mistake." He noted wryly that Goodyear "resolutely turned his back on the alluring summit" and descended by mule to "hold me up in my proper light."[11]

King also attributed his grave error to local magnetic deviation caused when he took a bearing on Mount Whitney from Mount Tyndall in 1864; the inaccuracy had been incorporated into the map used by him on the climb.

By such fortuities King's nine-year liaison with the highest pinnacle in the Sierra Nevada came to an end.

The ongoing polemic between the arrogant Whitney and Muir as to whether Yosemite's mighty walls and valleys had been created by glacial erosion or large-scale earth subsidences also involved King. Muir, derided as "that sheepherder" by King, adhered to the glacier theory, which ultimately prevailed. Whitney stoutly insisted that all such claims were based on ignorance. King actually had uncovered evidence of glacial presence in Yosemite and on Mount Shasta, but Whitney was not convinced, and King came to the defense of his former chief.

Verbal jousts between King and Muir enlivened the era. On reviewing King's daredevil account of the Mount Tyndall ascent, Muir pointedly commented, "He must have given himself a lot of trouble. When I climbed Tyndall, I ran up and back before breakfast."

From the austerity of science and mountaineering King ventured into cattle grazing. In short order he and a partner owned 30,000 head and were among Wyoming's largest grazers. He sold out at a handsome profit shortly before a weather freeze created havoc in the beef market.

In 1879, after a lively political battle, King was appointed by President Rutherford B. Hayes as the country's first Director of Geological Survey. One admirer called him the "most accomplished man of his age in the country."

King's standing among his peers was, indeed, unsurpassed. To John Hay, later secretary of state and coauthor of the monumental *Abraham Lincoln: A History,* King was, in a phrase that seems ironic today, "the best and brightest man of his generation."[12] Another intimate, eminent historian-author, Henry Adams, described him as a "bird of paradise rising in the sagebrush . . . an avatar."[13]

Commenting on King's energetic forays into the mountain, Adams wrote: "In the works like that of Mr. King the wonder always is that a day passes without accident. If he is not dragging or riding a mule up or down a perpendicular precipice, he is shooting at bears, getting struck by lightning, or catching a rattlesnake by the tail. There is no end to the forms in which life or health is risked in these adventures."[14]

Also: "No other young American approached him [King] for the combination of chances—physical energy, social standing, mental scope and training, wit, geniality, and science, that seemed superlatively American and irresistibly strong." Adams was certain that his friend would die "at eighty the richest and most many-sided genius of his day."[15]

King's acquaintances were wide and varied, ranging from ragged migrants and miners to the Prince of Wales, Theodore Roosevelt, and Baron Ferdinand James de Rothschild. His milieu also embraced the literary elite of the day, including Bret Harte, Henry James, James Russell Lowell, William Dean Howells, and John Ruskin. Yarns, epigrams, and persiflage fell in a stream from his lips, yet his actual literary output was not large, leaving his friends to lament that his impressive potential as a writer had not been tapped. His contribution on geology to James D. Hague's *Mining Industry* and a story called "The Helmet of Mambrino" were acclaimed. *Mountaineering in the Sierra Nevada* can fittingly share the same shelf with Leslie Stephen's *The Playground of Europe*. He authored many magazine articles. But the great novel some felt was within his power never materialized.

Resigning as head of the Geological Survey in 1881, King tried his luck as a mining promoter and prospector. "I have enough for my necessities," he observed. "What I wish now is enough for my eccentricities." He developed the Las Priestas mine near Sonora, and the Las Yedras and Sombrerete in Mexico. Frequently he was retained to testify as a mining expert in legal battles over conflicting claims. But his many enterprises typically foundered on the shoals of ill luck, and the financial fortune he sought remained beyond his grasp. Still, in those early times, he foresaw that conservation and energy would pose two of civilization's foremost challenges.

King was largely responsible for introducing a system for using contour lines to denote topography on maps. He also promulgated a theory of modified catastrophism to explain that geological changes occur more rapidly than previously believed, a principle advanced in a paper presented to the Sheffield School called "Catastrophism and the Evolution of Environment." His latter years were marked by a double life, kept secret from his genteel friends, caused by his having married an attractive black woman by whom he sired five children. Such a relationship, if revealed, would have been scandalous at the end of the nineteenth century.

Frustrated by financial reverses and a spinal injury, as well as the lingering effects of malaria, King eventually suffered an emotional breakdown and, with his own consent, was committed for a spell to an asylum. He passed away, with a characteristic quip on his lips, on December 24, 1901.

In solving one controversy about the High Sierra, King generated another. Since it was not he, who in fact first climbed majestic Mount Whitney? No surefire answer can be given. Three local fishermen—Charley Begole, Johnny Lucas, and Albert H. Johnson—supposedly made the climb on August 18, 1873. Camping in Kern Canyon, they hiked up Sheep's Rock (Mount Langley) first but, on reaching the top, spotted the higher summit across the way. They rode by horseback down Rock Creek and up a steep ravine to the north, reaching a campsite at Ramshorn Springs. Traversing two passes, they climbed the southwestern buttress, attaining the top at noon and erecting a monument.

The story was vigorously contested by one Tom McDonough, who claimed that he and four others had made the summit first, and that the fishermen could not have ascended Mount Whitney within the time described. An equally plausible claim was advanced by Bill Crapo and Abe Leyda.

A local newspaper joined issue: "Some people are now trying to take credit of their being the first there away from them, but they won't succeed. Prof. Whitney's agent finds fault with the people here for their lack of romance in calling it 'Fisherman's Peak.' Ain't it as romantic as 'Whitney'? The fishermen who found it looked mighty romantic on their return to Soda Springs. Wonder who the old earthsharp thinks is running the country, anyhow?"[16]

The dispute was never definitively settled. Today's most widely accepted version—perhaps partly for reasons of local sentiment—gives the nod to the fishermen. But the evidence is not conclusive, and the story seems to have gained stature by the undoubted desire of the local community to cleanse its horizon of the name Whitney, a less than popular figure at the time. The Dome of Inyo was once suggested as a name, but it never caught on. Legislation was introduced to officially designate it Fisherman's Peak, and then Fowler's Peak after a politician.

The governor had the last say, vetoing the bill. In due time the appellation Mount Whitney gained acceptance.

During the autumn of 1873 Muir also made his first ascent of the peak via Lone Pine Creek, after having climbed Sheep's Rock. Muir followed the mountaineer's route as it is known today; this is acknowledged to be one of the best climbs on Mount Whitney. Muir started from Independence, fourteen miles north of Lone Pine, and proceeded entirely by foot—a rugged journey by any standard.

The mule trail to the summit was completed in 1904, and even then it attracted a daily horde of hikers. Five years later a stone house was erected on top to provide a base for scientific observations.

The popular trail from Whitney Portal to the top is twenty-one miles roundtrip. It winds upward through an immense canyon past Lone Pine Lake until, after four miles, the campsite at Mirror Lake is reached. Then it passes through a luxurious green meadow to Trail Camp which, at 12,039 feet, represents the last spot where water is assured and which is commonly used as an overnight spot. Directly ahead is a 1,561-foot rise featuring 97 switchbacks that slowly curl over a 2.2-mile stretch, leading up to Trail Crest, which opens to the westerly side. A junction is made here with the John Muir Trail, which weaves up from Crabtree Meadows, and more long, gentle switchbacks lead to the 14,494-foot summit plateau, with its spectacular vista that oversees the

A snow camp in the High Sierra

Owens Valley. The climb may be readily made by anyone in sound health, with allowance for adjustment in the altitude. The vertical gain, from portal to summit, is 6,135 feet. Mount Whitney rises about 10,000 feet above its surrounding plateau—almost as much as does Mount Everest. A runner once completed the ascent in two hours, twenty-nine minutes.

Because of its easy access, Mount Whitney often is accused of not being a climber's mountain. However, the prodigious 2,000-foot escarpment that forms the east face presents interesting variations. It may be reached via a canyon that follows North Fork Creek and wends upward through boulder fields and talus past Clyde Meadows to Iceberg Lake, at the base of the palisades. Several of the routes here are class five plus, and pose challenges for the ablest.

Still, as one guidebook suggests, a main hazard may be rocks, bottles, and tin cans thrown down from above by summit hikers!

* * *

We arrived at the jagged crest of North Dragon Pass at midday. The early sunshine had faded to a blustery gray, but there was only a slight pause before we plunged down the long, snow-tousled scree slope. It was the end of October, late to be hiking in the Sierra. No one wished to contemplate, much less mention, the deteriorating weather. In our eagerness, we failed to cross the ridge northerly to a minor knoll before descending toward Rae Lakes, thus forcing ourselves to tackle a huge boulder-strewn field of snow that proved to be strenuous.

The five of us, Andy Fried, Gerard Furbershaw, Ed Lubin (the organizer), Ben Preyer, and I, had carefully brought winter gear—snowshoes, heavy down parkas, mittens, and the like—to the roadhead at Onion Valley above Independence; when it dawned clear, however, the snowshoes were left in an automobile trunk since we doubted their suitability for the type of terrain we would be crossing.

From our 12,400-foot col a mixed pageant of ermine and sable spires and defiles ranged about us. Mount Rixford and the colorful Painted Lady stood as massive sentinels overlooking the jumble of waterways that filled Kings Canyon; in the distance loomed the solid hulk of Fin Dome. To our rear lay Golden Trout Lake and Kearsarge Peak. Even in the gloom it presented an eerie, yet dazzling perspective.

The light snow flurries continued, and this, coupled with our slight routing error, caused us considerable loss of time. After an all-day pull, we set up camp at Rae Lakes rather than Sixty Lake Basin.

Our objective was the isolated pyramid of Mount Clarence King, which, at 12,905 feet, constitutes a dominant peak north of the Great Kings-Kern Divide. It was this saddle that King and Cotter navigated en route to their seminal ascent of Mount Tyndall.

With blithe optimism our plans also embraced possible climbs of Mount Gould, Mount Cotter, and maybe Mount Rixford, all within a three-day scramble. In our unbounded imaginations we contemplated knocking off pinnacles left and right, like beads on an abacus. In fact, when all was done, our bag of peaks would come up as empty as a cracked vase.

The next morning blossomed beautifully. A luminous sky accompanied us northward toward Mount Clarence King. However, we started quite late. The route was straightforward, passing through a lush checkerboard of lakes, the only delay resulting when we approached the wide canyon beneath the south ridge on the near instead of the far side. The granite slabs unfolded in thick layers above us, and our probes to the left or right were usually well rewarded. We had been informed that the key to the top section was a small hole in line with the summit, Mount Stanford and Mount Cotter. We found no such hole, and debated at length about whether the summit was on the north or south end of the peak, a neat puzzle since each looked similar in height. In fact, we shortly were standing on the south buttress, right beneath the top.

We pushed up a slanting tile roof, a not too difficult class four, and eventually reached a rock platform below a large granite block. We were now only 15 feet below the summit—a fact about which, due to our position, we could only speculate.

Mount Clarence King (12,905 ft.) in the center, as viewed from Sixty Lake Basin.

Snow-trimmed valley leading to Mount Clarence King

Andy now spotted a blanket of blackly ominous clouds wafting in fast from the north. Strung out as we were, we calculated that at least another hour would be required for everyone to solve the tricky summit block. It was 5:00 P.M. and, due to the approaching storm and the hour, we abandoned the attempt, promising to return to finish it on another occasion. It was a painful, maddening decision. Our late start had cost us the peak.

The long haul back was punctuated by light flurries, with the Fin Dome serving as a guardian in the oily darkness. We reached our tents at 10:30 P.M. Gerard became separated from us, but eventually was guided in by our light. We slumped into our sleeping bags, confident that conditions would somehow improve.

All night the snowflakes thudded against the tents, and we awoke to a thick shag of snow, up to our shins. Warming some tea and oatmeal, we held a "confab."

The immediate issue was whether to start hiking that day, through the gathering drifts, or stay at our campsite, wait a day or two, and hopefully have the advantage of exiting over a frozen, consolidated crust. I was reminded that the snowpack in the Sierra once reached seventy-three and two-thirds feet. Concluding that another storm might be moving in, we made the obvious choice; soon all our gear was assembled, and with buoyant spirits we embarked on the long hike out.

The Muir Trail was obliterated, and the pallid overcast and raw wind made pathfinding difficult. I favored doubling back over North Dragon Pass, urging that it was a much shorter and direct route. On this I was outvoted, for the other members of the group sensibly felt that, with the freshly piled up snow, the pass would be too long and steep, and we might not be able to surmount it at all. Instead, the safer course lay over the Glen and Kearsarge Passes—almost double the length, a good many miles in fact, but hopefully more feasible.

The spindrift thickened; perhaps it seemed heavier than it was. While the hiking generally was easy, on some of the slopes the fluff had massed up so that we were kicking through it at knee level.

Two or three times an hour we gathered around our map (Mt. Pinchot quadrangle, 15' series) and, like tacticians in a bunker, attempted to unravel the riddle of exactly where we were and where we were going. All around us murky turrets poked their stony arms into the struggling, half-lit sky. Mount Rixford shone thinly through the inky mist, forming an airy escort past which we threaded toward Glen Pass. In front of us lay the beautifully carved and aptly named Painted Lady, standing like a flaming 11,693-foot lighthouse illuminating the trail.

On the open, exposed slopes the gusts blew stronger, and the morning warmth turned into a persistent chill. But we made solid progress and by mid-afternoon were at the base of Glen Pass, standing

Taking a break on the outbound trail after the storm hit

Hiking toward Glen Pass

around with a slight numbness, the only heat being generated by our tireless discourse about where the pass really began, and the way we should tackle it. Glassy whiteouts played havoc with our compass calculations. Finally, we confirmed that the pass was located right in front of us, and the best approach was simply to start up it. Gerard had remembered Glen Pass from his previous summer's month-long trek along the Pacific Crest Trail, and his recognition of its features, in the bleary light, helped immeasurably.

On any normal day the hike over Glen Pass is a lovely half-day idyll. It is a small matter as most Sierra cols go, a lovely romp among blossoming wallflower and heather, and favored by a well-defined trail that kids fairly race up. From its summit a picturesque view usually is obtained of the granite phalanxes that populate the Kings Canyon and Kearsarge regions. Now the trail was nonexistent, and sometimes the only forms we saw were those of each other. The drifts were deep, wet, and heavy, and we often halted amid the foggy obscurity.

As we waded through the snow on the north or exposed slope, we lost the trail entirely but were successfully able to feel our way over the outer lips of the ridges, winding back and forth along windswept snow bulges and troughs that represented the best available guidemarks. The pass was simply a gigantic heap of quicksand. By sunset we had reached the crest, at 11,978 feet, and paused for our first truly good rest of the day. Strips of dried beef jerky tasted like porterhouse steak. While the long pull up—about three hours—had been slow and fatiguing, it had served to keep us busy and warm. Actually, I think that we all enjoyed it. Our fitness level was high.

The light snowstorm was cold—Andy's beard was frozen—yet collectively we often seemed to be cloaked in sweat. I had committed the inexcusable gaffe of not having brought enough wool or down clothing, and my garments were soaked through. Somehow it did not seem to matter. Andy possessed the heaviest pack, with spare rope, crampons, and woolens, and the straps bit smartly into its carrier's shoulders. It was akin to hoisting a steamer trunk.

The horizon was purply dark by the time we plunged down the lee side of the col. A hazy moon lit up the snow and helped steer us down. We could not relocate the trail, but this proved to be of little moment, since the southerly flank was much more lightly dusted with snow than the thick pockets we had cut through during the ascent. Unthinkingly, we bypassed a chance to replenish our canteens at a lake outlet. By 10:30 P.M. we were played out, and up went the tents in a cluster of sparse vegetation that served as a windbreak. A tent pole broke, so we strung a line for support.

Ed energetically cooked up a sumptuously hot fare of tea, spaghetti, and chicken bouillon. We had virtually exhausted our fuel and patiently boiled water from the snow. More fuel was wasted by using gas-contaminated snow for the first pot of water. Our eyelids would not stay open. We wriggled into our bags. There was only the sound of a sharp wind blowing through the lean trees amid billowing wisps of snow.

Our little community started stirring again at 4:15 A.M. Chilled, like sleepwalkers stomping to keep warm, we agonizingly pulled down the guylines, and here and there munched on "gorp" (nuts, raisins, etc.) and dried fruit. We did not move out until 6:00 A.M.

By now we were quite dehydrated. Our canteens were empty, and no spring or lake water was at hand. After an hour the sun poked through; by a toss of luck the day was to be as brilliant as a Chagall painting. We headed toward Bullfrog Lake, now encountering the same heavy build-up of drifts that we had met on the way up Glen Pass. My boots were completely waterlogged. Ben lent me a pair of new nylon windpants; they kept me half-dry and probably helped prevent the complications about which one tends to worry. Slipping up and down, we got off-line in a tangle of trees, made a couple of minor retreats and loops, and finally reached a ridge above the lake, to which we directly headed. What a feast! I gulped down four quarts of water, and probably would have lapped up that entire liquid wonderland had not my companions coaxed me away.

We now were a strong, happy group. The sky was spotless, and we moved at a rapid pace following deer tracks toward Kearsarge Pass. Occasionally we sank well into the snow, nearly being stymied as we went in full to our hips; after a few tugs we usually were able to break free. The Kearsarge ramparts were visible in the distance and our enthusiasm grew. Once again Gerard smartly was able to remember the route that followed the midline of the ridge.

After eleven straight hours of hiking, we attained the summit of the 11,823-foot pass at 5:00 P.M. We found the register but no pencil with which whimsically to inscribe ourselves as the "Trans-Sierran Mount Clarence King Winter Expedition." (We were, it should be added, only too keenly aware that we had neither crossed the range nor scaled the

Deep snowdrifts en route to Kearsarge Pass

High Sierra

peak, nor, strictly speaking, was winter at hand.) We noted that two other backpackers had passed through earlier in the day heading into the Sierra, and wondered how well provisioned they were.

A panoply of stars splashed across the sky, and again the hazy moon served as a flare as we strode down the easterly side of Kearsarge, taking slopes in rhythmic bounds, often detouring around obscure obstacles. The hours spun by, but even near the bottom the snow lay densely about us. By 9:30 P.M. we were finally down, sitting contentedly alongside our cars, having plodded some twenty-eight hours in two days.

We checked into the sheriff's substation in Independence and learned that several parties had been reported lost or stranded in this first heavy storm of the season. In fact, we had gone four days without seeing a soul. Yes, my office had telephoned. It stiffly desired to know, the deputy sheriff said, whether I was aware that I'd missed several engagements, and what did I wish to do about it. From the sublime to the inane, I thought, and tersely informed the officer that such an irrelevancy had, by a remarkable phenomenon, utterly escaped my attention. We drove home that night, reaching Los Angeles at sunrise.

Reviewing the hike, we felt that it had gone well. Moving over steep passes in the autumn when the weather can be fickle entails risks, but except for the lack of snowshoes and a few other items, our supplies and equipment had been adequate. We truly had enjoyed the skirmish, and, of course, we were back in the Sierra at the first hint of spring. Ed, Andy, and Gerard—and later Ben—returned to Mount Clarence King and, using a more exposed and difficult approach, finished off those last fifteen feet. Andy also scaled Mount McKinley and the Mexican volcanoes.

Following in the wake of Clarence King and, coincidentally, John Muir, I previously had climbed Mount Ritter and Mount Whitney, the latter via both the trail and the beautiful mountaineer's route, a nice bracer even for the robust.

Mount Ritter, 13,157 feet, one of the most impressive pinnacles in the region, forms part of the residue of an old mountain system that came into being more than one hundred million years before the present range was uplifted. Together with Banner Peak, 12,945 feet, to which it is linked by a snow saddle, it provides a spectacular backdrop for the nearby Mammoth Mountain ski area.

For eight miles we packed through bright greenery and waterways to Lake Ediza, after which we passed the afternoon lolling beneath the Minarets. Up at 4:00 A.M., we ascended a long easterly snow basin to the saddle. While cramponing up a glacier below some stone chutes, one of the group suddenly slipped and went shooting down the icefield, tumbling, gathering speed, and desperately trying to dig in his ax tip. He spun to a halt about fifty feet above a swatch of spiky granite. Although shaken, and with hands and elbows cut badly, he completed the climb.

Turning the buttress above the chutes to the left, and circling up and around a high gable, we attained the top by noon. Few views in the Sierra compare with those seen from Mount Ritter. They extend from Yosemite to the Whitney region, a span of about a hundred miles. All in all the climb was delightful and not difficult.

The scramble up Mount Whitney's mountaineer's route also consumed two glorious days, starting from the portal above Lone Pine and following North Fork Creek to a campsite at 12,500-foot-high Iceberg Lake. The route entails much bouldering with backpacks through thick brush to a plateau where the canyon opens up, then curves southerly around large hummocks and up a series of stacked shelves to the lake. The next morning we went up a wide, slanting couloir of heavy scree and talus adjoining the east buttress, reaching a notch that divides the crest from the north arête. From here we clambered up 400 to 500 feet of ledges that led directly to the broad summit of the Sierra.

Now, seasons later, I ambled up the gentle rock slopes of Mount Langley and stood, at 14,027 feet, on the same spot reached by Clarence King and Paul Pinson that stormy, leaden day of their misfortune more than a century before.

Directly across, in austere profile, rose the granite helmet and bold square bluff of Mount Whitney, just as it had been described from the north. But I enjoyed a decided advantage over the famous geologist mountaineer, for the sky was now clear and pristine, and shone with a radiant azure sparkle.

7

La Haute Route: Crossing the Western Alps on Skis

> *'Tis morn: with gold the verdant mountains glows*
> *More high, the snowy peaks with hues of rose.*
> *Far-stretched beneath the many-tinted hills,*
> *A mighty waste of mist the valley fills,*
> *A solemn sea! whose billows wide around*
> *Stand motionless, to awful silence bound.*
>
> —William Wordsworth, *Descriptive Sketches*

> *It would be impossible to imagine a wilder passage than the narrow gap through which we were now crossing the main chain of the Pennine Alps. We were amongst the most shattered rocks I ever saw, and on either hand aiguilles towered above our heads in every fantastic shape . . . . The gap itself was not more than four or five feet wide, so narrow and so definite, that, on W.'s calling it 'la fenêtre,' we adopted the name at once as being the most descriptive we could give it.*
>
> —Alfred Wills, *The Passage of the Fenêtre de Salena,* in *Peaks, Passes, and Glaciers*

It is an immense, unspoiled silence, where nature's harshness reigns. The silken whiteness warps itself into buckling crust, storms swirl in and out like errant missiles, temperatures are either subzero or blazing hot, the going is tedious, and the season for doing it is abysmally short. In its classic form, it traverses eleven glaciers and eighty miles, and features 65,000 vertical feet of ascending and descending.

Icy north face of Les Droites (13,124 ft.) overlooking Argentière hut

This is *la Haute Route,* or the High Level Route. The grandest ski tour in Western Europe, it offers the most memorable and breathtaking of alpine experiences.

Chamonix, France, and Zermatt, Switzerland historically have been the continent's principal climbing centers, and Mont Blanc, the Matterhorn, and Monte Rosa stand as the granite anchors of the Western Alps. It was not surprising that the snowy links between them should become so notable.

The British were quick to make the discovery. Rev. John F. Hardy, an original member of the Alpine Club, led the first complete passage of the route by foot in the summer of 1861. Others in the party were J. A. Hudson, E. B. Prest, and G. R. Johnson. They hiked from Zermatt to the Great Saint Bernard pass, crossing the Cols de Valpelline, Reuse de l'Arolla, and Sonadon, and eventually reached the south side of Col d'Argentière above Chamonix. Hardy, Prest, and Johnson, joined by Frederick W. Jacomb, then ascended Mont Blanc from Saint Gervais.

Hardy, a steward and prelector at Cambridge University, also made the initial ascent of the 14,692-foot Lyskamm, the first English climbs of the 13,284-foot Piz Bernina and 14,022-foot Finsteraarhorn, and the

Rocky turrets of the Aiguille du Chardonnet (12,546 ft).

third ascent of the 13,026-foot Eiger; in 1862 he joined Leslie Stephen, A. W. Moore, and three others in the initial passage of the Jungfraujoch.

A solicitor by profession, Jacomb was especially interested in solving the puzzles of the Haute Route. In 1860 he made the first traverse of the Col de Valpelline shortly before reaching Zermatt, the initial crossing of the Col de Sonadon a year later, and in 1864 discovered the Col des Planards, a link in the direct path from Chamonix to Zermatt. Other key figures in piecing together sections of the route included William Mathews, F. F. Tuckett, Stephen Winkworth, and T. Fowell Buxton. A 113-page description of it, with an introduction by Jacomb, appeared in 1862 in *Peaks, Passes, and Glaciers,*[1] the predecessor of the *Alpine Journal.*

Previously, travelers going from Zermatt to Chamonix had proceeded via Visp and the Rhone valley to Martigny, and then over the Tête Noir or Col de Balme; alternatively, they followed the Théodule pass to Châtillon, Aosta, and Courmayeur, and, if spirited, the Col du Géant to Chamonix. Others adopted the Saint Bernard pass. Thanks principally to the explorations of Scottish glaciologist J. D. Forbes and Swiss geologist B. Studer, adventurous tourists increasingly began to use the Col d'Erin in the east, and the Col du Géant or Saleina glacier in the

Aiguille d'Argentière (12,795 ft.), left, and Tour Noir (12,589 ft.)

west. Ascents of the Grand Combin and Vélan further opened up the region. Still, fully three-quarters of the intermediate terrain was left untouched until 1860 and 1861.

According to Jacomb, the Chamonix-to-Zermatt hike could be achieved during the summertime in four stages: first, via the Col d'Argentière to Orsières or Bourg Saint Pierre; second, up the Col de Sonadon and down the Mont Durant glacier; third, from Chermontane to Prerayen via the Chermontane glacier and the Col de Reusse de l'Arolla; and, fourth, by the Col de Valpelline to Zermatt, passing either the Dent des Bouquetins or Tête Blanche. Stated Jacomb: "Thus the new 'High Level' route is complete, and a *grand course* of inexhaustible interest, traversing, as it does, almost throughout its entire length, a series of the most magnificent glaciers and snow-fields."[2]

Joined by Johann Kronig of Zermatt and a guide named Gabriel, Jacomb was defeated by a heavy mist on his initial effort to cross the Col de Valpelline to Zermatt. Fog-lost, floundering through treacherous snow, encircled by a maze of crevasses, Jacomb said his cowardly guide was terrorized, and ready to abandon them, when "a shout mingled with the noise of the falling ice, and Kronig's form, looming out huge and spectre-like from the mist, appeared, and he bade me wait. He carefully descended, and explained that he had been to the top of the couloir, and some distance on the plateau beyond; but the mist there

Aiguille d'Argentière, first climbed by Whymper party in 1864

was still more dense, and he had not been able to obtain any view. I could now, therefore, no longer refuse to admit to myself that we must return."[3]

Later the party attempted the passage again and made its way safely to Zermatt.

Following the conquest of the major peaks, the alpine pioneers concentrated on winter climbing expeditions. Mont Blanc was scaled in winter by Mary Straton in 1876, and the Matterhorn by Vittorio Sella, the famous mountain photographer, in 1882. Contrary to expectations, climbers found that snow tended to consolidate not in winter, but in spring. Skis proved to be the key to winter attempts, and ski ascents became the vogue. The Dufourspitze, highmost point on the Monte Rosa, was climbed on skis in 1898; likewise, the Breithorn in 1899, Mont Blanc in 1904, and the Grand Combin in 1907. Of such exploits, more later.

Ski mountaineering and touring, as exemplified by the Haute Route, is directly descended from the sport of skiing, which itself enjoys a lengthy genealogy. The need to hunt and gather wood long ago made necessary the development of a primitive wooden version of what today is known as the modern fiberglass ski, with its pointed, shovel-like tip, sidecut, camber, metallic edges, variable flexes, torsional rigidity, and

The Chardonnet glacier—first stage of the Haute Route

groove along the bottom. Evidence of such early skis, crude but with tips and thong bindings, have been found in the peat bogs of Sweden, Norway and Finland, in Siberia dating back to 2,500 B.C., and in southwest Asia 2,000 years old. The Hoting ski was about three feet, seven inches long and eight inches wide. Other early forms were in the shape of snowshoes.

The annual Birkebeiner in Norway, a ski race of twenty-one miles, honors the rescue in 1206 of an infant king, Haakon Haakonson, from murder at the hands of the rebel Baglern. Two bodyguards, who wore birch-bark leggings to protect themselves in the deep drifts, carried the child to safety, from Guldbrandsdal to Østerdal, across the Dovre mountains. The race was established in 1932.

One of the world's longest ski marathons is the Vasaloppet, a competition of fifty-three miles between Mora and Sälen, Sweden, held annually since 1922. This celebrates the return of Gustav Vasa who, in 1520, inspired a Swedish revolt against the Danes, established the Vasa dynasty, and gave birth to the Swedish reformation. Although his true name was Gustavus Eriksson, he is known as Vasa, an adaptation from the bundle of sticks that appeared in the family coat of arms. After the Danes occupied Sweden, many of its citizens, including Gustav's father, were slaughtered in the "Stockholm Bath of Blood," designed to force consolidation of a Scandinavian Union. Narrowly eluding pro-Danish police, the hot-blooded Gustav traveled from village to village vainly trying to rouse the peasants to fight; they were apathetic and dubious. Deciding to seek asylum in Norway, he was within a short distance of the frontier when a messenger from Mora overtook him and persuaded him to return. The populace now had heard of the mass murders, new levies were being imposed, and gallows were being rigged in every major city. Using bows, arrows, axes, javelins, and pikes with iron heads, the spirited Swedes, led by Gustav, turned on the Danish garrisons and drove them out of their country.

A French doctor reported the following curious sight in 1671 after a visit to Lapland:

> We saw a Lapp hunting, sliding on snow as quickly as our sledge without foundering, thanks to his skates of bark, some seven feet long and four inches broad, flat underneath and hollowed out on top to place the foot. He held a spear in one hand and a bow in the other; on his back was a quiver full of arrows and he was followed by a huge black cat.[4]

Ascending steep section of the Chardonnet glacier

Nearing the top of the Col du Chardonnet

By 1716 the Norwegians had formally organized a contingent of ski troops.

One of the most remarkable skiing sagas was that of John B. "Snowshoe" Thompson, who, beginning in January 1856, carried mail across the High Sierra in midwinter for a period of twenty years. Born in the Telemark region of Norway, originally known as Jon Tostensen, Thompson migrated to the United States at age ten and to California at twenty-four. Wagons, horses, and pack mules transported mail across the Sierra chain then, but snowdrifts up to fifty feet in height rendered this impossible during the winter. Thompson commenced running the route on heavy, ten-foot, handmade skis.

The trip covered ninety miles, from Placerville, California, to Carson City, Nevada. Thompson often took three days going and two to return. He carried fifty to eighty pounds, charged two dollars per letter (but often went unpaid), and used neither blankets nor a heavy overcoat, relying upon his exertions to keep him warm and camping by fire at night. Although he often helped rescue others in distress, he never experienced a serious problem himself. During the Civil War Thompson was the only winter link between northern California and the Union. Eventually he submitted a claim to Congress; its response was a polite letter of thanks, but no money. His gravestone stands today at Genoa, Nevada.

Modern ski design is credited to a Norwegian, Sondre Norheim, from Morgedal in the Telemark region. The ablest skier in the area, Norheim popularized the telemark turn, in which the skis are split at a V-like angle, with one moving ahead of the other, serving as a forerunner to the stem turn; he also developed the christiania, which is similar to the later parallel turn. Norheim's design innovations in the 1860s and 1870 included the use of sidecut or "waisting," bindings that featured strap combinations (made of twisted willow twigs) for toes and heels, giving more precise control, and shorter skis (eight feet) than previously had been employed. In 1868, at the age of forty-two, he dominated the annual Christiania (now Oslo) jumping and touring competition against a field largely composed of youths twenty years his junior. This championship evolved into the famed Holmenkollen. Norheim is regarded as the father of modern skiing.

Public interest in skiing was awakened in 1888 when Fridtjof Nansen of Norway crossed the Greenland icecap in forty-three days. A zoologist, oceanographer, and statesman as well as an explorer, Nansen

Looking eastward toward the Pennine Alps

dragged sledges 300 miles to a height of 8,800 feet, using oakwood skis with three grooves, but no toe irons. Instrumental in repatriating prisoners and obtaining food for a starving Russia after World War I, he was awarded the Nobel Peace Prize in 1922.

In 1880 an Englishman, Cecil Slingsby, headed a ski expedition through Norway's 5,085-foot Keiser Pass. The Pragel pass in Switzerland, of similar height, was traversed by Colonel Christoph Iselin in 1893. Wilhelm Paulcke, a German, led what has been called the first great ski mountaineering expedition across most of the Bernese Oberland, from Grimsel pass to Brig, in January 1897. With Robert Helbling, Paulcke also climbed high on the Monte Rosa on skis in 1898. Dr. Henry Hoek, of Dutch-English extraction, crossed the Bernese Oberland in 1901, scaling the Finsteraarhorn and Mönch, and two years later achieved the initial ski climb of the 12,142-foot Wetterhorn. On February 25, 1904, Hugo Mylius, a German, with three guides, reached the summit of Mont Blanc on skis. During World War I, Arnold Lunn and Josef Knubel, his guide, made a ski ascent of Switzerland's 14,911-foot Dom.

It thus was inevitable that the Haute Route would be essayed on skis. In January 1903, the first winter traverse was attempted, and largely completed, from Chamonix to Zermatt. The group included a colorful local guide, Joseph Ravanel, Dr. Paul Payot, who introduced skiing to

Aiguille Verte (13,524 ft.) as seen from the Col du Chardonnet.

Aiguilles Dorées (11,542 ft.) guard the Plateau du Trient

Chamonix, as well as Alfred Simond, Camille Ravanel, Jean Ravanel, and Jules Couttet, the latter three carrying forty-two pounds of camera equipment to record the event.

Forced to change the summer route due to winter conditions, the party crossed the Col du Chardonnet and Fenêtre de Saleina to Orsières, then reached the Chanrion hut via Val de Bagnes, thereby circumventing the Grand Combin massif. Foul weather caused the party to abandon the tour near the Col de l'Evêque (no Vignettes cabin existed then). Instead, it traveled by road to Les Haudères, and continued across the Col d'Hérens to Zermatt.

Joseph Ravanel, called Ravanel-le-Rouge because of his flaming red hair and moustache, was a compelling, rambunctious figure. More than two dozen first ascents and new routes in the Mont Blanc range were pioneered by him. With Dr. Payot he crossed the Col du Géant on skis in the winter of 1897, a feat that was doubted until their tracks were seen on Mont Fréty above Courmayeur. He scaled the Grépon fifty-seven times.

Since Ravanel climbed mainly in his own region, his reputation, unlike that of some of his contemporaries, did not extend to the far parts of the Alps. Yet he was regarded as a first-rate mountaineer, and the Aiguille Ravanel perpetuates his name. He would noisily charge up the rocks, muttering oaths and moving with more brute force than grace. He suffered numerous mishaps but always survived them.

Ski party passes beneath Aiguilles Dorées.

Cut where massive snowpack avalanched

Trient hut—terminus for the second stage of the Haute Route

Passing through snow-clad forest near Champex

In 1899 he was seriously injured by a falling stone on the Petit Dru. While descending to his chalet in the dark, he and his wife once narrowly eluded death from nearby blasting operations. In 1900, having achieved the second ascent of the Aiguille du Géant, he witnessed the death of a second guide, Joseph Simond, who was struck by lightning during the descent. (Viewing the charred, severed rope, Ravanel's friend and client, Emile Fontaine, said simply, "Would to God it had been I."[5]) Ravanel again sustained serious injury in 1904 when a boulder collapsed while he was scaling the Aiguille sans Nom. Most of his life he suffered from phlebitis, which never seemed to slow him on the mountain. He once climbed the Aiguille Verte during the early hours, returning to Montenvers by 8:30 A.M. the same morning.

During his later years Ravanel and his wife took charge of the Couvercle hut. He ran it with an iron hand, delighted in regaling aspirants with tall tales, and became a renowned personality in the valley.

A successful Haute Route variant, via Arolla, also was executed in February 1903, by Robert Helbling and F. Reichert, with Anatole Pellaud. They skied the Pennine Alps from Val de Bagnes to Zermatt, traversing the north side of the Grand Combin, and making a dangerous descent to the Chanrion hut. Pellaud lost a ski during a slip, and had to return to the valley. Helbling and Reichert continued alone via a unique line over the Cols du Mont Rouge, de Cheilon, and de Reidmatten to Arolla, and then across the Col d'Hérens to Zermatt. It was an exceptional expedition.

In 1909 another winter crossing from Chamonix to Zermatt was made by M. Beaujard with Joseph Ravanel. In April of 1910 Alf von Martin, H. Rumpelt, Oscar Supersaxo, and Herman Kronig skied from Zermatt to Saas-Fee, via Adler pass, ascending the 13,747-foot Strahlhorn en route.

The present-day classic route was opened in January 1911 when Marcel Kurz of Neuchâtel, Switzerland and Genevan Professor F. F. Roget skied directly across the Western Pennines from Bourg Saint Pierre to Zermatt. They proceeded by the Valsorey hut to the Plateau de Couloir, south of the Grand Combin, to the Col de Sonadon and Chanrion cabin, and then to the Bertol hut via the Col Collon. En route they accomplished the first winter ascent of 14,295-foot Dent Blanche. The entire trip took four days.

Tall, gaunt, laconic, Kurz was one of the first outstanding ski mountaineers. Pairing up mainly with Roget, he crossed the Diablerets to the Wildstrubel, toured the Bernina region, and climbed the 14,154-foot Grand Combin and 12,546-foot Aiguille d'Chardonnet on

The grand massif of Mont Blanc

skis. His other ski ascents included the Rimpfischorn, Gabelhorn, and Täschhorn, and he completed the first crossing from the Simplon to Saint Gothard passes. In 1926 Kurz traversed Mount Tasman in New Zealand, and in 1930 joined an expedition to Kangchenjunga in the Himalayas, where, with four others, he reached the summit of 24,518-foot Jonsong Peak, the highest mountain scaled up to that time. A noted topographer, Kurz developed into a prolific and meticulous writer on mountains and skiing. He collaborated with his father, Louis, on a well-known guidebook to the Mont Blanc chain and authored a four-volume text on the Valaisian alps, as well as several books on the Himalayas, which was visited by him three times and became a central interest of his life. For several years he served as editor of *The Mountain World*.

Another ski route connecting Chamonix and Zermatt was discovered by Kurz in 1926. This began at Verbier, crossed the Rosablanche group from Mont Fort to the Dix hut, and joined the classic way via the Pigne d'Arolla.

Though now commonplace, the complete traverse remained an extraordinary achievement for many years. Numerous well-trodden ski peaks owe their popularity to their proximity to the route. No guideless party of Britons is believed to have made the entire crossing prior to the

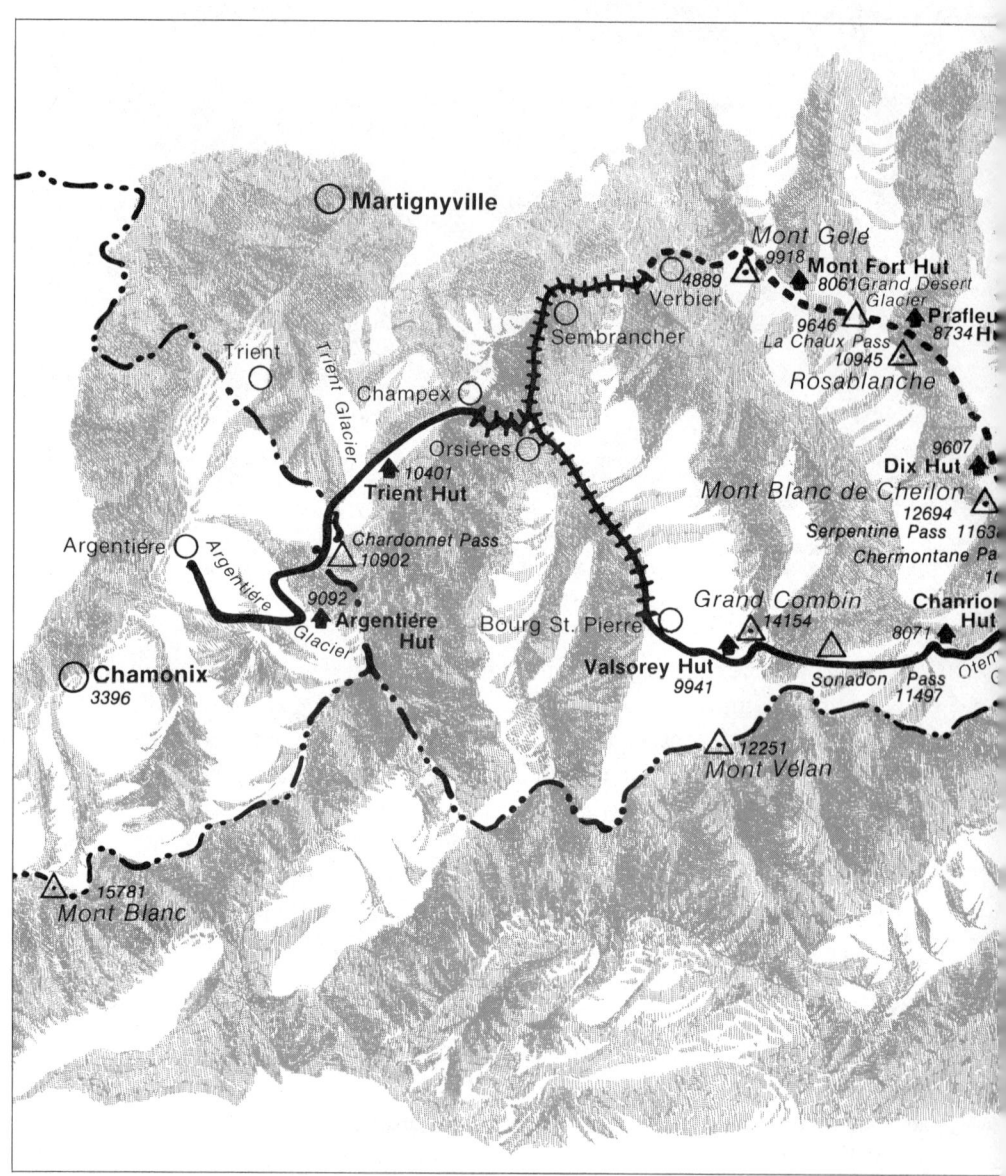

Illustrated by Erika Oller

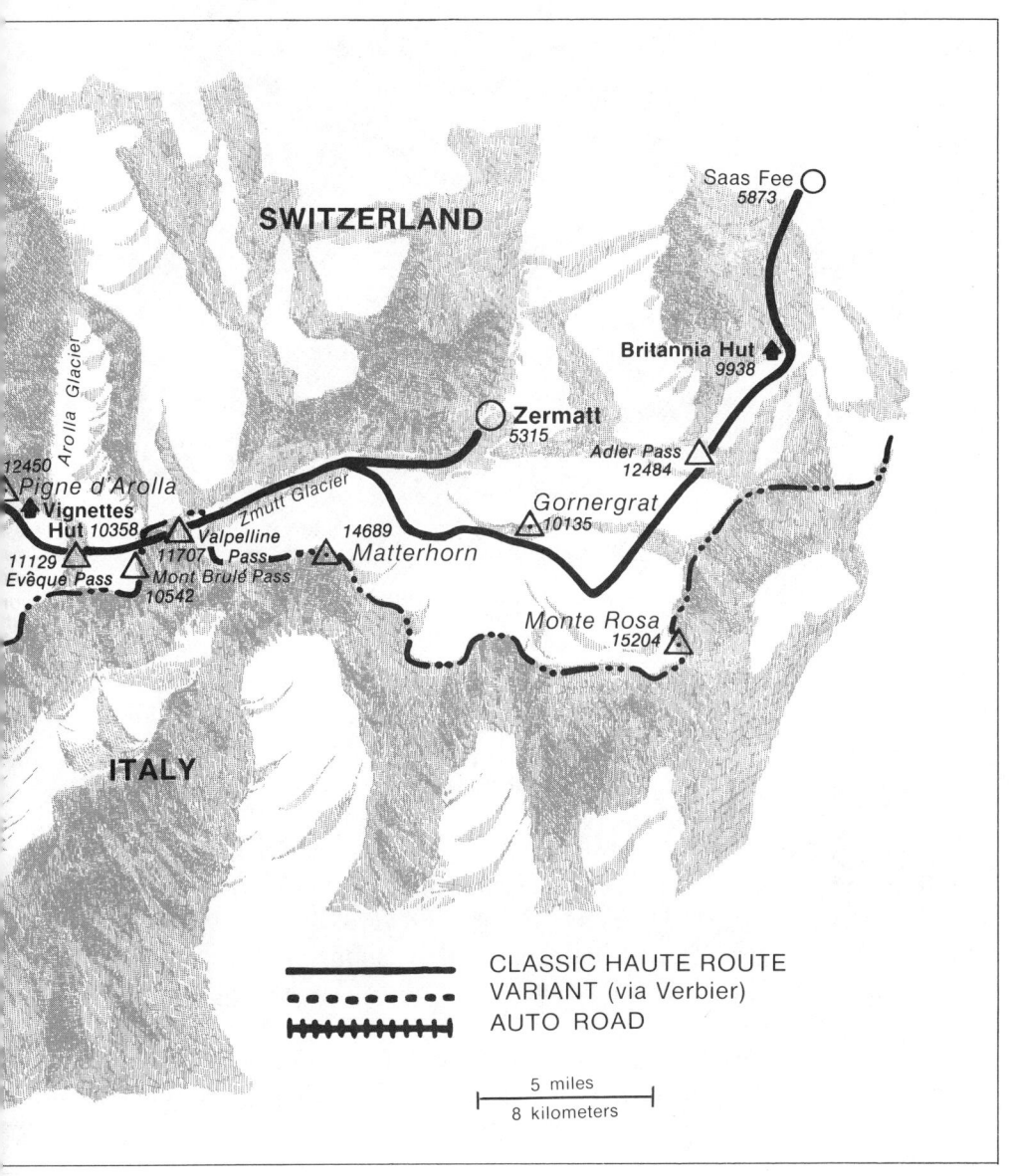

Grand Combin (14,154 ft.) is the dominant peak along the Haute Route.

1950s, a fact that illustrates the importance of knowing how to navigate amid such untamed surroundings. Yet, in 1934 a Frenchman, Leon Zwingelstein, was able to ski the route alone. In 1979 Jean-Pierre Bernard completed the Chamonix-to-Zermatt stretch in an astonishing, record-setting twenty-four hours flat.

Portions of the Haute Route were utilized in accomplishing significant ascents and journeys in the early days of alpine exploration. Probes by Alfred Wills, James D. Forbes, Edward Whymper, A. W. Moore and Emile Javelle helped to make the regions more accessible and led to the ultimate consolidation of the route. The setting always was a source of wonder.

Making a tour from Chamonix via the Glacier du Tour, over the Fenêtre de Saleina to the Glacier de Saleina in 1857, Alfred Wills stated that:

> ... Of all the countless aiguilles, named and nameless, which rise in rugged majesty throughout the whole range of Mont Blanc, and constitute so curious and characteristic a feature of the Mont Blanc scenery, few are to be compared with the Aiguille d'Argentière. It is not only of great elevation, towering far above any neighbouring summit, but is remarkable for the ruggedness of its sides, and for the number and varied aspects of the glaciers which literally stream

Skiing across wide snowfields

down its base, while above, it is broken into fantastic and inaccessible precipices, or clothed with a glittering mantle of snow.[6]

Farther on Wills found the "most wonderful part of the prospect" to be the towering "chain of rocks" that Professor Forbes had named the Aiguilles Dorées. Wills also made the traverse from Saas-Fee to Zermatt, via Adler pass, and from Arolla to Zermatt. He crossed the Col du Géant, a small matter today, but considered a feat in his time. Apart from the epochal ascent of the Wetterhorn, he scaled such peaks as the Monte Rosa and Mont Blanc, the latter three times, once with Forbes and John Tyndall.

Born in 1828, Wills made his first visit to the Alps, at Chamonix, at age eighteen. He was admitted to the bar in 1851 and appointed judge of the Queen's Bench thirty-three years later. Revising and updating his father's respected treatise on criminal law, "Principles of Circumstantial Evidence," absorbed much of his time and energy. In his last years he succeeded the Duke of Wellington as president of Hartley University College in Southampton.

An animated, no-nonsense type, slight in stature, possessed of a sharp and practical intellect, Wills found the mountains to be a haven from the strict rigors of the courtroom. Although not a trained scientist, he was knowledgeable about botany, and sided with Forbes in the latter's

The long dotted line up a pass.

running feud with Tyndall respecting the nature and effects of glaciers.

Wills fought against, and often was able to avoid, many of the onerous trade-union regulations that controlled guided climbs in those embryonic days. The first man on the rota, no matter how incompetent or unqualified, had to be engaged by the next client, even for a virgin or dangerous ascent. The number of guides per trip was rigidly prescribed, often resulting in an expedition incurring unnecessarily exorbitant costs.

Wills developed a lasting friendship with the revered guide, Auguste Balmat (grandnephew of Jacques Balmat), with whom he made most of his notable ascents. When the judge became the first outsider to build a summer chalet, called the Eagle's Nest, in the Sixt valley, north of Chàmonix, Auguste was placed in charge. Wills had to overcome strong opposition to buy the property. The Wills family was Unitarian, and arguments were advanced by local citizens that its presence would compromise religious orthodoxy or domestic purity; further, it was said that the hills would become marred with buildings, and that such a locale would better be devoted to the mining of gold ore or cutting of

Alfred Wills (right) with Auguste Balmat, shown in Chamonix in August 1857. *By permission of* The Alpine Club

Zigzagging up a steep snow ridge past Dix Lake

trees. A stormy, acrimonious session ensued before the Council of the Commune, and a vote resulted in a seven-to-seven tie, broken in favor of Wills by the syndic, or mayor. Wills took possession of the land in 1858, and any doubts about how he would be received by his neighbors were quickly put to rest; now that the public debate was finished, he was greeted with hospitality and offers of assistance. He and his family occupied the cottage for more than forty years.

As was previously indicated in chapter three, Wills's elegant writings, exemplified by *Wanderings Among the High Alps,* immensely helped to popularize mountaineering. His narratives were unsentimental and realistic in style, yet he was keenly aware of the surpassing beauty of the Alps, to which he was repeatedly drawn until his death in 1913.

Edward Whymper ascended the Col du Chardonnet several times in the course of making four attempts on 12,795-foot Aiguille d'Argentière. He attained its summit with Michel Croz, Anthony Adams-Reilly, and Henri Charlet on July 15, 1864, one year before the fateful tragedy on the Matterhorn. As vividly related by Whymper in *Scrambles Amongst the Alps,* an accident was narrowly avoided on one attempt:

'My feet are getting suspiciously numbed,' cried Reilly; 'how about frost-bite?' 'Kick hard, sir,' shouted the men; ''tis the only way.' I followed their example too violently, and made a hole clean

Nearing the crest after a three-hour effort

through my footing. A clatter followed as if crockery had been thrown down a well.

I went down a step or two, and discovered in a second that all were standing over a cavern (not a crevasse, speaking properly) that was bridged over by a thin vault of ice, from which great icicles hung in groves. Almost in the same minute Reilly pushed one of his hands right through the roof. The whole party might have tumbled through at any moment. 'Go ahead, Croz, we are over a chasm!' 'We know it,' he answered, 'and we can't find a firm place.'

In the blandest manner, my comrade inquired if to persevere would not be to do that which is called 'tempting Providence.'[7]

There being no dissent, they spent the night at Montenvers. Shortly thereafter they found a straightforward route to the summit of the Aiguille d'Argentière.

Neighboring Aiguille du Chardonnet, 12,546 feet, was initially ascended by an Irishman, Robert Fowler, with two guides, on September 20, 1865.

Pausing atop a col

A companion of Whymper's on one such climb was A. W. Moore, another of the originals of the Alps. Adolphus Warburton Moore was born in 1841, attended Harrow, served as private secretary to Lord Randolph Churchill, and was appointed to the important post of political secretary of the government's India office shortly before his untimely death in 1887. An advocate of winter climbing, Moore made a difficult first ascent of the Brenva ice ridge on Mont Blanc in 1865 and, three years later, climbed 18,442-foot Mount Elbruz (east peak) in the Caucasus with the Douglas W. Freshfield expedition. The latter represented the first major mountain exploration outside the Alps. Moore also reached the higher, 18,841-foot west summit in 1874. All told, he made at least ten first ascents of peaks and cols, including the Piz Roseg, Ober Gabelhorn, Les Écrins, and Jungfraujoch. Although nearsighted, he moved quickly. He once climbed from Kleine Scheidegg to the summit of the Mönch, and returned to Grindelwald, in one day (instead of the usual two or three days); on another occasion he crossed Mont Blanc, from Courmayeur to Chamonix, in a day.

Clever, lively, unselfish, possessed of what fellow climber Horace Walker called a "good natured cynicism and affectation of egotism,"[8] Moore twice refused the presidency of the Alpine Club because of the press of official duties. Freshfield considered Moore's diaries, first published privately under the title *The Alps in 1864,* to be the "most authentic, exact and vivid record of what climbing was to early explorers in the High Alps."[9] He will be mentioned again later.

A. W. Moore. *By permission of The Alpine Club*

Step-by-step down a sheer snowslope

Émile Javelle, a Swiss teacher, rhetorician, and philosopher, became enamored of the mountains at a young age, and eventually achieved the first ascent of the 12,509-foot Tour Noir, which stands immediately to the southeast of the Aiguille d'Argentière. He died of a lung disease at the early age of thirty-six, but left a decided, if not altogether positive, impact on Alpine literature. Javelle wrote in a flatulent, symbolistic style that was haplessly emulated by a succeeding generation of French and Swiss writers; hence, his ornate description of how a non-mountaineer would react to the beauty and chaos of alpine glaciers and crevasses makes one feel he or she is being seduced by a horror show. Recalling his climb of the Tour Noir, he wrote with awed religious fervor:

> Oh, how great and noble, how austere and magnificent, it all was! How had I the heart to descend from that height? Why did I not remain there like those Brahmins of ancient India, who could, it is said, live a thousand years without meat or drink, buried in their ecstasy in the midst of the lofty solitude of the Himalayas?
>
> ... Men, my brothers, who shall come here, I also, a living and loving soul, have seen for one moment what you see. I also have trembled with emotion gazing upon this mysterious beauty. Oh! whilst you are in the light pronounce my name; let me live again one moment in your thought! Rocks, you who shall exist so long, let this memory of me last as long as you can keep it alive![10]

Tiny figures cross a broad plain of snow after descending steep embankment.

Then in a less desperate mood:

> ... I can still see—and even the imagination of it makes me shudder—the formidable chain which composes this unparalleled crescendo: the Courtes, the Droites, the Aiguille Verte, offering on one side an uninterrupted wall five kilometres (3 miles, 560 ft.) in length, streaked everywhere from top to bottom with nearly perpendicular snow couloirs, of which the last—those of the Aiguille Verte—are the most terrible in the Alps. And lastly, quite close to us and scarcely above our level, with its splendid rocks rising like a sheaf of great organ-pipes, I see the Aiguille d'Argentière so dazzling in the sun that it seemed as if made of snow and gold.[11]

In its purest form the Haute Route extends from Chamonix (or nearby Argentière) to Saas-Fee, a way that was open by 1911. The route proceeds via the Col du Chardonnet, Champex, and Bourg Saint Pierre, across the back of the Grand Combin, over the Col de Sonadon to the Chanrion hut, via the Otemma glacier to the Vignettes hut, over the Cols de Evêque, du Mont Brule, and de Valpelline, to Zermatt; or, bypassing Zermatt, on to the Monte Rosa hut, Adler pass, the Brittania hut, and Saas-Fee. Nine stages typically are required for the entire passage.

Traversing large snowfields between Mont Fort and Dix hut

Originally the route extended to Zermatt only, and that frequently is an end destination today. The variants are many. One of the most popular is via the Pigne d'Arolla, which is considered to be part of the classic route. A west to east approach, from Chamonix toward Zermatt and Saas-Fee, generally is favored since it offers more downhill skiing.

Further information:

When: April and May are the best months. Winter is risky; one must contend then with short days, severe cold, unguarded huts, and crevasses concealed by unconsolidated snow.

Weather: The critical factor. Snowstorms and whiteouts strike suddenly. Frostbite can occur. Rescues may be foiled. Even the slightest mishap can become serious. A map and compass, with the skills to use them, are essential. Approximately one-half of the parties that commence the route are forced to turn back by weather alone.

Huts: Often they are open the year around. Wardens usually occupy cabins commencing about Eastertime. Joining an alpine club of a West European country is wise; it is a valuable source of information about routes, huts, and conditions.

Clothing: Heavy, warm clothing is needed just in case. The new breathable jackets are ideal. Also: balaclava, long gaiters, mittens, suncream, goggles, widebrim hat, woolen sweater, warm underwear, and the like.

Party wends over vast snow expanses.

Equipment: Essentials include: convertible touring bindings; ski skins; metal (or *harsch*) blades to gain additional purchase on steep slopes; double boots (old leathers or new plastics); and flexible powder skis, not too long, with a notch at the rear for attaching skins. Narrow cross-country skis, useful for flat terrain, are *not* suitable here.

Maps: Swiss maps (Carte Nationale de la Suisse) nos. 282, 283, 284, and 294, in the 1:50,000 scale series, cover the entire route; for more detail a 1:25,000 series is available.

* * *

"Like a feather," said Gilbert in rough-cut English, holding up my bright red pack. "Here, you carry this." He thrust out ten extra pounds of food and gear. Guess I have to make up for what the others do not tote, I thought. Just then a German lass strode up. She was shouldering a Mount Everest of a backpack. Another myth exploded.

We were assembling at the Chamonix guide bureau for a week-long dash across the Alps—the Haute Route. It was the end of April. The air was crisp and the sky like a reflector. We were warned that the weather might turn sour, a prophecy we too eagerly ignored.

We blithely boarded a bus that rattled off toward Les Houches—this, despite the unassailable fact that our destination was exactly in the opposite direction, to Argentière, on the outskirts of town. There we would take the Grands Montets tram to the top of the Lognan ski area.

Spring day on the Haute Route

"A great start," yelped Eddy, a thin, bearded lad from Belgium. Everybody speaks English, I noted. "Does anyone know French?" came a worried voice from the rear.

Our party was a mix of seven men and two women from the Netherlands, Austria, Belgium, Germany, and the United States. The first day's outing was short. We had only to reach the Argentière hut at 9,092 feet. A bagatelle, I told myself.

As soon as we gathered at the 10,719-foot level of the Grands Montets, from which commence some of Europe's finest ski runs, there was the usual panic. Someone forgot sunglasses. Mittens were too thin. A rucksack was too small, too heavy, or just plain lopsided. In my case, the rented equipment did not fit. My plastic double-boots were so big that it did not matter which foot went where. My convertible Marker bindings were serviceable, but I occasionally clamped them down when trying to kickslide uphill, and fastened them into touring position while attempting a schuss. "Not ze way," said René Guilini, the tough, trim apprentice guide who was to become the spark of the group. Moving with a heavy pack proved to be awkward and unsettling, even on gentle terrain. It definitely was not the same as bursting helter-skelter, free and unencumbered, down the groomed pistes that were only a glance away. No fancy wedelns or jet turns here.

All my skiing life I had dreamed of traversing the Haute Route. I had come from the slopes of Val d'Isere and Courchevel to Chamonix for an

Nearing the Dix hut; in the right background, Mont Blanc de Cheilon (12,694 ft.).

Easter holiday. I skied the Vallée Blanche from Pointe Helbronner, ten miles of marvelously scenic terrain, laced with crevasses but generally flat. Then I learned of the ski tour to Zermatt.

We kicked into the Argentière hut around 6 P.M. Seventy bunks were available, and at least a pair of grimy bodies occupied each one. The nearby pinnacles gleamed like fluorescent streaks. Facing us was the sheer north wall of Les Droites, 13,124 feet, one of the premier snow-and-ice faces that the irrepressible René had scaled among his many alpine heroics.

The night was an indelible horror. I had the runs—woefully and unrelentingly. I went through two sets of France's finest underwear, used rolls of paper, splattered the snow, froze my bare parts, and otherwise passed the time madly sprinting from one personal crisis to the next. Others slept.

We started at 4 A.M. Breakfast was a continental tea-and-roll quickie. We plunged out into the frosty darkness. René wore a lamp. The metallic ski edges rasped sharply against the hard ice. A chill wind stung

Sun-splashed pyramidal form of Mont Blanc de Cheilon

our faces. The barren spires of 13,524-foot Aiguille Verte were wrapped in a thin, gray mist.

Slowly we circled along the edge of the Argentière glacier. This long ice stream is dominated and encircled by Mont Dolent, Aiguille Verte, and Aiguille d'Argentière, each of which was first surmounted by a party led by Edward Whymper in 1864 and 1865.

In the darkness someone's ski came off and shot down the glacier several hundred yards. Only by luck was it retrieved. Now we started up the Chardonnet glacier. This proved to be as long and rugged as any section of the route. "A nice bracer," said Simon, a ruddy mountaineer from Holland.

Tirelessly we cut z-tracks up the glistening snowfield, holding to its midline, carrying skis on our shoulders on the steep sections near the bottom, switching to ski skins thereafter. Gradually the Alps were caressed by the morning sun, and silvery snow slants opened wide and high above us. Spread far apart, we stopped little, talked less, and metronomically plodded upward, our skins gripping well. After three

Early morning traverse toward the Col de la Serpentine

hours on the glacier we attained the Col du Chardonnet, which, at 10,902 feet, neatly divides the Aiguille d'Argentière and the Aiguille du Chardonnet. Here, on the Swiss-French border, we paused to survey the blazing majesty of our surroundings.

A. W. Moore, joining Edward Whymper in an attempt on the Aiguille d'Argentière, reached this col in 1864. The experience was special:

> We were now immediately opposite the foot of the lateral glacier leading up to the depression between the Aiguille d'Argentière and the Chardonnet, from which we supposed the former peak to be accessible, and whither we were therefore bound. Our first step was to cross the glacier towards the Chardonnet, making for a point just to the south of the spur coming down from that peak, which forms the right bank of the lateral glacier, whose left bank is protected by a similar spur from the Argentière. This operation was quickly performed, and by 4:35 we were on the other side, and halted a few moments to contemplate the wonderful precipices of the Verte,

Gaping crevasses near Mont Blanc de Cheilon

Heading toward the Col de Breney

which towered up magnificantly on the side of the glacier we had just quitted....

... Scrambling up the rocks of the Chardonnet, we found a tolerable sheltered position, and settled ourselves to study carefully the appearance of our enemy. ... in calculating so surely on the accessibility of the Aiguille from the col, we had reckoned without our host. Instead of an ordinary arête, as we had expected, of good rock succeeded by snow, we found the lower and most considerable portion to consist of a steep ridge of splintered, rocky pinnacles, the interstices of which were filled with snow and ice, completely cutting us off from the evidently practicable part higher up ...

As each party had plenty of time before it we were in no hurry to leave our refuge, and sat contemplating the spotless fields of névé at the head of the Saleinaz Glacier at our feet, the towering mass of the Grand Combin in the middle distance, and more remote, but not so much so as to be hazy, the grand forms of the Weisshorn and Dent Blanche. The sky was perfectly cloudless, a state of things which rendered us only more savage at the wind, which prevented our taking full advantage of so glorious a day.[1,2]

On the far side of the Col du Chardonnet we found a slippery forty-five-degree slope, partially overhanging and falling abruptly to the Saleina glacier (spelled "Salena" by Wills and "Saleinaz" by Moore, no doubt reaping confusion among the uninitiated). Gingerly we abseiled down, watchful of a nearby ice blue bergschrund. "This will wake us up," I told Eddy. A member of another party froze on the rope and could not, or refused to, move either up or down; an Austrian guide helped relieve his paralysis.

As we traversed a high snow basin, sparkling new vistas came into view. Strapping our skis to our backs, we scrambled up another plumb-line slope to the Fenêtre de Saleina—the narrow, rock-lined passage which so mesmerized Wills during his tour from the Col de Balme to the Val Ferret in 1857, as set forth at the head of this chapter.

Already it was noon. We relaxed, ate snacks, and circulated a chilled bottle of Chablis that someone thoughtfully had dropped into a pack. We felt quite alone and satisfied until a small ski-plane skidded to a halt right in front of us on the Plateau du Trient. Out stepped a group of skiers. Without breaking a sweat they glided right off.

Now we pushed and kicked over lovely flat terrain to the distant Trient hut, marked by a large Swiss flag, perched just beyond the elegant 11,542-foot Aiguilles Dorées (one of whose summits is fittingly named after Émile Javelle).

Sprawling snowfields lead to Pigne d'Arolla (12,450 ft.)

Traditionally one tours in the early hours, and tries to reach the destination by midday. This minimizes avalanche danger as well as the early afternoon heat, which can be formidable.

I flopped down on the first available bunk. "Not there," barked the warden, shooing me into my proper hole. In a Swiss cabin everything must be just so. For every aspect of human conduct there are an equal number of rules. The place was smartly kept, and violators were given unholy hell for the slightest transgression.

We carried part of our own food. The attendant helped us cook it. In the spring, after the huts are stocked, one usually can buy staple items such as potatoes, sauerkraut, and schnitzel.

The Trient cabin was spacious but crowded. There was just enough room to accommodate the wave of humanity that swept in from the slopes—a pattern that was to repeat itself throughout the trip. Everyone seemed to find a bunk, but there was never a spare. And the parties always came from a variety of directions—in this case, from Le Tour, Champex, Trient, La Forclaz, and Argentière.

Surprisingly, there was little intermingling. Everyone remained with his own group and problems—fixing broken straps, adjusting bindings, treating sunburn, and ministering to a wide assortment of other hurts. Foot blisters were unavoidable. "You can tape them until the glaciers melt, and still they thrive," I commented, standing in a swatch of blood.

Pigne d'Arolla—a crux of the Haute Route

The third day took us to Mont Fort. Initially we skied beneath Pointe d'Orny, near the head of an icefall, then crossed the Col des Ecandies and the upper portion of the Apette Valley. Here we tracked through sparse, idyllic woodlands, with generous open slopes and light powder, until we eventually encountered chairlifts. The mid-morning skiing was superb. After four hours we reached Champex, a small lakeside village. Lunch was at a nifty chalet that caters to Swiss Alpine Club members. After emptying the kitchen, and every beer mug within reach, none of us could surmount a staircase, much less an alp.

From there we were transported to Verbier, a normal interruption in the purity of the route, then boarded Les Attelas téléphérique later in the afternoon. Three parties banded together here, but a thick whiteout descended, and we each led the other in concentric circles while vainly trying to fathom the way to the Mont Fort cabin. Normally this is a pleasurable traverse from the top of the tram. We had dropped too low, and two hours of skin-climbing ensued before we stumbled into the one-hundred-bed refuge. "Murky stuff," someone observed.

Saddle below the Pigne d'Arolla

"No game today," I announced the next morning, and sank back beneath a pile of blankets. A storm had broken, and our planned excursion to the Prafleuri hut, west of Mont Blava, was cancelled. We were snowbound—and stymied. One more day like this and the trip would be abandoned.

We passed the time drying out woolens, de-icing mittens, hammering crampons, and straightening out sealskins. During mid-afternoon the weather lifted slightly so, to prevent our laziness from becoming too habitual, we hiked up a nearby slope. The fog closed in, and again we had to find our way back to the hut by compass and by guess.

René shouted us out of the bunks at 3 A.M. on the fifth day. We faced a double march to make up for yesterday's sitout. "Hard, long pull," he enthused, as though that made it all worthwhile. The horizon was clear. We now would be following a route pioneered by Marcel Kurz in 1926.

Above us, a moon-lit three-hour pull, loomed the boundless snowfields of La Chaux glacier, leading to the 9,646-foot pass of the same name. It was a muscle-wrenching ascent, cold and steep, one of

Matterhorn (14,689 ft.), middle left, and Dent d'Hérens (13,684 ft.), as seen from the Pigne d'Arolla

the longest on the tour. Beyond it lay the Grand Desert glacier. I never felt any danger on the route; it seemed entirely safe. Bur during the early hours, east of the Mont Fort hut, we spent a long time edging down a narrow snow-throat, walled on all sides like an elevator shaft, several hundred feet steep. A spew of avalanches caromed down adjacent embankments. Everyone seemed nervous. Talk was muted. Impulsively, I tried some mogul bashing. Gilbert almost punctured me with a pole, yelling, "No! no!" It was the riskiest place we encountered.

After that we traversed a string of snowfields, gaining altitude, dropping sharply, then climbing, an endless cycle. It usually required two or three hours to kick to the summit of a pass or slope, and only fifteen minutes to ski down the opposite side. The downhill skiing usually was neither interesting nor good. Mostly we encountered breakable crust, late-morning slush, or crud. A few times we floated on nice, dry powder, with its invigorating spray teasing our beards and faces, the most tantalizing of skiing sensations; but these moments were rare. The magic of the Haute Route consists of its glorious environment. It is a visual and aesthetic feast.

Weisshorn (14,780 ft.), middle left, and Dent Blanche (14,295 ft.), right

Crossing the Col de la Blava at 9,200 feet, we attained Dix Lake, where we stopped for a lunch break. After reaching the base of a sheer snow ridge we were forced to employ our *harsch* blades for the only time. The strung-out line swerved back and forth like a pendulum, slowly, inexorably gaining height, some of the group having difficulty on the steep turns, others halting frequently; all was quiet except for the labored breathing and the rhythmic scratchings of ski bottoms and blades on the wet slush and ice.

By noon we were being scorched by the sun. The sweat poured. I had a floppy cap, an invaluable possession, for those who had no head cover were almost stopped by the searing heat.

It was after 2 P.M. when we lurched around and up a prominent rock barrier and into the Dix cabin.

Each of us experienced nagging problems that day. Simon could not ski downhill without falling every few turns. A German couple, who once had hiked to Uhuru Point atop Kilimanjaro, suffered mild dehydration. One skier's binding plate came loose, and the afternoon was spent screwing it back into place. Simon was a magician with the pliers and screwdriver. Equipment repair was a prime preoccupation on the route. Every spare minute was passed checking one's gear for the next stage.

The succeeding morning we skied down to the Cheilon glacier and pushed southeasterly, past some nasty-looking crevasses, to a glacial ridge that paralleled the sharp, triangular, 12,694-foot Mont Blanc de

Cheilon. Enormous hanging glaciers sprouted above us, and we kept a respectful distance. In several places one could see where tons of snow had collapsed onto a glacier or cirque, leaving the rock skin-bare. Two hours later we attained the Col de la Serpentine (originally called the Col de Breney by Moore), and crossed the intersection of a pair of moraine-trimmed glaciers.

A large vertical slope soon appeared below us, and we side-slipped down, one at a time, moving cautiously on the icy surface. Then we ascended the true Col de Breney at the head of the main glacier, and, tracking across a tilted snowfield several miles square, headed toward a wide saddle. The excitement grew. Hurriedly we pressed on, gaining height, until at last we stood on the summit of Pigne d'Arolla at 12,450 feet.

This was our high point, literally and figuratively. It was worth every slogging step. A sea of peaks danced in and out of the sunlit horizon. The Weisshorn, Dent d'Herens, and Dent Blanche shot up in stony bulwarks, seemingly only a touch away. Blocking the east was the elephantine form of the ponderous 15,204-foot Monte Rosa, bringing to mind Alfred, Lord Tennyson's famous quatrains from "The Daisy," written from the vantage of the Milan cathedral after his visit there in 1852:

> I climb'd the roofs at break of day;
> Sun-smitten Alps before me lay.
> I stood among the silent statues,
> And statued pinnacles, moot as they.
>
> How faintly-flush'd, how phantom-fair
> Was Monte Rosa, hanging there
> A thousand shadowy-pencill'd valleys
> And snowly dells in a golden air.

The Pigne d'Arolla was crowded. It is a popular spot. Although listed as a peak, it is an easy hike up and quite accessible, and seems to be the lip of a long ridge or even a buttress. It forms the start of one of the most spetacular high mountain ski runs in the Pennine Alps. Some regard it as a crux of the Haute Route.

Pigne d'Arolla was first ascended in 1865 by the unflagging A. W. Moore, who wrote:

> At 8:55 we turned up towards the Pigne d'Arolla, and, after surmounting the first steep slope, found outselves on an undulating plateau, crowned on the further side by two low snow-humps, the highest of which was our peak, though we did not at first realize the fact. . . .

Whatever may be its inferiority as a mountain, as a point of view the Pigne d'Arolla more than holds its own with many loftier and more striking rivals. Placed almost midway between Mont Blanc and Monte Rosa, the Combin and Dent Blanche, and with nothing higher than itself between the Oberland on the north and the Graian Alps on the south, it stands in the one position most favorable for a comprehensive view of those great ranges. The weather was anything but perfect, but we saw enough to satisfy us of the grandeur of the panorama, which can scarcely be surpassed unless from the adjoining and slightly higher summit of the Ruinette. . . . We had long been of opinion that it was discretible to the Club that so considerable a peak [Ruinette] should remain unscaled, and had decided that, being in the neighbourhood, we were bound to attempt to reduce it to the same state of subjection as its neighbours. This, however, would involve passing a night at the dirty châlets of Chanrion, on very short commons, and a probability of absolute starvation on the ensuing day—a prospect

Vignettes hut (10,358 ft.)

which, I almost blush to confess, had so few charms for us, that it was with supreme satisfaction we discovered on the summit of the supposed virgin peak an unmistakable stone man. There was no doubt whatever about it, and we promptly moved a vote of thanks to the unknown individual (afterwards found to be Mr. Whymper) who had anticipated our views, and left us free to make our way to Aosta and the fleshpots of the Hotel Mont Blanc....[13]

"Tomorrow Zermatt," we shouted after hacking, cartwheeling, and stemming through wicked windslab to reach the Vignettes cabin in the shadow of Petit Mont Collon. Set on a remote ledge at 10,358 feet, the stone hut is architecturally striking, featuring tunnels and guiderails outside and wood paneling inside. Later a slight pall was visible.

Our usual wakeup left us thwarted. A snowstorm had broken upon us; visibility was nil. "Must go down," said Gilbert. A couple of us noisily protested. He and others knowledgeable about conditions

L'Evêque (12,194 ft.), center, and Petit Mont Collon, right foreground, encircle Mont Collon glacier, viewed from Vignettes hut

adamantly insisted there was no choice but to descend; they would wait no longer. From the Vignettes hut to Zermatt was, frustratingly, only one day's stage, although a long one, crossing three passes and the Stockji, Tiefmatten, and Zmutt glaciers. Ski tours in the Alps frequently are waylaid by foul weather, and we caught our allotment on this, our seventh and last day.

It ended all too abruptly. Yet we were grateful for having been able to cover most of the route. Should the opportunity occur again, we agreed that we would resume by starting at the opposite end, Saas-Fee, and traverse westerly over Adler pass.

By 8 A.M. we already had skied down the chalky, windblown slopes to tiny Arolla. Nobody was about. A burly old cow looked at us sullenly, then shuffled on.

Glossary

ARÊTE: A sharp, rugged ridge.
BELAY: Securing of rope to a firm anchor or projection, so as to protect climbers attached to it; or the projection itself.
BERGSCHRUND: Large crevasse at upper end of a glacier, separating the latter from mountain slopes above.
BIVOUAC: Temporary overnight camp without a tent.
CARABINER: Metal snap-links usually attached to a piton or rope.
CHANG: Sherpa beer brewed from rice (or millet or corn).
CHORTEN: Small Buddhist shrine or monument.
COL: A pass, or a depression in a ridge (e.g., South Col).
CORNICE: Overhanging mass of snow or ice, shaped by wind, and often dangerous.
COULOIR: Gully or gorge in a mountainside (frequently filled with ice or snow).
CRAMPON: Metal frames, with projecting spikes (usually 10 or 12 points), lashed to boots by straps for gripping on ice or hard snow; or, to move wearing such spikes.
CREVASSE: Fissure or cleft in glacial ice; often very deep and wide.
CWM: Deep hollow at head or flank of a valley; a cirque (e.g., Western Cwm).
GENDARME: Rock tower or pinnacle.
GOMPA: Buddhist monastery.
ICEFALL: Steep, jumbled mass of ice in a glacier; formed when a glacier passes over a change in angle or direction of the ground beneath it, or by bends in the glacier (e.g., Khumbu icefall).
MOGUL: Bump of snow on a ski slope, often on steep, narrow terrain.
MORAINE: Collection of stones and debris carried down by a glacier.

PITCH: Difficult stretch of climbing between belay points or ledges.

PITON: Metal spike, with ring or eye in its head, through which a rope may be passed; when driven into rock or ice, it typically is used to support a belay.

RAKSHI: Alcoholic spirit distilled from rice (Nepal).

RAPPEL: Moving down a steep incline or past an overhang by means of a double rope secured above and wrapped around the body; to descend in such a manner.

SCREE: Slope of small, loose stones.

SÉRAC: Pinnacle of ice, typically formed by movement or melting of ice, shaped by wind, and found on a glacier; often collapses and is hazardous.

SHERPAS: Hillmen of Tibetan stock who migrated to Eastern Nepal.

SIRDAR: Sherpa chief or leader.

SPINDRIFT: Spray of snow caused by wind or avalanche.

TRAVERSE: Crossing a slope diagonally or horizontally; also, crossing a peak or pass from one side to the other; or, the place where one traverses.

VERGLAS: Veneer of ice; glasslike ice.

Notes

Chapter 1 Genesis: To the Top of Mont Blanc

1. Douglas W. Freshfield, *The Life of Horace Benedict de Saussure* (London: Edward Arnold, 1920), p. 83.
2. Ibid., p. 187.
3. T. Graham Brown and Gavin de Beer, *The First Ascent of Mont Blanc* (New York and London: Oxford University Press, 1957), pp. 195-96.
4. Ibid., pp. 210-11.
5. Douglas W. Freshfield, *Alpine Journal* 19 (February 1899) :341.
6. Charles Edward Mathews, *The Annals of Mont Blanc* (London: T. Fisher Unwin, 1898), p. 96.
7. Brown and de Beer, *The First Ascent of Mont Blanc*, pp. 331-35.
8. From de Saussure's *Voyages dans les Alpes*, quoted in R. L. G. Irving, *The Romance of Mountaineering* (London: J. M. Dent and Sons Ltd., 1935), p. 21.
9. From de Saussure's *Voyages dans les Alpes*, quoted in Claire Eliane Engel, ed., *Mont Blanc–An Anthology* (London: George Allen and Unwin Lted., 1965), pp. 65-66.
10. From Goethe's *Reisen,* quoted in Engel, ed., *Mont Blanc–An Anthology,* p. 69.
11. From Ruskin's *Praeterita,* quoted in Engle, ed., *Mont Blanc–An Anthology,* p. 70.
12. From Hugo's *La Legende des Siecle,* quoted in Engle, ed., *Mont Blanc–An Anthology*, p. 112.
13. John Tyndall, *Glaciers of the Alps & Mountaineering in 1861* (London: J. M. Dent & Co.; New York: E. P. Dutton & Co., Inc., 1906), p. 169.
14. From Michelet's *La Montagne*, quoted in Engel, ed., *Mont Blanc–An Anthology*, pp. 59-60.
15. From Twain's *A Tramp Abroad*, quoted in Engel, ed., *Mont Blanc–An Anthology*, p. 168.

Chapter 2 The Matterhorn Revisited: In the Tracks of Whymper

1. Quoted in Ronald W. Clark, *The Day the Rope Broke* (New York: Harcourt, Brace & World, Inc., 1965), p. 60.
2. Edward Whymper, *Scrambles Amongst the Alps* (London: John Murray, 1971), p. 50.
3. Ibid.
4. Ibid., p. 123.
5. Ibid., pp. 249-50.
6. Ibid., p. 301.
7. Guido Rey, *The Matterhorn* (London: T. Fisher Unwin, 1907), p. 133.
8. Ibid., p. 134.
9. Whymper, *Scrambles Amongst the Alps*, p. 306.

10. Ibid., p. 310.
11. Ibid., pp. 314-15.
12. Rey, *The Matterhorn*, pp. 137-38.
13. Whymper, *Scrambles Amongst the Alps*, p. 322.

Chapter 3 The Bernese Trinity

1. In R. L. G. Irving, The Romance of Mountaineering (London: J. M. Dent and Sons Ltd., 1935), p. 52.
2. Alfred Wills, *Wanderings Among the High Alps* (London: Richard Bentley, 1856). pp. 216-17.
3. Charles Barrington, in *Alpine Journal* 11 (London: Longmans, Green & Co., 1884): 173.
4. Ibid, pp. 173-74.
5. Walter Unsworth, *Because It Is There* (London: Victor Gollancz Ltd., 1968), p. 126.
6. *Alpine Journal* 50 (1938) :9
7. Heinrich Harrer, *Seven Years in Tibet* (New York: E. P. Dutton and Company, Inc., 1954).
8. Heinrich Harrer, *The White Spider* (London: Rupert Hart-Davis, 1968), p. 99.
9. Ibid., p. 21
10. Ibid., p. 108.
11. Ibid., P. 119.
12. Ibid., p. 123.
13. In *Mountain Magazine* 16 (July 1971) :33-34.
14. Lionel Terray, *The Borders of the Impossible* (New York: Doubleday & Company, Inc., 1964), p. 168.
15. Gaston Rébuffat, *Starlight and Storm* (New York: Oxford University Press, 1968), pp. 197-98.
16. Harrer, *The White Spider*, pp. 170-71.
17. Jack Olsen, *The Climb Up to Hell* (New York and Evanston: Harper & Row, 1962), p. 90.
18. Ibid., p. 139.

Chapter 4 On the Edge of Everest

1. David Robertson, *George Mallory* (London: Faber and Faber, 1969), pp. 58-59.
2. Ibid., p. 90.
3. Francis Younghusband, *The Epic of Everest* (London: Edward Arnold & Co., 1926), pp. 27-28.
4. Ibid., p. 28.
5. Col. C. K. Howard-Bury, *Mount Everest—the Reconnaissance 1921* (London: Edward Arnold & Co., 1922), pp. 192-93.
6. Brig. Gen. C. G. Bruce et al., *The Assault on Mount Everest* (London: Edward Arnold & Co., 1923), p. 282.
7. Lt. Col. E. F. Norton, *The Fight for Everest: 1924* (London: Edward Arnold & Co., 1924), pp. 77-78.
8. Ibid., p. 88.
9. Ibid., p. 126.
10. Ibid., p. 130.
11. John Hunt and Edmund Hillary, *The Conquest of Everest* (New York: E. P. Dutton & Company, Inc., 1953), p. 202.

Chapter 5 A Pilgrimage on Fujisan

1. Frederick Starr, *Fujiyama—The Sacred Mountain of Japan* (Chicago: Covici-McGee Co., 1924), p. 108.

2. Lafcadio Hearn, *Exotics and Retrospectives* (Boston: Little, Brown & Co., 1910), pp. 3-4.
3. Ibid., pp. 35-36
4. Rutherford Alcock, *The Capital of the Tycoon* (New York: Harper & Brothers, 1877), pp. 340-41.
5. Ibid., pp. 369-70.

Chapter 6 Excursions in the High Sierra

1. Clarence King, *Mountaineering in the Sierra Nevada,* 5th ed. (Boston: James R. Osgood Co., 1875), p. 70.
2. William H. Brewer, *Up and Down California in 1860-1864* (New Haven, Conn.: Yale University Press, 1930), p. 525.
3. King, *Mountaineering in the Sierra Nevada*, p. 71.
4. Ibid., pp. 93-94.
5. Ibid., p. 95
6. Thurman Wilkins, *Clarence King* (New York: The Macmillan Company, 1958), p. 134.
7. Ibid., p. 165 n.
8. King, *Mountaineering in the Sierra Nevada*, p. 286.
9. Ibid., p. 288.
10. W. A. Goodyear, in *Proceedings of the California Academy of Sciences* 5, pp. 139-44.
11. King, *Mountaineering in the Sierra Nevada*, p. 292.
12. Henry Adams, *The Education of Henry Adams* (Boston and New York: Houghton Mifflin Company, 1918), p. 416.
13. Ibid., p. 311-12.
14. Wilkins, *Clarence King*, pp. 181-82.
15. Adams, *The Education of Henry Adams*, pp. 313, 346.
16. Francis P. Farquhar, *History of the Sierra Nevada* (Berkeley and Los Angeles, Calif.: University of California Press, 1966), p. 174.

Chapter 7 *La Haute Route:* Crossing the Western Alps on Skis

1. E. S. Kennedy, *Peaks, Passes, and Glaciers* 2d series, vol.1 (London: Longman, Green, Longmans and Roberts, 1862), pp. 227-340.
2. Ibid., p. 229.
3. Ibid., p. 325.
4. Claire Eliane Engel, *Mountaineering in the Alps* (London: George Allen & Unwin, Ltd., 1971), p. 172.
5. *Alpine Journal* 44 (1932) :338.
6. John Ball, ed., *Peaks, Passes, and Glaciers* (London: Longman, Green, Longman, & Roberts, 1860), p. 8.
7. Edward Whymper, *Scrambles Amongst the Alps* (London: John Murray, 1871), p. 204.
8. *Alpine Journal* 13 (1887) :261.
9. A. W. Moore, *The Alps in 1864* (Oxford: Basil Blackwell, 1939), p. xii.
10. Émile Javelle, *Alpine Memories* (London: T. Fisher Unwin, 1899), pp. 379-80; 384-85.
11. Ibid., 382.
12. Moore, *The Alps in 1864*, pp. 199, 201, 202.
13. *Alpine Journal* 5 (1872): 318-19.

Selected Bibliography

Mont Blanc (Chapter 1)

Bernstein, Jeremy. *Ascent.* New York: Random House, 1965.

Bonatti, Walter. *On the Heights.* London: Rupert Hart-Davis, 1964. Chapters 8, 9, 10, 13, and 17.

Brown, T. Graham. *Brenva.* London: J. M. Dent & Sons Ltd., 1944.

Brown, T. Graham, and de Beer, Gavin. *The First Ascent of Mont Blanc.* New York and London: Oxford University Press, 1957.

Collomb, Robin G. *Chamonix-Mont Blanc.* London: Constable & Company, Ltd., 1969.

Collomb, Robin G., and Crew, Peter. *Selected Climbs in the Mont Blanc Range.* London: The Alpine Club, 1967 and 1976. Volumes 1 and 2.

Dumas, Alexandre. *Impressions de Voyage* (1833) and *Travels in Switzerland.* London: Peter Owen Ltd., 1958.

Engel, Claire Eliane, ed. *Mont Blanc—An Anthology.* London: George Allen and Unwin Ltd., 1965.

Freshfield, Douglas W. *The Life of Horace Benedict de Saussure.* London: Edward Arnold, 1920.

Frison-Roche, Roger. *Mont Blanc and the Seven Valleys.* Grenoble: Arthaud, 1961.

Gos, François. *Rambles in High Savoy.* London: Longmans, Green & Co., Ltd., 1927.

Lepiney, Jacques and Tom de. *Climbs on Mont Blanc.* London: Edward Arnold & Co., 1930.

Mathews, Charles Edwards. *The Annals of Mont Blanc.* London: T. Fisher Unwin, 1898.

Milner, C. Douglas. *Mont Blanc and the Aiguilles.* London: Robert Hale, Ltd., 1955.

Rébuffat, Gaston. *The Mont Blanc Massif—The 100 Finest Routes.* London: Kaye & Ward; New York: Oxford University Press, 1974.

Smith, Albert. *The Story of Mont Blanc.* London: David Bogue, 1853.

Tissot, Roger. *Mont Blanc.* London: The Medici Society Ltd., 1924.

Whymper, Edward. *A Guide to Chamonix and the Range of Mont Blanc.* London: John Murray, 1911.

The Matterhorn (Chapter 2)

Bonatti, Walter. *The Great Days.* London: Victor Gollancz Ltd., 1974. Chapter 10.

Clark, Ronald W. *The Day the Rope Broke.* New York: Harcourt, Brace & World, Inc., 1965.

Collomb, Robin G. *Selected Climbs in the Pennine Alps.* London: The Alpine Club, 1968.

___. *Zermatt and District.* London: Constable & Company Ltd., 1969.

Gos, Charles. *Alpine Tragedy.* New York: Charles Scribner's Sons, 1948. Chapters 4, 11, and 15.

Gos, François. *Zermatt and Its Valley.* London: Cassell and Company Ltd., 1926.

Lunn, Arnold. *Matterhorn Centenary.* Chicago: Rand McNally & Company, 1965.

___. *Zermatt and the Valais.* London: Hollis & Carter, 1955.

Mummery, A. F. *My Climbs in the Alps and Caucasus.* Oxford: Basil Blackwell, 1936. Chapters 1 and 2.

Rébuffat, Gaston. *Men and the Matterhorn.* New York: Oxford University Press, 1967.

Rey, Guido. *The Matterhorn.* London: T. Fisher Unwin, 1907.

Smythe, Frank S. *Edward Whymper.* London: Hodder and Stoughton Ltd., 1940.

Tyndall, John. *Hours of Exercise in the Alps.* New York: D. Appleton & Company, 1875. Chapters 3, 10, 14, 21, and 24.

Unsworth, Walter. *Matterhorn Man.* London: Victor Gollancz Ltd., 1965.

Whymper, Edward. *Scrambles Amongst the Alps.* London: John Murray, 1871.

___. *The Valley of Zermatt and the Matterhorn.* London: John Murray, 1897.

Williams, Cicely. *Zermatt Saga.* Brig, Switzerland: Rotten-Verlag, 1964.

The Eiger (Chapter 3)

Bonington, Chris. *I Choose to Climb.* London: Victor Gollancz Ltd., 1973. Chapters 4, 12, and 14.

___. *The Next Horizon.* London: Victor Gollancz Ltd., 1973. Chapters 11, 12, and 13.

Gillman, Peter, and Haston, Dougal. *Direttissima.* New York and Evanston: Harper & Row, 1966.

Harrer, Heinrich. *The White Spider.* London: Rupert Hart-Davis, 1968.

Haston, Dougal. *The Eiger.* London: Cassell & Company Ltd., 1974.

___. *In High Places.* London: Cassell & Company Ltd., 1972. Chapters 4 and 6.

Heckmair, Anderl. *My Life As A Mountaineer.* London: Victor Gollancz Ltd., 1975.

Hiebeler, Toni. *North Face in Winter.* Philadelphia and New York: J. B. Lippincott Company, 1963.

Olsen, Jack. *The Climb Up to Hell.* New York and Evanston: Harper & Row, 1962.

Rébuffat, Gaston. *Starlight and Storm.* New York: Oxford University Press, 1968. Pp. 168-218.

Terray, Lionel. *The Borders of the Impossible.* New York: Doubleday & Company, Inc., 1964. Chapter 5.

Ullman, James Ramsey. *Straight Up—The Life and Death of John Harlin.* New York: Doubleday & Company, Inc., 1968.

Unsworth, Walter. *North Face.* London: Hutchinson Junior Books Ltd., 1969. Chapters 7 and 8.

Whillans, Don, and Ormerod, Alick. *Don Whillans—Portrait of a Mountaineer.* London: William Heinemann Ltd., 1971.

Mount Everest (Chapter 4)

Ahluwalia, Major H. P. S. *Faces of Everest.* New Delhi, Bombay, Bangalore, Calcutta, and Kanpur: Vikas Publishing House Pvt. Ltd., 1978.

———. *Higher Than Everest.* New Delhi, Bombay, Bangalore, Calcutta, and Kanpur: Vikas Publishing House Pvt. Ltd., 1975.

Bonington, Chris. *Everest the Hard Way.* New York: Random House, 1976.

———. *The Ultimate Challenge.* New York: Stein and Day, 1973.

Bruce, Brig. Gen. C. G. et al. *The Assault on Mount Everest.* London: Edward Arnold & Co., 1923.

Carr, Herbert R. C., ed. *The Irvine Diaries—Andrew Irvine & The Enigma of Everest.* Goring, England: Gastons-West Col, 1979.

Denman, Earl. *Alone to Everest.* New York: Coward-McCann, Inc., 1954.

Dittert, Rene; Chevalley, Gabriel; and Lambert, Raymond. *Forerunners to Everest.* New York: Harper and Brothers, 1953.

Eggler, Albert. *The Everest-Lhotse Adventure.* London: George Allen & Unwin Ltd., 1957.

Fleming, Jon, and Faux, Ronald. *Soldiers on Everest.* London: Her Majesty's Stationery Office, 1977.

Habeler, Peter. *Everest—Impossible Victory.* London: Arlington Books, 1979.

Hagen, Toni; Dyhrenfurth, G. O.; von Fürer-Haimendorf, Christoph; and Schneider, Erwin. *Mount Everest—Formation, Population and Exploration of the Everest Region.* London: Oxford University Press, 1963.

Hillary, Edmund. *High Adventure.* London: The Companion Book Club, 1956.

Hornbein, Thomas F. *Everest—The West Ridge.* San Francisco, Calif.: Sierra Club, 1965.

Howard-Bury, Col. C. K. *Mount Everest—the Reconnaissance 1921.* London: Edward Arnold & Co., 1922.

Hunt, John, and Hillary, Edmund. *The Conquest of Everest.* New York: E. P. Dutton & Company, Inc., 1953.

Kohli, Comm. M. S. *Nine Atop Everest.* Bombay: Orient Longmans Ltd., 1969.

Lowe, George. *From Everest to the South Pole.* New York: St. Martin's Press, 1961.

Malartic, Yves. *Tenzing of Everest.* New York: Crown Publishers, Inc., 1954.

McCullum, John D. *Everest Diary.* Chicago and New York: Follett Pub. Co., 1966.

Messner, Reinhold. *Everest–Expedition to the Ultimate.* London: Kaye & Ward, 1979.

Miura, Yuichiro et al. *Japanese Everest Skiing Expedition.* Tokyo: Bungeishunji Ltd., 1970.

___ with Eric Perlman. *The Man Who Skied Down Everest.* San Francisco: Harper & Row, 1978.

Morin, Micheline. *Everest.* New York: The John Day Company, 1955.

Murray, W. H. *The Story of Everest.* London: J. M. Dent & Sons, Ltd., 1953.

Noel, John. *The Story of Everest.* Boston: Little, Brown & Company, 1927.

Norgay, Tenzing. *After Everest.* London: George Allen & Unwin Ltd., 1977.

Norton, Lt. Col. E. F. *The Fight for Everest: 1924.* London: Edward Arnold & Co., 1924.

Noyce, Wilfrid. *South Col.* New York: William Sloane Associates, Inc., 1955.

Pye, David. *George Leigh Mallory.* London: Oxford University Press, 1927.

Ridgeway, Rick. *The Boldest Dream–The Story of Twelve Who Climbed Mount Everest.* New York and London: Harcourt Brace Jovanovich, 1979.

Robertson, David. *George Mallory.* London: Faber and Faber, 1969.

Ruttledge, Hugh. *Everest 1933.* London: Hodder & Stoughton Ltd., 1934.

___. *Everest: The Unfinished Adventure.* London: Hodder & Stoughton Ltd., 1937.

Sayre, Woodrow Wilson. *Four Against Everest.* Englewood Cliffs, N.J.: Prentice-Hall, Inc., 1964.

Shipton, Eric. *The Mount Everest Reconnaissance Expedition 1951.* London: Hodder & Stoughton Ltd., 1952.

___. *Men Against Everest.* Englewood Cliffs, N.J.: Prentice-Hall, Inc., 1955.

Singh, Brig. Gyan. *Lure of Everest.* Delhi: Government of India, 1961.

Smythe, Frank S. *Camp Six.* London: Adam & Charles Black, 1956.

Somervell, T. Howard. *After Everest.* London: Hodder and Stoughton, 1936.

Styles, Showell. *Mallory of Everest.* New York: The Macmillan Company, 1967.

Steele, Peter. *Doctor on Everest.* London: Hodder, Stoughton Ltd., 1972.

Tilman, H. W. *Mount Everest 1938.* Cambridge: At the University Press, 1948.

Ullman, James Ramsey. *Americans on Everest.* Philadelphia and New York: J. B. Lippincott Company, 1964.

___. *Kingdom of Adventure: Everest.* New York: William Sloane Associates, Inc., 1947.

___. *Tiger of the Snows–Tenzing of Everest.* New York: G. P. Putnam's Sons, 1955.

Wibberley, Leonard. *Epics of Everest.* New York: Junior Literary Guild and Ariel Books, 1954.

Younghusband, Francis. *The Epic of Mount Everest.* London: Edward Arnold & Co., 1926.

___. *The Heart of a Continent.* London: John Murray, 1896.

Also of note:

Another Ascent of the World's Highest Peak–Qomolangma. Peking: Foreign Language Press, 1975.

Everest—The Swiss Expedition of Photographs. New York: E. P. Dutton & Co., Inc., 1954.

A Photographic Record of the Mount Jolmo Lungma Scientific Expedition. Peking: Science Press, 1974.

Fujisan (Chapter 5)

Alcock, Rutherford. *The Capital of the Tycoon.* New York: Harper and Brothers, 1877.

Hearn, Lafcadio. *Exotics and Retrospectives.* Boston: Little, Brown & Co., 1910.

Narazaki, Muneshige. *Hokusai—The Thirty Six Views of Mt. Fuji.* Tokyo, New York, San Francisco: Kodansha International Ltd., 1968.

Okada, Koyo. *Mt. Fuji.* Tokyo: Hobundo Co., 1959.

Starr, Frederick. *Fujiyama—The Sacred Mountain of Japan.* Chicago: Covici-McGee Co., 1924.

Weston, Rev. Walter. *The Playground of the Far East.* London: John Murray, 1918.

Also of note:

The Manyōshū (Collection of Myriad Leaves).

Mt. Fuji. Tokyo: The Japanese Times Ltd., 1970.

The High Sierra (Chapter 6)

Bowen, Ezra. *The High Sierra.* New York: Time-Life Books, 1972.

Brewer, William H. *Up and Down California in 1860-1864.* New Haven, Conn.: Yale University Press, 1930.

Century Association. *Clarence King Memoirs.* New York: G. P. Putnam's Sons, 1904.

Clyde, Norman. *Rambles Through the Range of Light.* San Francisco, Calif.: Scrimshaw Press, 1971.

Farquhar, Francis P. *History of the Sierra Nevada.* Berkeley and Los Angeles, Calif.: University of California Press, 1966.

Hutchings, J. M. *The Heart of the Sierras.* Oakland, Calif.: Pacific Press, 1886.

King, Clarence. *Mountaineering in the Sierra Nevada.* 5th ed. Boston: James R. Osgood Co., 1875.

Muir, John. *The Mountains of California.* New York: Century Press, 1894.

———. *The Yosemite.* New York: Century Press, 1912.

Roper, Steve. *The Climber's Guide to the High Sierra.* San Francisco, Calif.: Sierra Club Books, 1976.

Rose, Eugene A. *High Odyssey.* Berkeley, Calif.: Howell-North Books, 1974.

Rowell, Galen A. *The Vertical World of Yosemite.* Berkeley, Calif.: Wilderness Press, 1974.

Shebl, James M. *King, of the Mountains.* Stockton, Calif.: Pacific Center for Western Historical Studies, 1974.

Webster, Paul. *The Mighty Sierra.* Palo Alto, Calif.: American West Publishing Company, 1972.

Wheelock, Walt, and Condon, Tom. *Climbing Mount Whitney*. Glendale, Calif.: La Siesta Press, 1970.

Wilkins, Thurman. *Clarence King*. New York: The Macmillan Company, 1958.

La Haute Route (Chapter 7)

Darbellay, Michel. *Haute Route*. Lausanne: Marguerat, 1979. (French and German texts).

Flower, Raymond. *The History of Skiing and Other Winter Sports*. Toronto and New York: Methuen, 1976.

Heller, Mark, ed. *The Skier's Encyclopedia*. New York and London: Paddington Press Ltd., 1979. pp. 20-33; 58-64.

____. *The World Ski Atlas*. New York: A & W. Publishers, Inc., 1978. pp. 6-9; 18-30.

____ and Milne, Malcom, eds. *The Book of European Skiing*. New York, Chicago and San Francisco: Holt, Rinehart and Winston, 1966. pp. 29-35; 157-181.

Jacomb, F. W. *High Level Road. Peak, Passes, and Glaciers*. 2d series. London: Longman, Green, Longmans and Roberts, 1862.

Lund, Morten. *The Skier's World*. New York: Random House, Inc., 1973. pp. 37-47.

Lunn, Arnold. *A History of Ski-ing*. London: Oxford University Press, 1929.

____. *The Story of Skiing*. London: Eyre & Spottiswoode, 1952.

Miller, Peter. *Ski Almanac*. Garden City: Doubleday & Co., 1979. pp. 1-3; 183-199.

Moore, A. W. *Variations on the High Level Route*. Alpine Journal, Vol. 5. London: Longman, Green, Reader, and Dyer, 1872. pp. 309-329.

____. *The Alps in 1864*. Oxford: Basil Blackwell, 1939. pp. 191-217.

Pause, Walter. *Salute the Skier*. London: George C. Harrap & Co., Ltd., 1963. pp. 16-17; 26-27; 42-43; 46-53; 58-59.

Roberts, Eric. *High Level Route*. Goring, England: West Col Productions, 1973.

Scharff, Robert, ed. *Encyclopedia of Skiing*. New York, Evanston, and London: Harper & Row, 1979. pp. 1-51; 96-100.

Wills, Alfred. *The Passage of the Fenêtre de Salena. Peaks, Passes and Glaciers*. London: Longman, Green, Longmans, and Roberts, 1860. pp. 1-27.

Also of note:

America's Ski Book. New York: Charles Scribner's Sons, 1966. pp. 14-26; 115-119.

Edwards, Harvey. *The Great 'Haute Route.'* Ski Magazine, January, 1965. pp. 54 et. seq.

Jamieson, Bob. *Chamonix to Zermatt on Skis*. Skiing Magazine, February, 1974. pp. 61 et. seq.

The Alps

Ball, John, ed. *Peaks, Passes and Glaciers*. London: Longman, Brown, Green, Longmans and Roberts, 1859.

Clark, Ronald W. *The Alps*. New York: Alfred A. Knopf, 1973.

____. *The Early Alpine Guides*. London: Phoenix House, 1949.

____. *An Eccentric in the Alps*. London: Museum Press, 1959.

____. *The Victorian Mountaineers*. London: B. T. Batsford Ltd., 1953.

Conway, William Martin. *The Alps*. London: Adam and Charles Black, 1904.

___. *The Alps from End to End.* London: Archibald Constable & Co., Ltd., 1904.

Coolidge, W. A. B. *Alpine Studies.* London: Longmans, Green & Co., 1912.

___. *The Alps in Nature and History.* London: Methuen & Co., 1908.

de Beer, Gavin. *Early Travelers in the Alps.* London: Sidgwick and Jackson Ltd., 1930.

de Saussure, Horace Bénédict. *Voyages dans les Alpes.* Neuchâtel: Louis Fauche-Borel, 1779-96.

Engel, Claire Eliane. *Mountaineering in the Alps.* London: George Allen & Unwin, Ltd., 1971.

___. *They Came to the Hills.* London: George Allen & Unwin, Ltd., 1952.

Forbes, James D. *Travels Through the Alps of Savoy and Other Parts of the Pennine Chain; with Observations on the Phenomena of Glaciers.* Edinburgh: Adam & Charles Black, 1843.

Gervasutti, Giusto. *Gervasutti's Climbs.* Seattle: The Mountaineers, 1979.

Irving, R. L. G. *The Alps.* New York: Charles Scribner's Sons; London: B. T. Batsford, 1942.

Javelle, Émile. *Alpine Memoirs.* London: T. Fisher Unwin, 1899.

Kennedy, E. S., ed. *Peaks, Passes and Glaciers.* 2d series. London: Longman, Green, Longmans and Roberts, 1862.

Klucker, Christian. *Adventures of an Alpine Guide.* London: John Murray, 1932.

Kugy, Julius. *Alpine Pilgrimage.* London: John Murray, 1934.

Lukan, Karl. *The Alps and Alpinism.* New York: Coward-McCann, Inc., 1968.

Magnone, Guido. *The West Face.* London: Museum Press, 1955.

Moore, A. W. *The Alps in 1864.* Oxford: Basil Blackwell, 1939.

Noyce, Wilfrid. *The Alps.* London: Thames and Hudson, 1961.

Rey, Guido. *Peaks and Precipices—Scrambles in the Dolomites and Savoy.* London: T. Fisher Unwin, 1914.

Roberts, Eric. *High Level Route.* Goring, England: West Col Productions, 1973.

Skirakawa, Yoshikazu, and Wyss, Max A. *The Alps.* New York: Harry N. Abrams, Inc., 1973.

Stephen, Leslie. *The Playground of Europe.* New York and London: G. P. Putnam's Sons, 1909.

Tyndall, John. *Glaciers of the Alps & Mountaineering in 1861.* London: J. M. Dent & Co.; New York: E. P. Dutton & Co., Inc., 1906.

Unsworth, Walter. *North Face—The Second Conquest of the Alps.* London: Hutchinson, 1969.

Wills, Alfred. *Wanderings Among the High Alps.* London: Richard Bentley, 1856.

Young, Geoffrey Winthrop. *On High Hills.* London: Methuen & Co., Ltd., 1947.

The Himalayas

Armington, Stan. *Exploring Nepal.* Glendale, Calif.: La Siesta Press, 1975.

___. *Trekking in the Himalayas.* Australia: Lonely Planet Publications, 1979.

Banks, Mike. *Rakaposhi.* New York: A. S. Barnes and Company, Inc., 1960.

Barker, Ralph. *The Last Blue Mountain.* New York: Doubleday & Company, 1960.

Bates, Robert H.; Burdsall, Richard L.; House, William P.; Houston, Charles S.; Petzoldt, Paul K; and Streatfield, Capt. Norman R. *Five Miles High.* New York: Dodd, Mead & Company, 1939.

Bauer, Paul. *Himalayan Quest.* London: Nicholson and Watson Limited, 1938.

___. *Kangchenjunga Challenge.* London: William Kimber, 1955.

___. *The Siege of Nanga Parbat 1946-1953.* London: Rupert Hart-Davis, 1956.

Baume, Louis C. *Sivalaya.* Goring, England: West Col Productions, 1978.

Bechtold, Fritz. *Nanga Parbat Adventure.* New York: E. P. Dutton and Company, Inc., 1936.

Bernstein, Jeremy. *The Wildest Dreams of Kew.* New York: Simon and Schuster, 1969.

Bezruchka, Stephen. *A Guide to Trekking in Nepal.* Katmandu: Sahayogi Prakashan, 1976.

Boardman, Peter. *The Shining Mountain.* London: Hodder and Stoughton, 1978.

Bonington, Chris. *Annapurna South Face.* New York: McGraw-Hill Book Co., 1971.

Bonington, Chris; Boysen, Martin; Hankinson, Alan; Haston, Dougal; Sandhu, Balwant; and Scott, Doug. *Changabang.* London: William Heinemann Ltd., 1975.

Braham, Trevor. *Himalayan Odyssey.* London: George Allen & Unwin Ltd., 1974.

Buhl, Hermann. *The Lonely Challenge.* New York: E. P. Dutton & Company, Inc., 1956.

Chapman, Spencer F. *Memoirs of a Mountaineer: Helvellyn to Himalaya.* London: T. Fisher Unwin, 1951.

Collie, J. Norman. *Climbing on the Himalaya and Other Mountain Ranges.* Edinburgh: David Douglas, 1902.

Conway, William Martin. *Climbing and Exploration in the Karakoram Himalayas.* London: T. Fisher Unwin, 1894.

Curran, Jim. *Trango-The Nameless Tower.* Sheffield, England: Dark Peak, 1978.

Desio, Ardito. *Ascent of K2.* London: Elek Books, 1955.

Dyhrenfurth, G. O. *To the Third Pole.* London: Werner Laurie, 1955.

Eiselin, Max. *The Ascent of Dhaulagiri.* New York and Toronto: Oxford University Press, 1961.

Evans, Charles. *Kangchenjunga–The Untrodden Peak.* New York: E. P. Dutton & Co., Inc., 1957.

Fantin, Mario. *Sherpa Himalaya Nepal.* New Delhi: The English Book Store, 1974.

Filippi, Filippo de. *Karakoram and Western Himalaya.* London: Constable & Co., 1912.

Franco, Jean, and Terray, Lionel. *At Grips with Jannu.* London: Victor Gollancz Ltd., 1967.

Freshfield, Douglas W. *Round Kangchenjunga.* London: Edward Arnold, 1903.

Hagen, Toni. *Nepal.* Chicago: Rand McNally & Company, 1971.

Harrer, Heinrich. *Seven Years in Tibet.* New York: E. P. Dutton and Company, Inc., 1938.

Harvard, Andrew, and Thompson, Todd. *Mountain of Storms—The American Expeditions to Dhaulagiri.* New York: New York University Press, Chelsea House, 1974.

Herrligkoffer, Karl M. *Nanga Parbat.* New York: Alfred A. Knopf, 1954.

Herzog, Maurice. *Annapurna.* New York: E. P. Dutton & Co., Inc., 1952.

Hillary, Edmund, and Doig, Desmond. *High in the Thin Cold Air.* New York: Doubleday & Company, Inc., 1962.

Houston, Charles, and Bates, Richard. *K2—The Savage Mountain.* London: Collins, 1955.

Keay, John. *When Men and Mountains Meet—Explorers of the Western Himalayas 1820-75.* London: John Murray, 1977.

_____. *The Gilgit Game.* London: John Murray, 1979.

Kumar, Col. Narinder. *Kanchenjunga.* London and The Hague: East-West Publications, 1978.

Lambert, Raymond, and Kogan, Claude. *White Fury.* London: Hurst & Blackett, 1956.

Maraini, Fosco. *Karakoram—the Ascent of Gasherbrum IV.* New York: The Viking Press, 1961.

_____. *Where Four Worlds Meet—Hindu Kush.* New York: Harcourt, Brace & World, Inc., 1964.

Mason, Kenneth. *Abode of Snow.* New York: E. P. Dutton & Co., Inc., 1955.

Matthiessen, Peter. *The Snow Leopard.* New York: The Viking Press, 1978.

Messner, Reinhold. *The Challenge.* New York: Oxford University Press; London: Kaye & Ward, 1977.

_____. *Solo Nanga Parbat.* New York: Oxford University Press, 1980.

Mulgrew, Peter. *No Place for Men.* London: Nicholas Vane Ltd., 1965.

Mullik, B. N. *The Sky Was His Limit—The Life and Climbs of Sonam Byatso.* India: Palit & Duit, 1970.

Noyce, Wilfrid. *Climbing the Fish's Tail.* London: William Heinemann Ltd., 1958.

Peissel, Michel. *The Great Himalayan Passage.* Boston and Toronto: Little, Brown and Company, 1975.

_____. *Mustang—The Forbidden Kingdom.* New York: E. P. Dutton & Co., Inc., 1967.

Ridgeway, Rick. *The Last Step—The American Ascent of K_2.* Seattle: The Mountaineers, 1980.

Rowell, Galen. *In the Throne Room of the Mountain Gods.* San Francisco, Calif.: Sierra Club Books, 1977.

Schaller, George B. *Stones of Silence—Journeys in the Himalaya.* New York: The Viking Press, 1980.

Shipton, Eric. *Nanda Devi.* London: Hodder & Stoughton, Ltd., 1936.

Shirakawa, Yoshikazu. *Himalayas.* Tokyo: Tetsuo Oga, 1971; New York: Harry N. Abrams, Inc., 1976.

Smythe, F. S. *Kamet Conquered.* London: Victor Gollancz Ltd., 1932.

_____. *The Kangchenjunga Adventure.* London: Victor Gollancz Ltd., 1930.

Tichy, Herbert. *Cho Oyu.* London: Methuen & Co. Ltd., 1957.

___ . *Himalaya.* New York: G. P. Putnam's Sons, 1970.

Tilman, H. W. *The Ascent of Nanda Devi.* New York: The Macmillan Company, 1937.

___ . *Nepal Himalaya.* Cambridge: At the University Press, 1952.

___ . *When Men and Mountains Meet.* Cambridge: At the University Press, 1947.

Tucker, John. *Kanchenjunga.* New York: Abelard-Schuman, Ltd., 1955.

Verghese, B. G. *Himalayan Endeavor.* New Delhi: Times of India, 1962.

Von Fürer-Haimendorf, Christoph. *The Sherpas of Nepal.* London: John Murray, 1964.

___ . *Himalayan Traders.* New York: St. Martin's Press, 1975.

Ward, Michael. *In This Short Span.* London: Victor Gollancz Ltd., 1972.

Weir, Tom. *East of Katmandu.* London and Edinburgh: Oliver and Boyd, 1955.

Yamada, Keiichi. *The Himalaya from the Air.* Tokyo: Shinbun, 1975.

General and Other

Adams, Henry. *The Education of Henry Adams.* Boston and New York: Houghton Mifflin Company, 1918.

Beckey, Fred. *Challenge of the North Cascades.* Seattle: The Mountaineers, 1969.

Benuzzi, Felice. *No Picnic on Mount Kenya.* New York: E. P. Dutton & Company, Inc., 1953.

Brown, Joe. *The Hard Years.* London: Victor Gollancz Ltd., 1969.

Browne, Belmore. *The Conquest of Mt. McKinley.* Boston: Houghton Mifflin, 1956.

Bueler, William. *Mountains of the World.* Seattle: The Mountaineers, 1977.

Burdsall, Richard L., and Emmons, Arthur B. 3rd. (Contributions by Moore, Terris, and Young, Jack Theodore). *Men Against the Clouds—The Conquest of Minya Konka.* New York: Harper & Brothers, 1935.

Casewit, Curtis W. *The Mountain World.* New York: Random House, 1976.

Clark, Ronald W. *Men, Myths and Mountains.* New York: Thomas Y. Crowell Company, 1976.

Cleare, John. *Mountains.* New York: Crown Publishers Inc., 1975.

___ . *Collins Guide to Mountains and Mountaineering.* London: William Collins Sons & Co., Ltd., 1979.

Conway, William Martin. *The Bolivian Andes.* London and New York: Harper & Bros., 1901.

___ . *Mountain Memories.* New York: Funk and Wagnalls Company, n.d.

Craig, Robert W. *Storm & Sorrow in the High Pamirs.* Seattle and New York: The Mountaineers with the American Alpine Club, 1977.

Davidson, Art. *Minus 148°—The Winter Ascent of Mt. McKinley.* New York: W. W. Norton & Company, Inc., 1969.

Diemberger, Kurt. *Summits and Secrets.* London: George Allen & Unwin, Ltd., 1971.

Ferlet, Rene, and Poulet, Guy. *Aconcagua South Face.* London: Constable & Company Limited, 1956.

Filippi, Filippo de. *Ruwenzori: An Account of the Expedition of H. R. H. Prince Luigi Amedeo of Savoy, Duke of the Abruzzi.* London: Archibald, Constable & Co., 1908.

Finch, George I. *The Making of a Mountaineer.* London: J. W. Arrowsmith Ltd., 1924.

Fitzgerald, E. A. *The Highest Andes.* New York: Charles Scribner's Sons, 1899.

Freshfield, Douglas W. *The Exploration of the Caucasus.* London: Edward Arnold, 1896.

Gray, Dennis. *Rope Boy.* London: Victor Gollancz Ltd., 1970.

Gribble, Francis. *The Early Mountaineers.* London: T. Fisher Unwin, 1899.

Hillary, Edmund. *Nothing Venture, Nothing Win.* New York: Coward, McCann & Geoghegan, Inc., 1975.

___. *From the Ocean to the Sky.* London: Hodder and Stoughton, 1979.

Holder, Charles Frederic. *Louis Agassiz—His Life and Work.* New York: G. P. Putnam's Sons, 1893.

Hunt, John. *Life Is Meeting.* London: Hodder and Stoughton, 1978.

Huxley, Anthony, ed. *Standard Encyclopedia of the World's Mountains.* New York: G. P. Putnam's Sons, 1962.

Irving, R. L. G. *A History of British Mountaineering.* London: B. T. Batsford Ltd., 1955.

___. *The Romance of Mountaineering.* London: J. M. Dent and Sons Ltd., 1935.

Jerome, John. *On Mountains—Thinking About Terrain.* New York and London: Harcourt Brace Jovanovich, 1978.

Jones, Chris. *Climbing in North America.* Berkeley and Los Angeles, Calif.: University of California Press, 1976.

Kain, Conrad. *Where the Clouds Can Go.* New York: The American Alpine Club, 1979.

Keenlyside, Francis. *Peaks and Pioneers—The Story of Mountaineering.* London: Paul Elek Ltd., 1975.

Longstaff, Tom. *This My Voyage.* New York: Charles Scribner's Sons, 1950.

Lunn, Arnold. *A Century of Mountaineering.* London: George Allen & Unwin, Ltd., 1957.

Mazeaud, Pierre. *Naked Before the Mountain.* London: Victor Gollancz Ltd., 1974.

Meade, C. F. *Approach to the Hills.* New York: E. P. Dutton and Company, Inc., 1940.

Messner, Reinhold. *The Seventh Grade.* New York: Oxford University Press, 1974.

___. *The Big Walls.* London: Kaye & Ward; New York: Oxford University Press, 1978.

Milne, Malcolm. *The Book of Modern Mountaineering.* New York: G. P. Putnam's Sons, 1968.

Molenaar, Dee. *The Challenge of Rainier.* Seattle: The Mountaineers, 1971.

Moore, Terris. *Mt. McKinley & The Pioneer Climbs.* College, Alaska: University of Alaska Press, 1967.

Newby, Eric. *Great Ascents.* New York: The Viking Press, 1977.

Noyce, Wilfrid, and McMorrin, Ian. *World Atlas of Mountaineering.* New York: The Macmillan Company, 1970.

Patey, Tom. *One Man's Mountains.* London: Victor Gollancz Ltd., 1973.

Rébuffat, Gaston. *Between Heaven and Earth.* New York: Oxford University Press, 1970.

___ . *Mont Blanc to Everest.* Grenoble: Arthaud, 1956.

Roper, Steve and Steck, Allen. *Fifty Classic Climbs of North America.* San Francisco, Calif.: Sierra Club Books, 1979.

Rowell, Galen. *High and Wild.* San Francisco, Calif.: Sierra Club Books, 1979.

Scott, Doug. *Big Wall Climbing.* New York: Oxford University Press, 1974.

Sherman, Paddy. *Cloud Walkers.* Seattle: The Mountaineers, 1965.

Shipton, Eric. *Mountain Conquest.* New York: American Heritage Publishing Co., Inc., 1966.

___ . *That Untravelled World.* London: Hodder and Stoughton Ltd., 1969.

Snyder, Howard H. *The Hall of the Mountain King.* New York: Charles Scribner's Sons, 1973.

Stuck, Hudson. *The Ascent of Denali (Mount McKinley).* New York: Charles Scribner's Sons, 1914.

Styles, Showell. *On Top of the World.* New York: The Macmillan Company, 1967.

Thomas, Lowell. *Lowell Thomas' Book of the High Mountains.* New York: Julian Messner, Inc., 1964.

Tilman, H. W. *Snow on the Equator.* New York: The Macmillan Company, 1938.

Ullman, James Ramsey. *The Age of Mountaineering.* New York and Philadelphia: J. B. Lippincott Company, 1964.

Unsworth, Walter. *Because It Is There.* London: Victor Gollancz Ltd., 1968.

___ . *Tiger in the Snow–The Life and Adventures of A. F. Mummery.* London: Victor Gollancz Ltd., 1967.

Whymper, Edward. *Travels Amongst the Great Andes of the Equator.* London: John Murray, 1892.

Zurbriggen, Matthias. *From the Alps to the Andes.* London: T. Fisher Unwin, 1899.

Periodicals

The most important club publications that cover the areas described in this book are the *Alpine Journal, American Alpine Journal, Himalayan Journal,* and *Sierra Club Bulletin.*

Index

Italicized numbers refer to illustrations.

A

Aarau, 87
Abraham Lincoln: A History (Hay), 206
Adams, Henry, 207
Adams-Reilly, Anthony, 70, 240–41
Adelboden, 94
Adler Pass (Haute Route), 232, 237, 245, 262
Africa, 130
Agassiz, Louis, 198–99
Agelu, 132, 133, 137, 145, 155, 158, 159, 172
Aiguille Verte. *See* Verte, Aiguille.
Ainu, 179, 180
Akahito, Yamabe, 174
Alcock, Rutherford, 188
Aleutians, 179
Alexander, the Great, 52
Allmen, Albert von, 98, 100
Allmen, Hilti von, 59
Alluvial Epoch, 179
Almberger, Walter, 111
Almer, Christian, 69, 70, 72, 89, 90, 91
Alpine Club, 101, 117, 220, 242, 260
Alpine Journal, 29, 80, 116, 221
Alpine superstitions, 15, 66–67
Alps, 14, 16, 28, 44, 48, 50, 51, 55, 59, 65, 66, 68, 72, 82, 85, 91, 92, 93, 95, 96, 97, 107, 112, 116, 129, 229, 237, 240, 242, 245, 247, 250, 259, 263
Alps in 1864, The (Moore), 242
Ama Dablam, *133,* 149, 151, *151, 154,* 159, *159*
Amatter, Fritz, 92
Amazon River, 130
American Revolution, 14
Amsterdam, 203
Amundsen, Roald, 130
Ancien Passage, 22, 25, *26,* 44
Ang Chatter, 132, 146, 148
Ang Dawa, 132, 165, 169
Angerer, Willi, 98, 100, 101
Ang Tsering, 132, 135, 137, 161, 172
Ang Tshering, 129
Annals of Mont Blanc, The (Mathews), 30
Annapurna 42, 107, 113, 172, *172*
Annapurna, (Herzog), 137
Annapurna Sanctuary, 172
Antarctic, 155
Aosta (Italy), 221, 261
Apache tribes, 197
Apette Valley, 255
Arctic, 36
Argentière, 245, 247, 254
Argentière, Aiguille d', 69, *222, 223,* 236, 240, 241, 244, 245, 250, 251
Argentière, Col d' (Haute Route), 220, 222
Argentière Glacier (Haute Route), 250
Argentière Hut (Haute Route), 220, 248, 249

Armington, Stan, 131, 132, 139, 140, 145, 147, 155, 161
Arnold, Phil, 203
Arolla, Switzerland, 232, 237, 262
Arolla, Pigne d'. *See* Pigne d' Arolla.
Arun River Valley, 131, 168, *171*
Arve Gap, 36
Ashburner, William, 198
Asia, 224
Asiatic Plate, 163
Atlantic Ocean, 130
Augustianian Monks, 86
Austria, 102, 106, 248
Austrian Expedition (Everest), 130
Austro-Hungarian Empire, 68
Averill, Chester, 198

B

Badille, Piz, 59, 109
Baglern, 224
Balmat, Auguste, *40,* 89, 238, *239*
Balmat, Jacques, 16, 19, 21, *26,* 27, 30, 34, 45, 46ff., 238
 age, 16
 ascent of Mont Blanc, 13–14, 21–24
 attempt on Mont Blanc, 19
 dispute with Paccard, 24, 27, 28, 30, 31
 Dumas interview, 28–29
 hunter, 16
Balme, Col de, 221, 253
Banner Peak, 218
Barbary Coast, 197
Barrington, Charles, 90–91
Base Camp (Everest), 131, *133,* 153, 159, 161, 165
Basho, 185
Bathgate, David, 163
Bavaria, 107
Beaujard, 232
Beer, Gavin de, *The First Ascent of Mont Blanc,* 31
 passim, 62, 83
Begole, Charley, 208
Beich Pass, 87
Belgium, 248
Bellevue, 31
Belshaw, G. W., 205
Bennen, J. J., 69
Berlin, 106
Bernard, Jean-Pierre, 236
Bernese Alps, 85, 87, 89, 107, 111, 114
Bernese Oberland, 50, 85, 88, 91, 228, 260
Bernina, Piz, 196, 220, 232
Bertol Hut (Haute Route), 232
Bhadgaon, 126
Bhandar (Changma), 140, 142
Biener, Franz, 69, 70, 72
Bionnassay, Aiguille de, 32, 36
Bionnassay Glacier, 19, 31, 46
Birkbeiner, 224
Bishop, Barry, 115, 129
Biwa, Lake, 179
Blake, William, *Gnomic Verses,* 31
Blanc de Cheilon, Mont, *249, 250, 252,* 258
Blanc de Courmayeur, Mont, 24
Blanc du Tacul, Mont, 26, 39
Blanche, Dent, 61, 65, 69, 232, 253, *258,* 259, 260
Blanche, Tête, 222
Blanche, Vallée, 42, 249
Blanc, Mont, 13ff.
 first ascent, 13, *15,* 20, 23, 25, *26, 33, 38, 41, 44, 46,* 52, 55, 61, 73, 85, 96, 116, 155, 198, 220, 223, 228, 229, 233, *233,* 236, 237, 242, 260
 views, 34, 37, 38, 39, 40, 44–45.
 See also separate entries for other features of mountain.
Blava, Col de la (Haute Route), 258
Blava, Mont, 256
Boardman, Peter, 130
Bohren, Peter, 90, 91
Bonatti, Walter, 59, *82*
Bonington, Chris, 129
Borders of the Impossible, The (Terray), 84

Bortes, Joseph, 88
Bosses Ridge (Mont Blanc), 43, 44
Bossons Glacier (Mont Blanc), 18, *18,* 19, *26*
Boswell, James, 116
Bouquetins, Dent des, 222
Bourdillon, Tom, 127
Bourg Saint Pierre, 222, 232, 245
Bourrit, Isaac, 20
Bourrit, Marc-Théodore, 16, 19, 20, 21, 24, 25, 30, 31, 32, 34
Bozon, Charles, 42
Bozon, Norbert, 31, 32, 33, 36, 37, 42, 43, *44,* 45
Brahmins, 135, 244
Braithwaite, Paul, 129
Brasher, Chris, 155
Braward, Samuel, 92
Bregaglia, 109
Breithorn, 96, 223
Breney, Col de (Haute Route), 252, 259
Brenva Ridge (Mont Blanc), 242
Breuil, 67, 68, 72, 73, 74, 78, 82
Brevent, Le, 16, 21
Brewer, Mount, 199
Brewer, William H., 198, 199, 200, *201,* 202, 205
Brig, Switzerland, 228
British Expeditions (Everest)
 1921: 117–20
 1922: 120–21
 1924: 121–25
 1951: 125
 1953: 126–29
 1972: 151, 153, 154, 163–65, 168
 1975: 129–30
British-Nepal Expedition (Everest), 130
Brittania Hut (Haute Route), 245
Broad Peak, 107
Broderson, Tom, 131, 132, 134, 135, 146, 161
Brouillard Pillar (Mont Blanc), 45
Brown, Charlie, 50, 52–64
Brown, T. Graham, *The First Ascent of Mount Blanc,* 31
Bruce, Brig. Gen. C. G., 117, 120, 121
Brule, Col du Mont (Haute Route), 245
Bruneau, Jean, 106, 108
Buddhist customs and religion, 132, 140, 142, *143,* 182, 183, 184, 188
Buhl, Hermann, 106, 108, 109
Bullfrog Lake, 216
Bullock, G. H., 119
Bung, 168, 170
Bupsa Ridge 145, *146*
Burke, Mick, 130
Busti, 136
Buxton, T. Fowell, 221
Byrd, Bill, 51
Byron, Lord, *Manfred,* 38

C

Caesar, Julius, 52
California, 198, 206, 226
California Academy of Sciences, 205
California Geological Survey, 198, 199, *201*
Calvinist oligarchy, 16
Cambridge University, 115, 220
Capital of the Tycoon, The (Alcock), 188–89
Capitan, El, 85
Carrel, Caesar, 72
 Jean-Antoine, 68, *68,* 76, 81
  age 67
  attempts on Matterhorn, 68, 69
  meets Whymper, 67
  misleads Whymper, 72
  occupation, 67
  obsession to climb Matterhorn, 67, 68, 69
  race to summit, 52
  traits, 67

281

Capitan, El, *Continued*
   Jean-Jacques, 67
   Louis, 82
Carson City, Nevada, 199, 226
Cassin, Ricardo, 110, 111
Caucasus, 242
Central Dauphine Alps, 65
Cervin, Mont (Matterhorn), 67
Cervin, Tête du (Matterhorn), 60, 63, 76
Cervinia, 63, *74*
Chamberlain, Basil H., 180, 182
Chamlang, 144
Chamonix, 14, 16, 18, 19, 20, 21, *26*, 30, 31, 32, 34, 38, 40, 42, 46, 69, 70, 73, 82, 220, 221, 222, 228, 232, 233, 236, 237, 238, 239, 242, 245, 246, 247, 248
Champex, Switzerland, *231*, 245, 254, 255
Changma (Bhandar), 140, 142
Changtse (North Peak), 119, 154
Chanrion, Switzerland, 260
Chanrion Hut (Haute Route), 229, 232, 245
Chardonnet, Aiguille d', *221*, 232, 241, 251, 253
Chardonnet, Col du (Haute Route) *226*, 228, 229, 240, 245, 251, 253
Chardonnet Glacier (Haute Route), *224, 225*, 250
Charenge River, 134
Charlet, Henri, 240
Charmoz, Grand, 45
Charterhouse, 116
Chateaubriand, Francois, 38
Châtillon, Switzerland, 221
Chaunrikharka, 142, 146
Cheilon, Col de (Haute Route), 232
Cheilon Glacier (Haute Route), 258
Cheilon, Mont Blanc de. *See* Blanc de Cheilon, Mont.
Chermontane Glacier, 222
Chermontane, Switzerland, 222
Chetris, 135, 140
Chevalley, Dr. Gabriel, 126
Chiara, Giacoma, 82
Chicago, University of, 180
Chimborazo, 82
Chinese communists, 129
Chinese folk tales, 182
Chinese-Tibetan Expedition (Everest), 129, 130
Chisapani, 138
Choba Bhamare, 138
Chogolisa, 107
Chomolungma (Mount Everest), 119, 144
Cho Oyu, 119
Christiania, Norway, 227
Christiania Turn, 227
Chudo Circuit (Mount Fuji), 184
Churchill, Johnny, 51
Churchill, Lord Randolph, 242
Cima Grande, 59
Civil War, 226
Clarence King, Mount, 202, 210, 211, *211, 212*, 217
Clark, Mount, 202
Clark's Ranch, 202
Clyde Meadows, 210
Coleridge, Samuel Taylor, 38
Collon, Col (Haute Route), 232
Collon, Mont Glacier, *261*
Collon, Petit Mont, *261*, 261
Colorado, 113, 203
Columbus, Christopher, 28, 34
Combin, Grand, 45, 65, 116, 222, 223, 229, 232, 236, 245, 253, 260
Como, Lake, 109
Comstock Lode, 199
Congress (United States), 226
Cook, Dr. Frederick A., 190
Coq, Crête du (Matterhorn), 67, 68, *70*
Corcoran, Mount 205
Cornier, Grand, 69
Corridor (Mont Blanc), 44
Corti, Claudio, 109, 110, 111
Côte, Montagne de la (Mont Blanc), 19, 21, *23, 24, 26, 27*
Cotter, Mount, 211

Cotter, Richard, 198, 199, 200, *201, 202*, 210
Couloir, Plateau de (Haute Route), 232
Courchevel, 248
Courmayeur, 70, 221, 229, 249
Couronne, Hotel de la (Chamonix), 28, 29
Courtes, 245
Couttet, Jean-Marie, 20
Couttet, Jules, 229
Couvercle Hut, 232
Crabtree Meadows, 209
Crapo, Bill, 208
Cravate, 67, 69, *70*, 76
Crawford, C. G., 121
Creole Proverbs, 182
Crimea, 73
Cro-Magnon Man, 179
Croz, Michel-Auguste, 69, 70, 73, 75, *75, 76, 78, 78*, 79, 80, 81, 240–41
Cuidet, Francois, 20

D

Daimyo, 183, 188
Dainichi Temple, 184
Dalai Lama, 103, 117, 128
Dandapani, 172
Darbellay, Michel, 112
Darjeeling, 118
Darwinian Doctrine, 182
Day Needle, 204
Death Bivouac (Eiger), 97, 98, *99*, 113
Denman, Earl, 128
Dent Blanche. *See* Blanche, Dent.
Dent d'Hérens. *See* Hérens, Dent d'.
Descriptive Sketches (Wordsworth), 219
Desert Glacier, Grand (Haute Route), 256
Dhankuta, 168
Dharan, 131, 168, 172
Dhaulagiri, 110
Diablerets, 232
Diablerets Glacier, 96
Diamond Mesa, 203
Dickens, Charles, 38
Difficult Crack (Eiger), 97
Direttissima, 86, *99*, 112, 113
Disraeli, Benjamin, 38
Dix Hut (Haute Route), 233, 246, 249, 258
Dix Lake (Haute Route), *240*, 258
Dolent, Mont, 69, 250
Dom, 65, 228
Dôme, Col du, 43
Dome of Inyo, (Mount Whitney), 208
Doré, Gemalde von G., 77, 78
Dorées, Aiguilles, *229, 230*, 237, 252
Douglas, Lord Francis, 73, *75, 76, 78, 79*, 80, 81
Dovre Mountains, 224
Droites, Les. *See* Les Droites.
Dru, 45
Dru, Petit, 232
Dübi, Dr. Henrich, 30
Dubost, Louis, 128
Dudh Kosi, 145, 147, 148
Dufourspitze (Monte Rosa), 73, 223
Duglha, 154
Dumas, Alexandre, 28, 29, 38
   Impressions de Voyage, 28
Durant, Mont, 222

E

Eagle's Nest (Wills), 238
East Face (Matterhorn), 70, 71, 72
East Face (Mount Whitney), *204*, 210
East Rongbuk Glacier, 119, 120
Ecandies, Col des (Haute Route), 255
Ediza, Lake, 218
Edo (Tokyo), 179
Eiger, 42, 50, 59, 61, 85, *85, 89*, 91, 94, 96, *100*, 101, *108*, 114, 163, 221. *See also* Eigerwand.
   first ascent, 90–91

   of Mittellegi ridge, 92
   of northeast side, 91, 92
   name, 85
   views, 96
Eigergletscher, 86, 111
Eiger, Mönch, and Jungfrau (Frothingham), 84
Eigerwand, 86, 92, 96–114, *97, 99, 100, 102, 104, 107*, 129
   deaths, 96, 98, 100–101, 111
   direttissima, 112–13
   fastest ascent, 113–14
   first ascent, 102–106
   first ascent solo, 112
   first winter ascent, 111–12
   rescue, 109–11
   views, 96.
   See also separate entries for other features of mountain.
Eiselin, Max, 110
Eismeer Station (Eiger), 86
Elbruz, Mount, 242
Emma Mines Scandal, 203
Emmons Glacier (Mount Rainier), 43
Engel, Claire Eliane, 38
England, 121
Ennogyoja. *See* Shōkaku, En-no-.
Ecuador, 82
Erin, Col d', 221
Eseltritte (Matterhorn), 58
Estcourt, Nick, 129
Etna, Mount, 17, 179
Etter, Paul, 99
Evans, Charles, 127
Eveque, Col de l', 229, 245
Eveque, l', *261*
Everest, George, 117
Everest, Mount, 113, 115, 117, *119, 123, 125, 126*, 132, *133*, 135, 146, 147, 150, 151, 152, 155, 158, *160*, 163, 165, 166, 168, 172, 210
   attempts from south, 125–26, 128, 138
   deaths, 118, 121, 130
   descriptions, 118–19, 144
   early attempts from north, 120–25, 128
   first ascent, 126–28
      by Americans, 129
      by female, 129
      by southwest face, 129–30, 155
      from north, 129
      solo, 130
      without supplementary oxygen, 130
   first traverse, 129
   reconnaissance, 117–20, 125
   solo ascent from high camp, 130
   total ascents, 130
   views, 144, 159.
   See also separate entries for other features of mountain.
Everest – The West Ridge (Hornbein), 115
Exit Cracks (Eiger), 97–98, *99*, 105, 110
Exotics and Retrospectives (Hearn), 182

F

Favre, 72
Finch, Capt. George, 120
Fin Dome, 210, 212
Finland, 224
Finsteraar Glacier, 88
Finsteraarhorn, 87, 96, *107*, 220, 228
First Ascent of Mont Blanc, The (de Beer and Brown), 31
First Icefield (Eiger), 97, 98, *99*, 100
First Pillar (Eiger), *97, 99*
First Step (Everest), 123–24, *124*, 125
Fisherman's Peak, 208
Flatiron (Eiger), 97, 98
Fonds, Glacier des, 47
Fontaine, Emile, 232
Forbes, James D., 21, 221, 236, 237
Fortieth Parallel Survey, 202, 203
Fort, Mont, 233, 246, 255
Fort, Mont Hut (Haute Route), 255, 257

Fou, Aiguille du, 113
Fowler, Robert, 241
Fowler's Peak, 208
France, 14, 42, 47, 94, 106, 220, 249
Franco-German Expedition (Everest), 130
French Expedition (Pumori), 152–54
French Revolution, 47
Freney Pillar (Mont Blanc), 45
Freshfield, Douglas W., 21, 29, 242
Fréty, Mont, 229
Fried, Andy, 210, 212, 215, 217
Frothingham, Nathaniel L., *Eiger, Mönch, and Jungfrau,* 84
Fubershaw, Gerard, 210, 214, 216, 217
Fuchs, Alfred, 86, 93, 94
Fujiko, 174, 180, 184, 193
Fuji, Mount. *See* Fujisan.
Fuji-no-Miya, 187
Fuji-no-Miya Trail (Mount Fuji), 190
Fujisan (Fujiyama), *176, 178, 178, 180, 181, 186, 187,* 190–96
  art, 174, 186–87
  eruptions, 179
  fast climb, 190
  first ascents
    by female (possibly), 189
    by foreigner, 188–89
    by male (possibly), 187
  formation, 179
  name, 179–80, 186
  passim, 192, 194
  poetry and verses, 174, 175, 177, 180–81, 185, 194, 196
  religious, cultural, mythological and historical aspects, 174, 175, 177, 183–86
  trails, 190
  views, 173, 175
  winter ascents, 189–90.
  See also separate entries for other features of mountain.
Fujisan-Ki (Miyako-no-Yoshika), 187
Fujisawa River, 180
Fujiyama — The Sacred Mountain of Japan (Starr), 180
Funatsu Trail (Mount Fuji), 190
Furggen Ridge (Matterhorn), 67, 69, *70,* 82
Furrer, Otto, 52
Furri, 83

G

Gabb, William M., 198
Gabelhorn, 73, 233
Gardiner, James T., 198, 199, 201, *201*
Gardiner, Mount, 202
Gauri Sankar, *133,* 138
Gautier, Theophile, 38
Géant, Aiguille du, 232
Géant, Col du, 17, *27,* 221, 229, 237
Géant, Dent du, 45
Geneva, 14, 16, 30, 36, 47
Geneva Academy, 15
Genoa, Nevada, 226
Geological Exploration of the Fortieth Parallel, 202
Geological Survey, 206, 207
Germany, 102, 106, 268
Gersdorf, Adolf Traugott von, 30
Gillman, Peter, 113
Giordano, Felice, 72, 76, 78
Glace, Mer de, 16, *17,* 42
Glacial Age, 179
Glatthard, Arnold, 101
Glen Pass, 213, 214, *214,* 215, 216
Gletscherhorn, 87
Gletschetstafel, 87
Glosser Aletschfirn, 87
Gnomic Verses (Blake), 31
Godiva, Lady, 52
Goethe, Johann Wolfgang, 38, 39
Golden Age of Mountaineering, 65, 88
Golden Trout Lake, 210
Gombu, Nawang, 129, 130
Goodyear, W. A., 205, 206

Gorak Shep, 126, 147, 155, 159, 161
Görlitz, 30
Gotemba, 173, 190
Gotemba Trail (Mount Fuji), 190
Gould, Mount, 211
Goûter, Aiguille du (Mont Blanc), 19, 20, 32–33, *33,* 34, *35,* 36
Goûter, Dome du (Mont Blanc), 18, 19, 20, 21, *26,* 32, 41
Goûter, Refuge du (Mont Blanc), 32, 36
Graian Alps, 260
Gramminger, Ludwig, 110
Grand Combin. *See* Combin, Grand.
Grand Desert Glacier. *See* Desert Glacier, Grand.
Grand Plateau. *See* Plateau, Grand.
Gratz, University of, 103
Graven, Alexander, 92, 93
Graves, Robert, 116
Great Tower (Matterhorn), 67, 68, *70*
Greenland, 14, 227
Grépon, 45, 229
Grimsel Pass, 87, 88, 90, 228
Grindelwald, 85, 88, 90, 91, 100, 103, 242
Gstaad, 96
Gudel, 168, 170
Guilini, René, 248, 249
Guldbrandsdal, Norway, 224
Gulu, Lama, 151
Gurkhas, 120
Gustavus, Eriksson. *See* Gustav Vasa.
Gustav, Vasa, King of Sweden, 224–25
Gyoja, 187

H

Haakon, Haakonson, King of Norway, 224
Habeler, Peter, 113, 130
Habran, Paul, 106
Hadow, Douglas, 73, 74, *75,* 76, *78,* 79, 80, 81
Hadrian, Emperor, 17
Hague, James D., *Mining Industry,* 207
Hakimondo, 189
Hakone Range, 188
Hannibal, 52
Hardy, Rev. John F., 220
Harlin, John, 86
  attempt on Eigerwand, 112–13
  death, 113
  direttissima, 86, 112, 113
Harrer, Heinrich
  ascent of Eigerwand, 103–106
  Seven Years in Tibet, 103
  student, 103
Harris, Wyn, 124
Harrow, 242
Harte, Bret, 207
Hartley University College, 237
Haston, Dougal, 113, 130, 163
Haute Route, La, 219ff.
  classic route, 245
  information on clothing, equipment, conditions, season, 246–47
  passim, 219ff., *220–61.*
  See also separate entries for passes, glaciers, and huts on route.
Hayes, Rutherford B. (president), 206
Hay, John, *Abraham Lincoln: A History,* 206
Hearn, Lafcadio, 181–83
  Exotics and Retrospectives, 182
  Japan — An Attempt at Interpretations, 182
Heckmair, Anderl
  age, 102
  ascent of Eigerwand, 102–106
  occupation, 102
Helbing, Robert, 228, 232
Hellepart, Alfred, 110
Hérens, Col d' (Haute Route), 229, 232
Hérens, Dent d', *257,* 259
Herzog, Maurice, *Annapurna,* 137
Hidden Peak, 114, 130
Hiebeler, Toni, 111

High Level Route. *See* Haute Route, La.
High Sierra, 43, 132, 197, 198, 199, 202, 205, 206, 208, *209,* 210, 212, *213,* 215, 217, *217,* 218, 226
Hile, 168
Hillary, Edmund, 126, 147, 155, 168
  age, 129
  ascent of Everest, 127–28
Hillary School and Bridges, 147, 148
Himalayan Range, formation, 161, 163
Himalayas, 42, 92, 103, 114, 126, 129, 131, 132, 135, 137, 138, 140, 143, *144,* 149, 150, 151, 155, 159, 166, *171,* 172, 233, 244
Hindustani, 120
Hinterstoisser, Anderl, 98, 100
Hinterstoisser Traverse (Eiger), 97, 98, *99,* 100, 109
Hiroshige, *One Hundred Views of Fuji,* 174
  Thirty-Six Views of Fuji, 174
Hitler, Adolf, 106
Hockett Trail, 202
Hoei Crater (Mount Fuji), 179
Hoek, Dr. Henry, 228
Hoffman, Charles F., 198, 199, 200
Hokkaido, 179
Hokusai, 186–87
  One Hundred Views of Fuji, 174, 186
  Thirty-Six Views of Fuji, 174, 186
  Three Lucky Things, 187
  Three Whites, 187
Holland. *See* Netherlands, The.
Holmenkollen, 227
Homer, 39
Horace, *Odes,* 128
Hongu Basin Peaks, 159
Hongu River, 168
Honshu, 179
Hood, Mount, 132
Hornbein, Tom, 129
  Everest — The West Ridge, 115
Hörnlihütte (Matterhorn), 50, 52, 63, 83
Hörnli Ridge (Matterhorn) 49, 52, *54,* 57, 60, 63, *64,* 67, *70,* 73, *82*
Hospice, 88
Hoting Ski, 224
Hours of Exercise in the Alps (Tyndall), 199
Howard, Dr. William, 32
Howard-Bury, Lt. Col. C. K., 117
Howells, William Dean, 207
Hudson, J. A., 220
Hudson, Rev. Charles, 43, 73, *75,* 76, *78,* 79, 80, 81
Hugo, Victor, 38, 39
Hunt, Col. John, 126
Hupfauer, Sigi, 113

I

Ice Age, 86
Iceberg Lake, 210, 218
Ice Hose (Eiger), 97
Imja Basin, 152, *153,* 168
Imja Khola, 150
Imperial University, 182
Impressions de Voyage (Dumas), 28
Independence, California, 209, 210, 217
India, 103, 118, 120, 131, 134, 172, 242, 244
Indian Expedition (Everest), 130
India Plate, 163
Interlaken, 86
International Expedition (Everest), 163
Inukhu Kosi, 168
Ionian Islands, 181
Irvine, Andrew, 123, 124, 125, *125*
Irving, R. L. Graham, 116
Iselin, Colonel Christoph, 228
Ishikawajozen, 196
Italian Expedition (Everest), 130
Italian Ridge (Matterhorn), 67, 70
Italy, 76
Ite Ibe. *See* Miroku.
Ito, 190

J

Jacomb, Frederick W., 220, 221, 222
   Peak, Passes, and Glaciers, 221
James, Henry, 207
Jangbo, 164
Jannu, 42, 172
Japan — An Attempt at Interpretations (Hearn), 182
Japanese Alps, 175
Japanese Expedition (Everest)
   1969: 129
   1975: 129, 130
Javelle, Émile, 236, 244, 253
Jerstad, Lute, 129, 132, 144
Jirels, 137
Jöchler, Sepp, 106, 109
Johnson, Albert H., 208
Johnson, G. R., 220
Jonction (Mont Blanc), 19, 21, *26*
Jonsong Peak, 233
Jorasses, Grandes, *17*, 44, *45*, 59, 65, 69, 107, 110
Jorsale, 149
Jubing, 127, 145
Junbesi, 127, *133*, 136, 142, 143, *144*, 145
Jungfrau, 50, 85, *85*, 86, 87, 88, 89, *89*, 90, 94, 96, *108*, 112, *112*, 114
   first ascent, 90–91
   north face, 91–92
   name, 85, 86–87
   views, 96
Jungfraujoch, 86, 93, 221, 242

K

Kado-no-Azuma-Maro, 194
Kakugyo (Takematsu), 184
Kala Pattar, 149, 155, 158, *158*, 166
Kampa Dzong, 118
Kangchenjunga, 172, 233
Kangshung Face, 127
Kantega, 143, 149, *150*, 151, 159, 163
Karakoram Range, 103, 107
Karma, 187
Karyolung, 143, 145, 149, 163
Kasparek, Fritz, 103, 104, 106
Katmandu, 126, 130, 139, 153
Kaufmann, Christian, 89
Kaufmann, Ulrich, 89
Kawaguchi, Lake, 175, 191
Kawaguchiko Trail (Mount Fuji), 190
Kaweah River, 202
Kearsarge Pass, 202, 213, 215, 216, *216*, 217
Kearsarge Peak, 210, 216
Keeler Needle, 204
Keiser Pass, 228
Kellas, Dr. A. M., 117, 118
Kengamine (Mount Fuji), 194, 195
Kennedy, E. S., 43
Kern Canyon, 208
Kern Valley, 203
Khari Khola, 145
Kharte, 145
Khimte River, 138, 139, 140
Khumbila, 146, 149
Khumbu Glacier (Mount Everest), 119, *126*, 131, 147, 151, 152, 154, *154*, *157*, *158*, 159, 161, *162*, *163*, 165, 167
Khumbu Icefall (Mount Everest), 126, *126*, 127, 159, 163, *163*, *164*, 165, 166
Khumbu Region, 127, 139, 140, *141*, 149, 158, 168, 172
Khumbutse, 154
Kilimanjaro, 258
King, Clarence, 198–208, 210, 218
   acquaintances, 207
   ascent of Mount Tyndall, 199–202
   attempts on Mount Whitney, 202, 203–206
   birth, 198
   death, 208
   education, 198
   Emma Mines scandal exposed, 203
   exploration of High Sierra, 199–202, *201*
   Fortieth Parallel Survey, 202–203
   head of Geological Survey, 206–207
   meets Brewer and Whitney, 199
   mistakes Mount Langley for Mount Whitney, 203–206
   Mountaineering in the Sierra Nevada, 197, 200, 207
   personal experiences, 199, 202
   quotes and writings, 197, 199–202
   reputation, 206–207
   Systematic Geology, 202
   traits, 198, 206
   trip west, 199
King, Mount Clarence. *See* Clarence King, Mount.
Kings Canyon, 210, 215
Kings-Kern Divide, Great, 200, 210
Kinshofer, Toni, 111
Kirantichap, *133*, 136
Kleine Matterhorn, 17
Kleine Scheidegg, 86, 92, 97, 98, *102*, 113, 242
Knubel, Josef, 92, 228
Kodari Highway, 130
Kolzow-Massalsky, Hélène (Dora d'Istria), 89
Kor, Layton, 113
Kronig, Herman, 232
Kronig, Johann, 222
Kunde, 155
Kuriles, 179
Kurz, Louis, 233
Kurz, Marcel, 232, 235, 256
   The Mountain World, 233
Kurz, Toni, 98, 100, 101
Kusushi Shrine (Mount Fuji), 193
Kwangde, 146, 149
Kyoto, 183

L

La Chaux Glacier (Haute Route), 256
La Chaux Pass (Haute Route), 256
Lachenal, Louis, 42, 106
La Forclaz, 254
Lambert, Raymond, 126
Lamjura Ridge, 142
Lamosangu, 130, 132, *133*, 147, 172
Langley, Mount, 205, 206, 208, 218
Lapland, 225
Las Priestas Mine, 207
Lassen, Mount, 198, 199
Las Yedras Mine, 207
Lauener, Ulrich, 88
Lauper, Hans, 91
   ascent of Eiger, 91, 92, 93, 96
   ascent of Jungfrau, 91, 92
   ascent of Mönch, 91,
   occupation, 91
Lauteraar Glacier, 88
Lauterbrunnen, 85, 86
Lavoie, Claire, 131, 132, 134, 140, 145
Lecco, 109
Leeches, 140
Le Fayet, 34
Lehne, Jörg, 113
Lehner, Richard, 52–64 *passim,* 62
L'Englishe, Place de, 29
Le Prarion, 31, 40
Le Prieuré, 42
Leroux, Pierre, 106
Les Attelas, 255
Les Droites, *220*, 245, 249
Les Écrins, 69, 242
Les Haudères, 229
Les Houches, 247
Les Pélerins, 16
Le Tour, 254
Letters on the First Journey to the Summit of Mont Blanc (Bourrit), 24
Leyda, Abe, 207
Leysin, 113

Lhakpa La, 119
Lhasa, 103, 128
Lho La, 159
Lhotse, 126, *126*, *133*, 144, 150, 155, 159, 160
Likhu River, 140
Lindbergh, Charles, 130
Lingtren, 154
Liniger, Max, 91
Lion, Col du (Matterhorn), 67, *70*
Lion, Tête du (Matterhorn), 67
Lobuje, *133*, 152, 155, 161, 166
Lognan, France, 247
London, 65, 203
London *Daily Telegraph,* 113
London *Observer,* 155
London *Times,* 80
Lone Pine, California, 203, 205, 209, 218
Lone Pine Creek, 209
Lone Pine Lake, 209
Longhi, Stefano, 109, 110
Longman, William, 65
Los Angeles, 217
Lowell, James Russell, 207
Lubin, Ed, 210, 215, 217
Lucas, Johnny, 208
Lukla, 147, 152
Lunn, Arnold, 101, 228
Lyskamm, 61, 65, 220

M

McDonough, Tom, 208
MacInnes, Hamish, 163
McKinley, Mount, 217
Magdalene College, 115
Magellan, Ferdinand, 130
Magg, Otto, 106, 108
Magg, Sepp, 106
Magnone, Guido, 106
Mainichi (Tokyo), 195
Makalu, 42, 128, 172
Maki, Yuko, 92
Mallory, George H. Leigh, 166
   attempts on Everest, 120–25, *123*, 128
   birth, 115
   climbs with Irving, 116
   death, 123–25
   describes Everest, 118–19
   descriptions of Mallory, 116, 117, 118, 121–22
   education, 115
   ice ax found, 125, *125*
   other climbs, 116
   reconnaissance of Everest, 117–20
   talents, 115, 116
   writings and quotes, 116, 123, 144, 150, 159
Mammoth Mountain, 218
Manang Valley, 172
Manaslu, 92, 130
Manfred (Byron), 38
Manidingma, 145
Mani Walls, 140, 142
Mannhardt, Anderl, 111
Männlichen, 112
Manyoshu, The (The Collection of Myriad Leaves), 173, 185
Marengo, 47
Mariana Trench, 130
Mariposa, 119, 202
Marquis of Queensberry, 73
Martel, Pierre, 16
Martigny, Switzerland, 45, 221
Martin, Alf von, 232
Mathews, Charles Edward, 30
Mathews, William, 221
Matsudai, 184
Matterhorn, 17, 42, 43, 45, 48ff.
   accident, *78*, 79–81, 240
   first ascent, 74–81, *77*
   by female, 55
   of Furggen ridge district, 82
   of north face, 59
   of Zmutt ridge, 82

Matterhorn, *Continued*
  first solo winter ascent, 59
  first traverse, 82
  passim, 49, 51, 53, 59, 70, 71, 74, 82, 85, 88, 90, 91, 94, 95, 107, 111, 115, 154, 199, 220, 257
  views, 61, 65, 66.
  See also separate entries for other features of mountain.
Matterhorngletscher, 54, 79
Matterhorn, The (Rey), 48
Mattervisp Gorge, 50
Maudit, Mont, 16, *26*
Mauna Loa, 179
Mauri, Carlo, 110
Mayer, Franz, 109, 110, 111
Mégeve, 34
Mehringer, Karl, 98
Meiji Restoration, 183, 189
Menlungtse, 138
Mer de Glace, 16, *17*
Messner, Reinhold, 113, 130
Mexican volcanoes, 217
Meyer, Gottlieb, 88
Meyer, Hieronymous, 87
Meyer, Johann Rudolf II, 87, 88
Meynet, Luc, 69
Michelet, Jules, 40
Midi, Aiguille du, 29
Milan, 259
Minarets, The, 202, 218
Mining Industry (Hague), 207
Miroku (Ite Ibe), 184
Mirror Lake, 209
Mishabels, 61
Mobberly, Cheshire, 115
Mönch, 65, 85, *85*, 86, *89*, 92, 93–96, *93, 95, 108, 112,* 113, 114, 228, 242
  first ascent, 89
  of north face, 91
  name, 85
  views, 95–96
Mongoloid extraction, 145
Monk (Mönch), 85
Monsoon, 121
Montagnier, H. F., 30
Mont Blanc. *See* Blanc, Mont.
Mont Blanc (Shelley), 13
Mont Cervin Hotel, 73
Monte Rosa. *See* Rosa, Monte.
Monte Rosa Hotel, 73, 79
Montenvers, 21, 232, 241
Montets, Grands, 247, 248
Moore, A. W., 221, 236, 242, *243,* 251, 253, 259
  The Alps in 1964, 242
Mora, Sweden, 224, 225
Morgedal, Norway, 227
Morshead, H. T., 120
Moseley Slab (Matterhorn), 58
Moslem, 117
Mother Lode, 197
Motosu, Lake, 178
Mount Everest. *See* Everest, Mount.
Mount Everest Committee, 117
Mount Fuji. *See* Fujisan.
Mountaineering in the Sierra Nevada (King), 197, 200, 207
Mountaineer's Route (Mount Whitney), 204, 209, 218
Mountains of California, The (Muir), 197
Mountain World, The, (Kurz), 233
Mudi, 134
Muir, John, 198, 202, 206, 209, 218
  The Mountains of California, 197
  Trail, 209, 213
Mulets, Grands (Mont Blanc), 19, 21, *23, 26,* 43, 45
Mulets, Petits (Mont Blanc), 22, 30
Mummery, A. F., 82
Munich, 98, 111
Munich School of Climbing, 97
Murayama, 188, 190
Mürren, 86, 114
Mushimaro Collection, The, 173
Mylius, Hugo, 228

N

Nagoud, 156, 159
Nai-in Sanctuary (Mount Fuji), 193
Namche Bazar, 126, 127, *133,* 139, 142, 146, 147, 148, 149, 153, 155, 166
Namdu, 136
Nanda Devi, 128
Nanda Devi East, 128
Nanga Parbat, 103, 106, 128, 130
Nansen, Fridtjof, 227
Napoleon Bonaparte, 46, 47
National Academy of Sciences, 203
Neanderthal Man, 179
Nepal, 118, 125, 130, *131,* 133, 134, 136, 146, 148, 152, *170, 171,* 172
  culture, customs, economy and language, 132, 134, 135, 137–38, 139–40, 149
Netherlands, The, 248, 250
Neuchâtel, Switzerland, 232
Newars, 135
New Zealand, 223
Nicheren, 184
Nigale, 134
Nihon Bridge, 187
Nihon-shoki (Chronicles of Japan), 185
Nile River, 130
Nill, Herb, 51
Nillerton, 202
Nippon Times (Tokyo), 195–96
Nixon, Richard M. (president), 165
Nobel Peace Prize, 228
Noel, Capt. John B., 117, 118
Noir, Tête, 221
Norgay, Tenzing
  age, 129
  ascent of Everest, 127–28
  attempts on Everest, 126, 128–29
  birth, 128
  other climbs, 128
Norheim, Sondre, 227
Norsemen, 14
North Col (Everest), 119, 120, 121, 122, 123, 125, 128, 129
North Dragon Pass, 210, 213
Northeast Ridge (Everest), 120, 122, *124,* 125, *126*
North Face (Eiger). *See* Eigerwand.
North Face (Matterhorn), 59, 79
North Fork Creek, 210, 218
North Pole, 130
Norton, Major E. F., 120, 121, 122, 123, *123*
Norway, 224, 225, 227, 228
Nothdurft, Günther, 109, 110, 111
Numbur, 138, 142, 146, 163
Nuptse, *119, 126, 133,* 144, 150, 155, *156, 157,* 159, 161, *161,* 165, 166

O

Oberaar, Glacier, 88
Ober Gabelhorn, 242
Odell, N. E., 123, 124, 125
Odes (Horace), 128
Ogre (Eiger), 85
Olginate, 109
Olympus, 39
One Hundred Views of Fuji (Hiroshige), 174
One Hundred Views of Fuji (Hokusai), 174, 186
Ongchu, 132, 134, 151, 152, 172
Onion Valley, 210
Oppurg, Franz, 130
Oregon, University of, 51
Orellana, Francisco de, 130
Orsho, 151
Orsières, 222, 229
Osaka, 179
Oslo, 227
Østerdal, Norway, 224
Otemma Glacier (Haute Route), 245
Owens Valley, 210
Oxford, 123

P

Paccard, Michel-Gabriel, 16, 19, 20, 21, 24, *26,* 30, 31, 34, 45, 46, 47
  age, 16
  ascent of Mont Blanc, 13–14, 21–24
  attempt from Saint Gervais side, 20
  dispute with Balmat and Bourrit, 24
  occupation, 16
Pacific Crest Trail, 214
Pacific Ocean, 179, 189, 194
Painted Lady, 210, 213
Pakhar, *133,* 134
Pangboche, 151
Pangu, 168
Paradiso, Gran, 96
Parker Brothers, 67
Parkes, Lady, 189
Parkes, Sir Harry, 189
Passage of the Fenêtre de Salena, The (Wills), 219
Patagonia, 130
Paulcke, Wilhelm, 228
Payot, Dr. Paul, 228, 229
Peace Corps, 147
Peaks, Passes, and Glaciers (Jacomb), 221
Peary, Robert, 130
Pellaud, Anatole, 232
Pelvoux, Mont, 65
Pemba, 134
Pennine Alps, 48, *227,* 232, 259
Pertemba, 130, 164
Petit Plateau. *See* Plateau, Petit.
Perino, Alfredo, 82
Perren, Franz, 51, 83
Perry, Com. Matthew C., 183
Peru, 106
Phakding, 146
Phalong Karpo, 152, 153
Phanthog, 129
Phari, 118
Phedi, 169
Phijal, 140
Phorjal, 140
Piccard, Auguste, 130
Pic Tyndall (Matterhorn), 67
Pigne d'Arolla, 233, 246, *254, 255, 256, 257,* 259, 260
Pinson, Paul, 203, 205, 218
Placerville, California, 199, 226
Planards, Col des (Haute Route), 221
Plateau, Grand (Mont Blanc), 19, 22, *26*
Plateau, Petit (Mont Blanc), 19, 21
Plateau Rosa, 50, 60, 83
Playground of Europe, The (Stephen), 207
Playground of the Far East, The (Weston), 190
Pococke, Dr. Richard, 16
Pointe d'Orny (Haute Route), 255
Pointe Helbronner (Courmayeur), 249
Polo, Marco, 52
Popocatepetl, 179
Porges, Dr. Sigismund, 89
Powell, Kathy, 131, 132, 140, 145
Powell, Walbridge "Bo", 131, 132, 136, 138, 145, 146, 169, 172
Prafleuri Hut (Haute Route), 256
Pragel Pass, 228
Prerayen, Switzerland, 222
Prescott, Arizona, 202
Prest, E. B., 220
Preyer, Ben, 210, 217
Principles of Circumstantial Evidence (Wills), 237
Puiyan, *133,* 145
Pumori, 119, *133,* 152, *152,* 154, 155, *156,* 158, 159, 166, *167*

R

Rae Lakes, 210
Rainer, Edi, 98, 100
Rainier, Mount, 43
Rais, 145, 168

Ramp (Eiger), 97, 103
Ramshorn Springs (Mount Whitney), 208
Range of Light, 198
Rauje, 143
Ravanel, Aiguille, 229
Ravanel, Camille, 229
Ravanel, Jean, 229
Ravanel, Joseph, 228, 229, 232
Rebitsch, Hias, 102
Rébuffat, Gaston, 106, 107
　Starlight and Storm, 84, 108
Reichert, F., 232
Reidmatten, Col de, 232
Rembrandt, 186
Rensselaer, Dr. Jeremiah van, 32
Reuse de l'Arolla, Col de (Haute Route), 220, 222
Rey, Guido, *The Matterhorn*, 48
Rhone Valley, 221
Rimpfischorn, 233
Ritter, Mount, 202, 218
Rixford, Mount, 211, 213
Roaring River, 199
Roberts, Jimmy, 159
Rochers Rouges (Matterhorn), 60
Rochers Rouges (Mont Blanc), 19, 22, *23*, 25, *26*, 30
Roget, Professor F.F., 232
Rongbuk Glacier, 125, 128
Rongbuk Monastery, 118, 120, 121
Rock Band (Everest), *126*, 129, *160*, 163, 230
Rock Creek, 208
Rocky Mountains, 202
Roosevelt, Theodore (president), 207
Rosablanche, 233
Rosa, Monte, 17, *55*, 58, 65, 73, 89, 96, 116, 220, 223, 228, 237, 259, 260
Rosa Monte Hut (Haute Route), 245
Roseg, Piz, 242
Rote Fluh (Eiger), 103
Roter Turm (Matterhorn), 59
Rothschild, Baron Ferdinand James de, 207
Rouge, Col du Mont, 232
Rousseau, Jean-Jacques, 16, 38
Rousse, Tête (Mont Blanc), 19, 20, 32
Royal Geographical Society, 117
Ruinette, 260
Rumpelt, H., 232
Ruskin, John, 38, 39, 198, 207
Russia, 228
Ruttledge, Hugh, 125, 128

S

Saas-Fee, 232, 237, 245, 246, 262
Sacramento, 199
Sai, Lake, 175
Saint Bernard Pass, Great, 47, 220, 221
Saint Gervais, 19, 20, 21, 31, 32, 34, 43, 45, 220
Saint Gothard Pass, 233
Saint Joseph, Missouri, 197
Saint Moritz, 96
Sakhalin, 179
Saleina, Fenêtre de (Haute Route), 229, 236, 253
Saleina, Glacier de (Haute Route), 221, 236, 253
Sälen, Sweden, 224
Sallanches, 16
Salpa Pass, 168
Samurai, 180, 182, 183
San Joaquin Plains, 198
Sand, George, 38
San Francisco and New York Mining and Commercial Company, 203
Sanjin, Shoku, 177
Sans Nom, Aiguille, 232
Sardinia, 16, 42, 46
Saussure, Horace Bénédict de, 16, 21, *26*, *27*, 31, 34, 45, 46, 47, 198
　age, 15
　ascent of Mont Blanc, 25

　first visit to Chamonix, 16
　interest in Mont Blanc, 17, 20
　other climbs and explorations, 17
　quotes, 13, 18, 34, 39
　talents, 15
　Voyages dans les Alpes, 13, 17, 47
Savoy, 16
Scandanavian Union, 225
Schilthorn, *108*, 114
Schmid, Franz, 59, *82*
Schmid, Toni, 59, *82*
Schreckhorn, 96
Schumacher, Pierre de, 92
Schwarzsee, 50, 54, 55, 81, 83
Scott, Doug, 130
Scrambles Amongst the Alps (Whymper), 48, 65, 240-41
Seattle, 43, 54
Second Icefield (Eiger), 97, *99*, 103
Second Step (Everest), 123-24, *124*
Sedlmayer, Max, 98
Seiler, Alexander, 79, 80
Sella, Quintino, 72, 76
Sella, Vittorio, 223
Sengen Shrine (Mount Fuji), 175, 177, 190
Serobesi, 134
Serpentine, Col de la (Haute Route), 251, 259
Sete, 142
Seven Years in Tibet (Harrer), 103
Shasta, Mount, 199, 206
Shattered Pillar (Eiger), 97
Sheep's Rock (Mount Langley), 205, 209
Shelley, Mary, 38
Shelley, Percy Bysshe, 38
　Mont Blanc, 13
Shenandoah Valley, 197
Sherpas, 121, 124, 127, 128, 132, 134, 135, *136*, 137, 138, 140, 142, 143, 144, 147, 148, *148*, 149, 150, 153, 155, 159, 164, 166, 168, 169, *169*, 172
　culture, customs, language and qualities, 132, 134, 140-43, 146-47, 148
Shichiman, Mount, *187*
Shingon Sect, 188
Shintoists, 193
Shinto Religion and Mythology, 177, 183, 184
Shipton, Eric, *125*, 126, 128
Shizuaka, 194
Shoji, Lake, 175
Shōkaku, En-no (Ennogyoja), 187-88
Shungendō, 188
Siberia, 224
Sierra Nevada. *See* High Sierra.
Sikri, 139
Simond, Alfred, 229
Simond, Joseph, 232
Simplon Pass, 233
Sindar, Dawa, 132, 137, 142, 146, 147, 148, 161, 165, 172
Siwalik Range, 172
Sixt Valley, 238
Sixty Lake Basin, 210, *211*
Skillington, Lincolnshire, 73
Slack, John, 203
Slingsby, Cecil, 228
Smythe, Frank, 225
Soda Springs, California, 208
Solu Khumbu, 126, 132
Solu Region, 140, 142
Solu River, 145
Solvay (Matterhorn), 16, 54, 58
Sombrerete Mine, 207
Somervell, Dr. Howard, 120, 121, 122, 123
Sönam, 140
Sonadon, Col de (Haute Route), 220, 221, 222, 232, 245
Southampton, 237
South Col (Everest), 126, *126*, 127, 129, 159, *160*, 165
South Korean Expedition (Everest), 130
South Pole, 130
South Summit (Everest), *126*, 127, 160

Southeast Ridge (Everest), *126*
Southern Alps, 194
Southwest Arête (Matterhorn), 67, 71, 72
Southwest Face (Everest), *126*, 138, *160*, 163
Spider (Eiger), 97, *99*, 104, 105, 108, 113
Stäger, Werner, 111
Stanford, Mount, 211
Stanford, University, 112
Stanley, Henry, 130
Starlight and Storm (Rébuffat), 84, 108
Starr, Dr. Frederick, 180, 181
　Fujiyama—The Sacred Mountain of Japan, 180
Stephen, Leslie, 35, 221
　The Playground of Europe, 207
Steuri, Fritz, 98
Steuri, Fritz, Sr., 92
Stevens, Ernest N., 30
Stockholm, 225
Stockji Glacier (Haute Route), 262
Strahlegg, 90
Strahlhorn, 232
Straton, Mary, 223
Strobel, Gunther, 113
Studer, B., 221
Subashiri Trail (Mount Fuji), 180, 190, 195
Summit Icefield (Eiger), 98, *99*
Sun Kosi, 130
Supersaxo, Oscar, 232
Surke, 146
Swallow's Nest (Eiger), 17, 103
Sweden, 224, 225
Swedish Reformation, 224
Swiss Alpine Club, 255
Swiss Expedition (Everest), 125-28, 130, 152
Switzerland, 45, 50, 67, 85, 91, 94, 220, 228, 232
Systematic Geology (King), 202

T

Tabei, Junko, 129
Taconna Glacier (Mont Blanc), 18, 19
Takematsu. *See* Kakugyo.
Taketori Monogatari (Bamboo Cutter), 185
Takshindu, *133*, 138
Tamangs, 135, 140
Tamba Kosi, 136, 138
Tanabe, 184
Tanero, Sasakawa Collection, 185, 194
Täschhorn, 65, 233
Tasman, Mount, 233
Taugwalder, Friedrich, 79
Taugwalder, Joseph, 73, 76
Taugwalder, Peter (old), 73, *75*, 79, 80, 81, 79, 80
Taugwalder, Peter (son), 73, *75*, *75*, 76, 79, 80
Taweche, 152, 159
Tehachapis, 198
Telemark, Norway, 226, 227
Telemark Turn, 227
Tendai Sect, 188
Tengboche, *119*, 127, 128, *133*, 147, 149, 150, 151, *151*, 161, 166
Tenjo, Mount, 191
Tenno, Jimmu, 177
Tennyson, Lord Alfred, *The Daisy*, 259
Tenzing Norgay. *See* Norgay, Tenzing.
Terai, 172
Terray, Lionel, 42, 106, 110, 111
　The Borders of the Impossible, 84
Tête, Blanche. *See* Blanche, Tête.
Tête, Noir. *See* Noir, Tête.
Teton, Grand, 63
Teton National Park, Grand, 51
Thamserku, 143, 149, *150*, 151, 159
Théodule, Col, 17, 48, 63, 73, 221
Théodule Glacier, 71
Third Icefield (Eiger), 97, 98, *99*, 103
Thirty-Six Views of Fuji (Hiroshige), 174

286

Thirty-Six Views of Fuji (Hokusai), 174, 186
Thomas's Sawmill, 198
Thompson, John B. "Snowshoe," 226
Thorong La, 172
Those, 127, *130*, 139
Three Lucky Things (Hokusai), 187
Three Whites (Hokusai), 187
Tibet, 103, 117, 118, 125, 128, 129, 130, 140, 159, 172
Tibetan Language, 134
Tiefmatten Glacier (Haute Route), 262
Tilman, H.W. "Billy," 125, 128, 150
Tokugawa Era, 183
Tokyo, 175, 180, 182, 183, 190
Tostensen, Jon. *See* Thompson, John B. "Snowshoe."
Toulouse-Lautrec, 52
Tour, Glacier du, 236
Tour Noir, *222*, 244
Trail Camp (Mount Whitney), 209
Trail Crest (Mount Whitney), 209
Tramp Aboard, A (Twain), 40
Traverse of the Gods (Eiger), 97, *99*, 103, 110
Trélatête, Aiguille de, 69
Trient Hut (Haute Route), *231*, 253, 254
Trient, Plateau du (Haute Route), *229*, 253
Trient, Switzerland, 254
Trieste (Bathyscaphe), 130
Tsa-chu, 128
Tschuggen, *112*
Tsolatse, 152, 159
Tuckett, F.F., 221
Turin, 59, 72
Twain, Mark, 38
  A Tramp Abroad, 40
Tyndall, John, 40, 65, 69, 70, 82, 198, 237, 238
  Hours of Exercise in the Alps, 199
Tyndall, Mount, 198, 200, 205, 206, 210

U

Udet, Col. Ernest, 98
Uhuru Point (Kilimanjaro), 258
Ukiyo-Ye School of Art, 186
United States, 81, 135, 226, 248
United States Expedition (Everest), 129, 130
Umagaeshi (Mount Fuji), 175
Unsoeld, Willi, 129
Unter Dach (Matterhorn), 60

V

Valais, 49, 50, 73, 81, 92
Valaisian Alps, 233
Val de Bagnes, 229, 232
Val d'Isere, 248
Valpelline, Col de (Haute Route), 220, 221, 222, 245
Val Ferret, 253
Vallée Blanche (Chamonix), 249
Vallot (Mont Blanc), 43, 46
Valsorey Hut, (Haute Route), 232
Valtournanche, 67, 68, 69, 72, 77
Vasaloppet, 224
Vélan, Mont, 222
Verbier, 233, 255
Vercors, 42
Verte, Aiguille, 42, 45, 70, 73, *228*, 232, 245, 250, 251
Vesuvius, 179
Vicksburg, 197
Victoria, Queen, 80
Victoria (ship), 130
Vienna, 103
Vignettes Hut (Haute Route), 229, 245, *260*, 261, *261*, 262
Ville, Hotel de, 46
Virgin (Jungfrau), 85, 87
Visalia, 198

Visp (Switzerland), 221
Volcanoes, 179
Völker, Alois, 88
Voltaire, 16
Vörg, Ludwig, 102, 103, 105, 106
Votteler, Roland, 113
Voyages dans les Alpes (de Saussure), 13, 17, 27
Voza, Col de, 31
Vulcanism, 179

W

Wager, L.R., 124
Wales, 116
Wales, Prince of, 207
Walker, Horace, 242
Walker, Lucy, 55
Walker, Spur (Grandes Jorasses), 44, 110, 111
Wallis, Graham, 131, 132, 147, 148
Wanderings Among the High Alps (Wills), 88, 240
Wasatch Range, 199
Watzmann, 107
Waugh, Andrew, 117
Weisshorn, 61, 65, 199, 253, *258*, 259
Wellington, Duke of, 237
Wengen, 85, 86, 114
Wengern Alps, 90
Western Alps, 220
Western Cordilleras, 202
Western Cwm (Everest), 119, 126, *126*, 159, 165
Weston, Rev. Walter, 190
  The Playground of The Far East, 190
West Ridge (Everest), 129
Wetterhorn, 65, 88, 89, 96, 114, 228, 237
Wheeler, E.O., 119
Whillans, Don, 163
Whitney, Josiah Dwight, 198, 199, 202, 205, 206, 208
Whitney, Mount, 43, 132, 198, 202, 203, *204*, 218
  ascent by Muir, 209
  early attempts, 202, 203-206
  first ascent, 208
  mistaken for Mount Langley, 204-206
  trail, 209-210, 218.
  See also separate entries for other features of mountain.
Whitney Portal, Mount, 209, 217
Whitney, "Old" (or "False") Mount, 205
Whittaker, Jim, 129
Whymper, Edward, 30, 35, 42, 60, 64ff.
  accident, 63, *78*, 79-81
  ascent of Matterhorn, 52, 55, 74-80, *82*
  attempts on Matterhorn, 68-69
  attempts with Carrel, 68
  birth, 65
  death, 82
  description of Matterhorn, 65-66
  illustrator, 65
  meets Carrel, 67
  meets Croz, Hudson, Douglas, Hadow in Zermatt, 73
  misled by Carrel, 72
  obsession to climb Matterhorn, 67, 69
  other climbs, 65, 69, 70, 240-41, 261
  passim, *66*, *75*, 88, 115, 223, 236, 240-41, 242, 250, 251, 261
  quotations and writings, 48, 59, 65, 67, 71-72, 74, 75, 76, 79, 80
  Scrambles Amongst the Alps, 48, 65, 240-41
  traits, 65
Whymper, Josiah, 65
Wilde, Oscar, 89
Wildstrubel, 232
Wills, Alfred, 40, 65, 88, 89, 236-40, *239*, 253

Passage of the Fenêtre de Salena, The, 219
Principles of Circumstantial Evidence, 237
Wanderings Among the High Alps, 88, 240
Wilson, Maurice, 125
Winchester School, 115, 116
Windham, William, 16, 38
Winkelmatten, 50
Winkworth, Stephen, 221
Wordsworth, William, 38
  Descriptive Sketches, 219
World Health Organization, 147
World War I, 228
Wright Brothers, 14

Y

Yale Sheffield Scientific School, 198, 207
Yamabushi, 187
Yamanaka, Lake, 178, 191
Yamato Clan, 183
Yarsa, 137, 138
Yatsudo Fuyo (The Eight Petals of Fuji), 193
Yokohama, 194, 196
Yosemite Valley, 85, 86, 201, 206, 218
Yoshida, 173, 174, 177, 178, 190, 194, 195
Yoshida Trail (Mount Fuji), 184, 190, 195
Yoshika, Miyako-no, *Fujisan Ki*, 187
Young, Geoffrey Winthrop, 116
Younghusband, Francis, 117, 118
Yugoslavian Expedition (Everest), 130

Z

Zermatt, 48, 50, 51, 52, 63, 65, 67, 68, 73, 76, 77, 78, 79, 80, 81, 82, 83, 116, 220, 221, 222, 223, 228, 229, 232, 233, 236, 237, 245, 246, 249, 261, 262
Zmutt Glacier (Haute Route), 262
Zmutt Ridge (Matterhorn), 67, 82
Zurcher, Alfred, 92
Zurich, 91
Zwingelstein, Leon, 236